WATERCRY

THE OLDEST RIGVEDIC PRAYERS

AMRESH VASHISHT

Made with ♥ on the Notion Press Platform
www.notionpress.com

DEDICATED TO THE SAPT RISHIS

Contents

Preface

In an era where humanity faces unprecedented environmental challenges and a growing disconnect from the natural world, the wisdom of ancient texts such as the Rigveda offers profound insights that are more relevant than ever. *WATERCRY: The Oldest Rigvedic Prayers* is a humble endeavor to reconnect with this timeless wisdom, particularly focusing on the most ancient prayers of the Rigveda that invoke the life-giving waters, celebrate the sacredness of nature, and reveal the deep ecological consciousness of our ancestors.

The Rigveda, composed over three millennia ago, is not merely a religious scripture; it is a testament to the spiritual and intellectual heights achieved by the Vedic civilization. Among its numerous hymns, the prayers for water stand out for their poignant relevance to contemporary issues. The hymns resonate with the universal human experience of dependence on water—a vital element that sustains life, fosters growth, and maintains balance in the natural world.

This book is structured to guide readers through a journey of rediscovery, beginning with an exploration of the eternal wisdom contained within the Rigvedic prayers and a comparison of the old and new Mandalas. This comparison highlights how the Vedic seers, or Rishis, evolved in their understanding of the cosmos and their relationship with the divine, particularly in the context of the natural world.

We then delve into the world of the Rigvedic gods, those divine beings who were invoked during yajnas (sacrificial rituals) to bless and protect the people. These deities, embodiments of natural forces, were integral to the Vedic worldview, representing the interconnectedness of all life and the importance of maintaining harmony with the environment.

Central to the narrative of the Rigveda is the Saraswati River—a river that was once the cradle of Vedic civilization. The Saraswati, both a physical entity and a divine symbol, played a crucial role in the spiritual and material life of the Vedic people. The third chapter of this book is dedicated to this river, tracing its significance in the Rigveda and the profound prayers offered by the Rishis for its revival as it began to dry up.

Following this, the book presents an in-depth examination of the hymns found in Mandalas 2, 3, 4, 6, and 7, composed by the great Rishis Gratsmand, Vishwamitra, Vamadeva, Bharadwaja, and Vashisht. These Mandalas contain some of the oldest and most powerful prayers for water, reflecting the Rishis' deep understanding of the cosmic forces and their intimate connection with the natural world.

As we journey through these ancient hymns, we are reminded that the Rigvedic prayers are not just relics of a bygone era but living traditions that continue to offer guidance and inspiration. They speak to us across the ages, reminding us of our responsibility to protect the environment, to honor the sacredness of water, and to live in harmony with the natural world.

The concluding chapter of this book, titled *Eternal Echoes - The Legacy of the Rigvedic Waters*, brings together the themes explored in the previous chapters, emphasizing the enduring relevance of the Rig-Veda's ecological wisdom. It calls on us to heed the lessons of the past and to recognize that the legacy of the Rigvedic waters is eternal—a legacy that we must preserve and pass on to future generations.

I am deeply indebted to the ancient Rishis whose wisdom forms the foundation of this book and to my son, Animesh Vashisht, whose support and encouragement have been invaluable in bringing this work to fruition. It is my hope that *WATERCRY: The Oldest Rigvedic Prayers* will inspire readers to reconnect with the sacredness of water and the natural world, and to draw upon the timeless wisdom of the Rigveda in addressing the challenges of our time.

AMRESH VASHISHT
30.01.2025

ONE
THE ETERNAL WISDOM

The Rig-Veda is the oldest compilation of human wisdom and the cornerstone of Vedic literature. Unlike a single cohesive book, it is a compilation of several distinct texts composed over different periods. This anthology's varied language, style, and ideas reflect its evolutionary nature, with some hymns predating their systematic arrangement by centuries. The Rig-Veda's unique character lies in its natural and authentic expression, distinguishing it from other Samhitas.

As the earliest sacred text of India, the Rig-Veda is the oldest and largest of the four Vedas. It serves as the foundation of India's religious and philosophical development, encompassing the seeds of classical Sanskrit poetry. Its significance extends beyond Indian culture, providing insights into the languages, literatures, and cultures of ancient civilizations worldwide. The Rig-Veda is a vital source for anyone seeking to understand the roots of Indian spiritual and literary traditions.

The Rig-Veda, as it stands today, consists of ten Mandalas. However, few of the Mandalas are found to be the oldest parts of the Veda. The world of spirituality is populated with intellectuals who interpret the hymns in their unique ways. The ancient Mandalas focus significantly on the theme of water, particularly in the context of the river Saraswati. As the Saraswati River dried up, the inhabitants faced existential threats and displacement from their ancestral lands. The Rishis of that era endeavored to revive the mighty Saraswati by performing a Yagna at Mohenjo-Daro, where the Saraswati met the Sindhu River. Water was the central theme of this Yagna, symbolizing their hope for restoration and survival.

The Rig-Veda is a foundational text of ancient Indian civilization, representing one of the earliest and most significant records of languages and cultures. Composed of ten books, known as Mandalas, it contains 1,028 hymns (Suktas) and 10,552 verses (Ricas or Mantras). Despite its oral preservation for thousands of years before being committed to writing, the Rig-Veda is universally recognized by scholars as a text of unparalleled authenticity and accuracy. Its meticulous transmission has allowed it to serve as a verbatim preservation of the ancient world, preserving not only linguistic data but also historical, cultural, and religious material in its original form.

The importance of the Rig-Veda in understanding the early Indo-European presence in India cannot be overstated. As scholars like Michael Witzel have emphasized, the Rig-Veda is not just a literary text but a historical document of immense value. Its hymns are considered equivalent to inscriptions, faithfully preserved over millennia with no alteration to their content, making the Rig-Veda a unique source of ancient knowledge.

However, the Rig-Veda is not a monolithic text; it is composed of distinct parts that reflect different chronological and cultural eras. These parts are often referred to as the Old Rig-Veda and the New Rig-Veda. Understanding this division is crucial for comprehending the evolution of Vedic society, language, and religion.

Water was the main theme

In the vast expanse of Rigvedic hymns, water emerges as a recurring and vital theme. The hymns reflect a profound reverence for water, acknowledging it as the essence of life and the sustainer of all existence. The Vedic seers composed passionate prayers, invoking the gods to release the life-giving waters, often trapped or withheld by natural forces or demonic entities. These hymns not only highlight the physical necessity of water but also its spiritual significance as a divine blessing.

Water is personified and deified in the Rig-Veda, with various deities associated with different aspects of water. For instance, the hymns to Varuna emphasize his control over the cosmic waters and his role in maintaining the natural order. Indra's exploits often involve the release of waters, symbolizing the victory of life and fertility over drought and desolation. The Saraswati River, frequently mentioned in the hymns, is revered as a goddess, embodying purity, knowledge, and abundance.

The Rigvedic hymns express a deep connection between water and the sustenance of life. They recognize water as essential for agriculture, health, and overall prosperity. The prayers for rain and the pleas to release the rivers reflect the agrarian society's dependence on water for their livelihood and survival. These hymns also highlight the significance of water in rituals and ceremonies, where it is used for purification and consecration, symbolizing spiritual renewal and divine grace.

In essence, the Rigvedic hymns dedicated to water capture the essence of a civilization deeply attuned to the natural world. They reveal a profound understanding of water's vital role in sustaining life and a heartfelt plea for the divine to bestow this precious resource upon humanity. Through these ancient prayers, we glimpse the timeless reverence for water that continues to resonate in the hearts of people today.

About Rig-Veda

The Rig-Veda-Samhita is composed in verses known as Riks, designed to praise deities. This collection of Riks is called Rig-Veda-Samhita. Currently, only the Shaakala recension of the Rig-Veda is available, containing approximately 10,552 mantras. These are organized into ten books called Mandalas, each divided into Anuvakas (sections) and further into Suktas (hymns), which consist of several Riks (verses).

The structured division of the Rig-Veda into Mandalas, Anuvakas, Suktas, and Riks is methodical and widely accepted. Each Sukta is dedicated to specific deities, with an associated seer (Rishi), deity (Devata), and metre (Chandas). For instance, RV 3.16.7 refers to the seventh mantra of the sixteenth Sukta of the third Mandala. This meticulous organization aids in the precise reference and study of Vedic texts.

Among the 1028 Suktas of the Rig-Veda Samhita, several are particularly renowned and frequently referenced. These include:

1. **Purusha Sukta**: Describes the cosmic being and the creation of the universe.
2. **Hiranya-garbha Sukta**: Celebrates the golden embryo and the creation.
3. **Dhana-anna-dana Sukta**: Pertains to the giving of wealth and food.
4. **Aksha Sukta**: Hymns related to dice and gambling.
5. **Nasadiya Sukta**: Contemplates the origins of the universe.
6. **Duhsvapna-nashna Sukta**: Concerns the dispelling of bad dreams.
7. **Yama-yami-samvada Sukta**: Dialogues between Yama and Yami.

Additionally, there are Suktas dedicated to various deities like Indra, Maruta, Varuna, Usha, Surya, Bhumi, Soma, Agni, and others. These hymns cover a wide range of subjects narrated poetically, philosophically, and religiously by Vedic seers.

Chandas(Metres) , regarded as the feet of the Veda Purusha, form the metric structure of Vedic texts. Each mantra has a specific Chandas, akin to a presiding deity, ensuring proper reading and recitation. Texts dealing with Vedic meters include Rikpratishakhya, Shankhayana Shrauta-sutra, Nidana-sutra of Samaveda, and the Chandas-sutras of Pingala.

Nirukta, regarded as the ears of the Veda Purusha, deals with the etymology of Vedic words. Yaska's Nirukta is the only surviving work in this Vedanga, providing a commentary on the Nighantu (list of Vedic words). It categorizes Vedic words, explains ambiguous terms, and classifies deities according to their realms.

Yajnavalkya Smriti lists fourteen sources of knowledge, including the four Vedas and six Vedangas (Shiksha, Kalpa, Vyakarana, Nirukta, Chandas, Jyotisha). The Mundaka Upanishad divides knowledge into Para (spiritual) and Apara (worldly), with the Vedas covering both aspects. Vedic scriptures are complemented by auxiliary sciences like phonetics, grammar, and rituals.

The Vedas are integral to understanding Indian culture and civilization, encapsulating wisdom, science, and tradition. The Rig-Veda, with its poetic verses and philosophical hymns, remains a vital source of spiritual and cultural knowledge.

The Rig-Veda represents the earliest sacred book of India, the oldest and largest of all the four Vedas. It contains the seeds of India's religious and philosophical development, with features of classical Sanskrit poetry traceable to its verses. Thus, the Rig-Veda is essential for anyone seeking to understand Indian literature and spiritual culture. Its value today extends beyond India, as its well-preserved language and mythology offer insights into the languages, literatures, and cultures of the world.

The Structure of the Rig-Veda

The Rig-Veda is divided into ten Mandalas or books, each containing a varying number of hymns. Scholars have categorized these ten books into two primary groups: the family books (2-4,6 & 7) and the non-family books (1,5, 8-10). The family books are so named because they are associated with specific families of rishis (sages) who composed them. These books are generally older and were composed and compiled before the non-family books.

The non-family books, on the other hand, are more mixed in their composition, both in terms of the rishis involved and the content of the hymns. The distinction between these two groups of books is not just academic but also reflects significant differences in linguistic, cultural, and religious practices.

However, one of the family books, Book 5, exhibits characteristics more aligned with the non-family books than with the other family books. This has led scholars to reclassify the Rig-Veda into two broader categories:

1. **The Old Rig-Veda**: This includes Books 2-4 and 6-7, excluding the Redacted Hymns, which were later additions or modifications.
2. **The New Rig-Veda**: This includes Books 1, 5, 8-10, along with the Redacted Hymns, which represent a transitional phase between the Old and New Rig-Veda.

This reclassification allows for a more nuanced understanding of the Rig-Veda's composition, reflecting the chronological and cultural shifts that occurred over the centuries during which the text was composed.

Characteristics of the Old Rig-Veda

The Old Rig-Veda, consisting of Books 2-4 and 6-7, is marked by its linguistic and cultural antiquity. This part of the Rig-Veda is closer to the Proto-Indo-European stage and shares many linguistic features with other ancient Indo-European languages. This affinity is particularly evident in the vocabulary used in the Old Rig-Veda, which includes words that are common across various Indo-European languages.

For example, the word for "night" in the Old Rig-Veda is *nakt-*, a term found in several other Indo-European languages, including Avestan (*naxt-*), Greek (*nukhta*), Latin (*nocte*), German (*nacht*), and Lithuanian (*naktis*). This linguistic continuity underscores the Old Rig-Veda's connection to the broader Indo-European linguistic and cultural tradition.

The composers of the Old Rig-Veda were ancestral rishis, revered as the forefathers of Vedic knowledge. These rishis composed hymns in honor of their ancestors, reflecting a strong tradition of ancestral reverence that was central to Vedic society. The hymns in the Old Rig-Veda are meticulously organized, following a strict order based on the deity being addressed, the number of verses in each hymn, and the meter used. This structured approach reflects the Rig-Veda's role as a carefully preserved cultural and historical document.

The Old Rig-Veda also employs older diametric meters, such as Gayatri (8 + 8 + 8) and Anustubh (8 + 8 + 8 + 8), which are characteristic of this period. These meters are simpler and more traditional, reflecting the linguistic and poetic conventions of the time. The language of the Old Rig-Veda is also more archaic, free from many of the innovations that appear in the later sections of the Rig-Veda.

Moreover, the Old Rig-Veda lacks references to certain socio-religious concepts and stylistic features that become prominent in the New Rig-Veda. For instance, certain mythical and socio-religious concepts, such as Surya as an Aditya or Indra's identification with the Sun, are absent in the Old Rig-Veda. Similarly, stylistic features like alliteration and the use of comparatives and superlatives are less common in the Old Rig-Veda, further emphasizing its antiquity.

Characteristics of the New Rig-Veda

The New Rig-Veda, comprising Books 1, 5, 8-10, represents a more evolved linguistic and cultural stage. The language of the New Rig-Veda shows significant innovations and changes, marking a transition to post-Rig-Veda and later Sanskrit. These linguistic changes are evident in the vocabulary, with new words and expressions appearing for the first time in the New Rig-Veda.

One of the most notable linguistic changes is the introduction of the word *ratri* for "night." Unlike nakt, which is found across various Indo-European languages, ratri is unique to the New Rig-Veda and later Vedic texts. This word becomes the standard term for "night" in Classical Sanskrit and later Indo-Aryan languages, reflecting the linguistic evolution that occurred during the composition of the New Rig-Veda.

The New Rig-Veda also departs from the strict family structure of the Old Rig-Veda. In the New Rig-Veda, composers often compose hymns in their own names rather than in the names of their ancestors. This shift reflects a greater sense of individuality and personal expression among the rishis of the New Rig-Veda, indicating a cultural shift in Vedic society.

The meters used in the New Rig-Veda also show a broader range of poetic experimentation. In addition to the older diametric meters, the New Rig-Veda includes newer meters such as Pankti $(8 + 8 + 8 + 8 + 8)$ and Mahapankti $(8 + 8 + 8 + 8 + 8 + 8)$. These meters are more complex and reflect the evolving poetic conventions of the time.

Furthermore, the New Rig-Veda introduces new sacred numerical formulas, words associated with agriculture, certain occupations, and technologies, and a variety of personal names and grammatical forms not found in the Old Rig-Veda. These innovations suggest a society in transition, with evolving cultural practices and beliefs. For example, the emergence of certain agricultural terms in the New Rig-Veda indicates the growing importance of agriculture in Vedic society, a shift from the more pastoral and nomadic lifestyle reflected in the Old Rig-Veda.

The New Rig-Veda also reflects changes in religious practices and beliefs. For instance, the New Rig-Veda contains references to new socio-religious concepts, such as the identification of Surya as an Aditya or the depiction of Indra's weapon as a discus. These changes reflect the evolving religious landscape of Vedic society, with new deities and religious symbols gaining prominence.

The Redacted Hymns: A Transitional Phase

The Redacted Hymns represent a transitional phase between the Old and New Rig-Veda. These hymns were modified or added to the Old Rig-Veda during the composition of the New Rig-Veda, reflecting the linguistic and cultural changes that were occurring at the time.

The Redacted Hymns are inserted into the older books of the Rig-Veda, sometimes violating the original pattern of arrangement. These hymns are often found at the end of the Old Books, indicating that they were later additions. The language of the Redacted Hymns shows signs of the linguistic innovations that characterize the New Rig-Veda, including the introduction of new vocabulary and grammatical forms.

For example, the word ratri, which is a hallmark of the New Rig-Veda, appears in one of the Redacted Hymns in Book 7. This indicates that the Redacted Hymns were composed during the transition from the Old Rig-Veda to the New Rig-Veda, reflecting the linguistic and cultural changes of that period.

The Redacted Hymns also reflect the evolving religious practices and beliefs of Vedic society. For instance, these hymns contain references to new socio-religious concepts, such as the depiction of Indra's weapon as a discus, which are not found in the Old Rig-Veda. These changes suggest that the Redacted Hymns were composed during a time of significant religious transformation, when new deities and religious symbols were gaining prominence.

The Redacted Hymns thus serve as a bridge between the Old and New Rig-Veda, reflecting the transitional phase in Vedic society. They provide valuable insights into the linguistic, cultural, and religious changes that occurred during this period, offering a glimpse into the dynamic and evolving nature of Vedic civilization.

Linguistic Innovations and Cultural Shifts

The distinction between the Old and New Rig-Veda is not limited to linguistic and metrical differences. The two parts of the Rig-Veda also reflect significant cultural and religious shifts within Vedic society.

The old Rig-Veda concept has not been glorified for a simple reason that the hymns spoken as prayers for the water have failed. The Saraswati River didn't awake and failed to reflow again. That's why the concept of holding yagna for water has been lost. The massive migration after the failure of Yajna also contributed much to keep off the rig-Vedic prayers.

One of the most striking cultural shifts is the change in the social structure reflected in the New Rig-Veda. The Old Rig-Veda emphasizes the importance of ancestral rishis and their collective efforts for regeneration of mighty river Saraswati.

Preservation of the Rig-Veda

Despite its antiquity, the Rig-Veda has been preserved in its original form with remarkable accuracy. Vedic seers devised methods to protect and transmit the text letter by letter. Techniques like Samhita-Patha, Pada-Patha, and Krama-Patha ensured its precise memorization and transmission. The use of accents (Swara) and metrics (Chandas) helped maintain its integrity. This meticulous preservation effort is unparalleled in the history of literature.

Eternity of the Veda

According to Hindu tradition, the Veda is not a human creation but a divine revelation, visualized by ancient seers and transmitted orally. This concept of Apaurusheyata (non-human origin) underscores the Veda's eternal and universal nature. The Rig-Veda describes the Veda as eternal, akin to the breath of Brahman, the ultimate reality.

Age of the Rig-Veda

Determining the exact age of the Rig-Veda is challenging due to the lack of external evidence and the doctrine of Apaurusheyata. Various scholars have proposed different dates, ranging from several millennia BC to the beginning of creation. Despite these challenges, the Rig-Veda remains the most ancient and revered document of human civilization.

Family Book

The concept of the Family Book in this context revolves around Mandalas 2, 3, 4, 6, and 7 of the Rigveda, which are traditionally attributed to the families of specific Rishis—Gritsamada, Vishvamitra, Vāmadeva, Bharadwaja, and

Vashisht. These Mandalas are considered the core or "family books" of the Rigveda, as they preserve the hymns and prayers passed down through these Rishi families, reflecting their spiritual legacy and insights.

The notion of the Family Book aligns with the structure of the Rigveda itself, as well as the teachings found in the Ārṣeya Upanishad. Though the Ārṣeya Upanishad is not categorized as one of the principal Upanishads, it holds a significant place among the Vedānta-Upaniṣads. It captures the essence of Vedantic philosophy through dialogues between renowned seers such as Vishvamitra, Jamadagni, Bharadvāja, Gautama, and Vashisht.

These dialogues delve into the timeless and universal principles of Vedanta, particularly focusing on the nature of the Atman (the Self) and its eternal existence. The discussions underscore the interconnectedness and familial approach to Vedic wisdom, where the teachings are not isolated fragments but part of a broader, intergenerational discourse.

This family-oriented structure of the Rigveda, as reflected in the Upanishadic teachings, reinforces the idea that Vedic wisdom is a shared, communal heritage, passed down through generations of seers who contributed their unique spiritual insights. The concept of the Family Book, therefore, not only highlights the continuity of spiritual knowledge but also emphasizes the collective contribution of these Rishi families to the preservation and dissemination of Vedic wisdom.

In this way, the Family Book concept becomes a powerful symbol of the enduring legacy of these ancient seers, whose teachings continue to resonate through time, offering guidance and inspiration to those who seek to understand the deeper mysteries of existence.

TWO
RIG-VEDIC GODS

The Rig-Veda gods, known collectively as the Devas, represent various aspects of the natural and cosmic order. The gods are multifaceted and revered for their various attributes that contribute to the well-being and prosperity of their devotees. Agni, the fire god, acts as a divine mediator between humans and gods, essential in rituals and sacrifices. Indra, the king of the gods, is celebrated for his might and heroic deeds, particularly his victory over the demon Vritra, which released the waters. Varuna, the god of cosmic order and moral authority, oversees the law of the universe. Ushas, the goddess of dawn, brings light and dispels darkness, signifying new beginnings. The Ashwini Kumars, twin horsemen, are revered for their healing abilities and youthful vigor. Soma, both a god and a sacred plant, is associated with the ritual drink that grants immortality and divine inspiration. The Adityas, including deities like Mitra and Aryaman, uphold societal laws and moral values. Collectively, these deities embody the forces of nature and cosmic principles, guiding and protecting humanity through their divine influence. The hymns reflect a deep connection between the divine and the natural world, emphasizing the importance of protection, sustenance, and moral order. Through these deities, the Rig-Veda captures the essence of Vedic spirituality and the enduring relationship between humans and the divine.

AGNI (FIRE)

Agni, the fire god, holds a central and revered place in the Rig-Veda, where he is celebrated for his purity, brightness, and essential role in Yagya (sacrificial rituals). Agni's multifaceted nature is vividly portrayed in numerous hymns, highlighting his significance in both the physical and spiritual realms. His flames, symbolizing light, wisdom, and spiritual enlightenment, are praised for their radiant brightness, illuminating the heavens and earth. Agni's presence is considered purifying and sanctifying, making him indispensable in the sacrificial rites where he acts as the divine mediator, carrying offerings from humans to the gods. He embodies various divine roles, such as Hota (invoker), Prishata Adhvaryu (priest), and Brahma (prayer leader), underscoring his critical role in these rituals.

Agni is described as being born from water, reflecting his connection to all elements and his integral role in the natural processes that sustain life. He delights in nature, embodying the life force that nurtures all living beings. Revered as the guardian of homes, Agni protects the household and fulfills the wishes of its inhabitants, with his presence in the domestic hearth symbolizing safety, prosperity, and well-being. As a source of light and wisdom, Agni guides devotees toward the divine, bringing prosperity, wealth, and children to his followers, thereby ensuring their material and spiritual success. His power extends to embodying other deities such as Vishnu, Varuna, Rudra, and the Maruts, highlighting his versatility and supreme status among the gods.

Agni's dynamic nature is depicted through his travel on blood-colored horses, symbolizing his active and powerful presence in both celestial and terrestrial realms. His role as a protector of humanity is emphasized by his flames, which spread across the heavens and earth like the moon, establishing him as a constant guardian against evil forces. Agni also serves as a guide to devotees, acting as a bridge between the mortal and divine worlds, and ensuring the success of sacrificial rituals by facilitating communication between humans and gods.

In Yagya-mandaps (sacrificial enclosures), Agni serves as the host, illuminating the space and receiving offerings on behalf of the gods, further emphasizing his central role in Vedic worship. He is celebrated for bringing rain from the heavens, ensuring abundant grain harvests and providing essential resources for significant sacrifices. Agni's role as a divine messenger, known for his deep knowledge of human thoughts, ensures that the wishes of supplicants are fulfilled. He is also depicted as a revered guest in sacrificial ceremonies, deserving of hymns, offerings, and respect. As the sustainer of both humans and gods, Agni maintains the balance of the cosmos and ensures the continuous performance of Yagyas.

Agni is called upon to swiftly defeat enemies and remove obstacles, symbolizing his powerful and relentless nature through his bright and vigorous flames. Despite his eternal and inexhaustible energy, Agni remains ever youthful, with his flames likened to a horse's tail, underscoring his perpetual presence and vitality. His ability to bring light, wisdom, prosperity, and protection to his devotees solidifies his status as a powerful and benevolent deity in the Rig-Veda, making him a cornerstone of Vedic worship and mythology.

INDRA

Indra, one of the primary deities in the Rig-Veda, is celebrated for his immense power, heroic deeds, and supreme status among both humans and gods. His significance in Vedic mythology is underscored by numerous hymns that extol his various attributes and actions. Indra's strength is so great that it is said to have frightened the sky and earth, stabilized the trembling earth, calmed mountains, and supported the sky by creating space. His heroic deeds, such as killing the demon Vritra, are among his most celebrated feats. This act not only caused the seven rivers to flow but also freed the cows restrained by the demon, symbolizing the release of life-sustaining resources and prosperity.

Indra is often referred to as the creator of the world, subduer of the wicked, and conqueror of enemies' wealth. He commands horses, cows, and chariots, controls the sun and dawn, and inspires water, making him a key figure in maintaining the cosmic order. His presence is crucial in battles, where his strength, derived from drinking Soma, enabled him to kill the demon Ahi, stabilize the solar system, and bring light to earth and space. Indra's might is further symbolized by his thunderbolt, which he used to open river gates, ensuring their long flow and regulating natural phenomena.

As a protector, Indra played a significant role in safeguarding sages, defeating demons, and bestowing wealth upon his devotees. He helped people cross rivers safely, made the Indus River flow northwards, and restored the sight and mobility of Paravruk. His ability to remove obstacles and heal his followers further illustrates his benevolent nature. Indra's role in Yagyas (sacrificial rituals) is also celebrated, where he is recognized for his enemy-slaying capabilities and honored through Soma rituals. His thunderbolt, chariot, horse, and weapons are described as symbols of his might.

Indra is likened to a boat saving those at sea, emphasizing his role as a protector in battles. He is praised for his ability to prevent evil, grant greatness to his servants, and provide wealth, fame, good fortune, and protection. Indra's donations are believed to fulfill all wishes, making him worthy of Yagya. His actions, from slaying demons to ensuring the flow of rivers and protecting sages, illustrate his vital role in maintaining the cosmic order and supporting his devotees. Indra's strength, derived from the sacred Soma, his role in battles, and his presence in Yagyas further underscore his significance as a protector and benefactor, making him one of the most revered deities in Vedic mythology.

BRAHMINSPATI (BRIHASPATI)

Brahminspati, also known as Brihaspati, holds a significant and revered position in the Rig-Veda, where he is celebrated for his multifaceted divine attributes and powerful actions. He is praised for his ability to eliminate detractors and dispel the metaphorical darkness of ignorance and sin, bringing enlightenment and wisdom to his devotees. Often depicted riding a divine chariot capable of destroying enemies and clouds, Brahminspati symbolizes control over both terrestrial and celestial realms, swiftly acting to protect his followers and maintain cosmic order. He plays a crucial role in guiding sacrificers, ensuring that their rituals are performed correctly and effectively, and thereby upholding the sanctity of religious ceremonies. As a protector of righteousness, Brahminspati shields his devotees from sin and moral decay, while also granting them resplendent wealth and removing obstacles that hinder their prosperity. His nurturing role extends to ensuring the well-being and growth of children, underscoring his importance as a benefactor of families. Additionally, Brahminspati is invoked to destroy blasphemers, clear debts, and kill rebels, actions that reinforce his association with justice and the maintenance of social and cosmic harmony. In collaboration with Indra, he reveals hidden cows and releases blocked water, symbolizing his role in providing essential resources and ensuring the sustenance of his followers. Through his blessings, Brahminspati is dedicated to ensuring the overall prosperity and spiritual fulfillment of his devotees. As a powerful deity in the Rig-Veda, Brahminspati exemplifies the Vedic ideals of wisdom, righteousness, and prosperity, playing a crucial role in maintaining cosmic order and the well-being of those who revere him.

ADITYAS

The Adityas are a revered group of deities in the Rig-Veda, celebrated for their diverse attributes and divine qualities. Among the prominent Adityas, Mitra is known for his compassion, non-violence, and representation of friendship and harmonious relationships. He is often invoked alongside Varuna, who is a major deity depicted as self-illuminated and the creator of all living beings. Varuna is revered for his omnipresence, omniscience, and governance of cosmic law, as well as his association with the waters, symbolizing purity and sustenance. Aryama, another Aditya, embodies nobility and is associated with chivalry and social order, ensuring righteous conduct within society. Bhaga represents good fortune and prosperity, and he is invoked for blessings, success in endeavors, and the well-being of devotees. Daksha, known for his skill and intelligence, is associated with order and creative power, symbolizing ability and expertise. Ansha, linked to the distribution of wealth and resources, ensures that every being receives their due share and sustenance. Collectively, the Adityas symbolize protection, sustenance, and the maintenance of cosmic order, and they are revered for their divine qualities of compassion, glory, non-violence, and friendliness.

SUN

The sun, revered in the Rig-Veda as Surya or Savita, is acknowledged as a vital force central to the cosmology and daily life of the Vedic people. Praised for his life-giving energy and light, the sun plays a crucial role in sustaining all living beings. As a protector of all worlds, the sun ensures the stability and harmony of the cosmos, while his radiant light brings divine happiness and prosperity to all creatures. The sun's rays are essential for the sustenance of life on earth, nurturing plants, animals, and humans alike, and his illumination dispels darkness, bringing clarity and knowledge to the world.

SAVITA

Savita, a specific aspect of the sun deity in the Rig-Veda, is revered for his role in providing light, wealth, and divine protection. Hymns dedicated to Savita highlight his crucial role in supporting the world and ensuring the well-being of his devotees. As the provider of light, Savita symbolizes knowledge, purity, and the dispelling of ignorance, while also being invoked to bestow wealth and prosperity, ensuring the material well-being of his followers. Savita is described as a protector and guardian, offering divine protection and safeguarding his devotees from harm, with his blessings sought for the welfare and prosperity of the host and their descendants. Associated with the daily cycle of the rising and setting sun, Savita embodies the eternal nature of divine support and the perpetual cycle of life, symbolizing the consistency and reliability of his presence in the lives of the Vedic people. Through his life-giving energy and light, Savita nurtures all living beings, bringing divine happiness and ensuring the continued protection and sustenance of all worlds.

USHAS

Ushas, the goddess of dawn, holds a significant place in the Rig-Veda, celebrated as the bringer of light and life, and playing a crucial role in the daily renewal of the world. As the prominent goddess of dawn in Vedic literature, Ushas heralds the arrival of a new day, driving away the darkness and chaos of the night and bringing light to the world. Her appearance signifies the end of darkness and the beginning of activity and life, imbuing vitality into all beings as the "life of all life" and "breath of all breaths." Ushas is revered for her ability to revivify the earth each day, setting all things in motion and inspiring all living beings to perform their duties. By driving away chaos and darkness, she symbolizes the dispelling of ignorance and the illumination of the mind and spirit. Though Ushas may not be as central as the three primary male deities—Agni, Soma, and Indra—her role as the medium of awakening, activity, and growth of the other gods is indispensable. Ushas is the personification of dawn, depicted as a beautiful, youthful goddess whose light purifies and elevates human consciousness, guiding individuals toward spiritual enlightenment and the ultimate realization of Truth. Her presence in Vedic mythology underscores the continuous cycle of dawn and dusk, symbolizing hope, renewal, and the promise of a new beginning, making her a vital and revered figure in Vedic worship and literature.

SOMA

Soma in the Rig-Veda is a multifaceted concept that encompasses a god, a plant, and a ritual drink, each aspect deeply intertwined and contributing to its overall significance in Vedic rituals and mythology. As a god, Soma is revered for his divine powers and attributes, celebrated in 120 hymns that praise his greatness, supernatural abilities, and role as a heroic warrior victorious in all battles. Though not often depicted in human-like form, Soma is sometimes symbolized as a bull or bird, representing strength and transcendence, and is considered a bringer of health, wealth, and vitality. The Soma plant, central to Vedic rituals, is the source of the sacred drink that shares its name, revered for its mystical qualities and association with the divine essence. This sacred beverage, yellow-golden in color and often identified with light, is believed to bestow supernatural powers and immortality, sustaining the gods and granting mortals divine abilities. Soma also acts as a bridge between the profane and divine realms, enhancing the spiritual experience of rituals. The intimate association between Soma and Indra, the king of the gods, is particularly significant; the drink empowers Indra to perform his mighty deeds, including the slaying of the demon Vritra, and is essential for his strength and divine courage. Thus, Soma represents a complex and essential entity in the Rig-Veda, embodying divine power, mystical nature, and the profound connection between the earthly and the divine.

VISHWADEVAS

The Vishwadevas, or "All-Gods," hold a significant and revered place in the Rig-Veda, representing the collective divine power and invoked for their protection, strength, and benevolence. As a unified group, the Vishwadevas embody the collective power of all gods, symbolizing the comprehensive nature of divine intervention and support in Vedic rituals and prayers. They are praised for their ability to protect devotees from harm, provide strength, and erase sins, offering a path to redemption and spiritual cleansing. The Vishwadevas are celebrated for their unwavering friendship and companionship, providing comfort, support, and guidance to their followers. As trustworthy allies, they stand by their devotees in times of need, ensuring well-being and success. Hymns directed to the Vishwadevas often seek their favor and assistance in achieving prosperity and overcoming enemies and obstacles. Their collective blessing is believed to ensure the overall well-being and triumph of their devotees. Thus, the Vishwadevas, as the embodiment of collective divine power, play a crucial role in Vedic rituals, symbolizing the unity and comprehensive support of the divine realm.

ASHWINI KUMARS

The Ashwini Kumars, celebrated as divine twin horsemen in the Rig-Veda, are revered for their numerous attributes and significant roles in Vedic mythology. As twin deities, they symbolize duality and balance, often depicted riding horses that emphasize their swiftness and power. They are invoked as protective guardians, ensuring the safety and well-being of their devotees, particularly from violence and old age, while also granting strength and fulfillment to help overcome obstacles. The Ashwini Kumars are associated with divine favor and are praised for bestowing wealth and pleasure, ensuring both material and spiritual prosperity. Described as swift and inexhaustible, they embody perpetual motion and energy, symbolizing eternal youth, health, and vitality—qualities they generously bestow upon their followers. Known as healers, they are closely associated with health and healing, often called upon in times of illness and distress to cure diseases and restore vitality. Their presence, likened to the visibility of mantras, reflects their omnipresence and readiness to assist in times of need. The Ashwini Kumars' dual nature, swiftness, and healing powers make them prominent figures in Vedic hymns, symbolizing balance, rejuvenation, and the eternal support of the divine.

APANPAT

Apanpat, a lesser-known deity in the Rig-Veda, is celebrated for his vital role in sustaining life and enhancing prosperity. Revered for his connection to water, Apanpat is praised for his ability to nourish both the land and its inhabitants, ensuring the fertility and abundance necessary for agricultural success. His presence in all waters symbolizes his omnipresence and integral role in sustaining life, while his contributions to increasing water volume highlight his significance in supporting rich food production and overall prosperity. In addition to his life-sustaining qualities, Apanpat is also admired for his beauty, reflecting an aesthetic appreciation of nature's bounty. The hymns attribute the production of medicines to him, emphasizing his role in health and healing alongside his agricultural importance. By ensuring the prosperity of his devotees through abundant water and successful harvests, Apanpat occupies a vital place in Vedic hymns, symbolizing the essential relationship between water, sustenance, and well-being.

THREE

NADITAMA SARASWATI (THE LIFEBLOOD OF THE RIG-VEDA)

The Rig-Veda presents Saraswati as a multifaceted entity, reflecting the Vedic seers' holistic and overlapping perception of the divine and natural world. Saraswati is celebrated primarily as a river, a life-giving force flowing across the physical landscape, yet she is also visualized as descending from the heavens, symbolizing a divine origin. This duality places her among the revered river-deities, acknowledging her sacred and earthly significance.

Additionally, Saraswati is worshiped as a deity in her own right, beyond her riverine identity. Her divine aspect extends to her role in the Vedic rituals, where she is invoked as an **Apri** deity, essential to the sacrificial ceremonies (yajñas). This emphasizes her integral presence in the spiritual and ritualistic practices of the Vedic society.

Saraswati's association with intellect (dhi) and speech (vāk) further deepens her significance. She embodies the essence of wisdom, knowledge, and communication, foreshadowing her later evolution into a full-fledged goddess presiding over learning and the arts. This intellectual aspect of Saraswati highlights the Vedic seers' reverence for the creative and cognitive faculties, positioning her as a source of inspiration and enlightenment.

The Rig-Veda does not strictly compartmentalize these varied facets of Saraswati; instead, these aspects fluidly interweave, reflecting the complexity and richness of her character. The overlap of her roles as a river, a divine force, a ritual deity, and a symbol of intellect and speech exemplifies the Vedic worldview, where divinity permeates all aspects of existence.

The Saraswati as a River

The Rig-Veda venerates the Saraswati as a mighty river, highlighting its prominence in the Vedic landscape through several hymns. One of the most quoted is the **Nadi-stuti hymn (10.75)**, where Verses 5 and 6 list a series of rivers, stretching from the Ganga in the east to the Sindhu (Indus) in the west. Notably, the Saraswati is positioned between the Yamuna and the Sutlej, emphasizing its significance in the geographical and spiritual milieu of the Vedic civilization.

Nadi-Stuti Hymn (10.75.5-6) : In these verses, nineteen rivers are named, including major rivers like the Ganga, Yamuna, Saraswati, Sutlej, Ravi, Chenab, Jhelum, and the Indus along with its tributaries. The hymn calls upon these rivers to listen to and accept the poet's praise, underlining their revered status. Although the hymn mentions nineteen rivers, a reference in Verse 1 to **sapta-sapta tredha** suggests twenty-one rivers, leaving two rivers unlisted, possibly including the Beas (Vipāś).

Saraswati Origin and Course : Verses 7.95.1 and 7.95.2 provide vital information about the Saraswati origin and course. The Saraswati is described as a powerful river, starting in the mountains and flowing to the ocean. This river is not only a geographical feature but also a protective force, likened to a metal fortress and a mighty charioteer surpassing all other rivers.Saraswati is portrayed as pure, vibrant, and essential to the world's prosperity, offering sustenance in the form of milk and ghee.

The Power of Saraswati: Further hymns emphasize Saraswati's strength and grandeur. For instance: Verse 6.61.2 describes how Saraswati waves shatter mountain peaks with their force, akin to uprooting lotus stems, highlighting her physical power. Verse 6.61.8 speaks of her boundless and tempestuous floodwaters, underscoring her dynamic and impetuous nature.

Tributaries and Association with Other Rivers: Saraswati is also described as having numerous tributaries, indicated by epithets such as **saptasvasā** (having seven sisters). Although identifying these seven sisters is challenging, **Driṣadvati** (modern Chautang) and **Āpayā** are two likely candidates, as mentioned in Verse 3.23.4. The hymns suggest that many peoples and kings lived along the Saraswati, further attesting to the river's importance as a life-sustaining force in the region.

Kings of the Saraswati Valley: The valley of the Saraswati was home to various peoples and rulers. For instance:Verse 6.61.12 refers to the river as the "promoter of five peoples.Verse 7.96.2 mentions the Pūrus, a prominent tribe, inhabiting the Saraswati's banks.Verse 8.21.18 acknowledges King **Chitra**, who ruled along the Saraswati, bestowing gifts and being contrasted with lesser rulers in the region.

The hymns of the Rig-Veda thus depict Saraswati as more than just a river; she is a central figure in the Vedic worldview, representing both a physical and a divine force that nurtures, protects, and sustains life and civilization.

Rig-Vedic Hymns: The oft-quoted Nadi-stuti hymn (10.75) mentions a series of rivers from the Ganga to the Indus, with verses 5 and 6 highlighting the Saraswati. O Ganga, Yamuna, Saraswati, Sutudri (Sutlej) and Parusni (Ravi), O Marudvridha with Asikni (Chenab), O Arjikiya with Vitasta (Jhelum) and Susoma (Sohan), please listen to and accept this hymn of mine. [5]O Sindhu (Indus), you first meet the Tristama, then the Susartu, the Rasa, and the Sveta, and thereafter the Kubha (Kabul), the Gomati (Gomal), the Krumu (Kurram) with the Mehatnu; and you move on in the same chariot with them (i.e., carry their waters with you). [6]In these verses, nineteen rivers are mentioned, placing Saraswati between the Yamuna and Sutlej. This suggests her geographical and spiritual significance. Verses 7.95.1 and 2 further describe her origin and course:This Saraswati gushes forward with her waters, protecting all like a metal fortress; with her might, like a charioteer, she surpasses all other waters. [1]Purest among rivers, vibrant, the Saraswati flows from the mountains to the ocean, manifesting immense riches and providing milk and ghee to Nahusha. [2]These verses clearly depict Saraswati as a powerful river originating in the mountains and flowing to the ocean, sustaining and nourishing life along her course.

The Saraswati as a River-Deity

The Rig-Vedic hymns elevate the Saraswati from a mere river to a revered deity, reflecting the profound respect and spiritual significance she held for the Vedic Aryans. Originating from the high mountains and descending into the plains where the Vedic people lived, Saraswati was seen not just as a physical river but as a divine entity with a celestial origin. This transformation from a river to a deity is articulated through various hymns, where she is invoked and worshiped with the highest reverence.

Celestial Origin and Reverence: The Vedic Aryans, in their deep reverence, considered Saraswati a heavenly deity. This is evident in several hymns, where Saraswati is invoked to descend from the heavens to bless the sacrifices (yajñas) of the devotees. For instance, **Verse 5.43.11** highlights this belief:The verse calls upon Saraswati to come from the heavens and the lofty mountains to partake in their sacrifice. She is described as being filled with ghee, a symbol of purity and nourishment, and is asked to listen to their hymns with favor.This invocation underscores her dual nature as both a river flowing on earth and a divine force connected to the heavens, bridging the gap between the earthly and the divine realms.

Saraswati as the Best of Mothers, Rivers, and Deities: The Rig-Veda further amplifies Saraswati's status by extolling her as the greatest among rivers and goddesses. **Verse 2.41.16** is particularly illustrative of this sentiment:The verse acclaims Saraswati as **"ambitame, nadītamā, devītamā"**—the best of mothers, the best of rivers, and the best of goddesses. This triple superlative reflects the deep affection, respect, and divine status accorded to her by the Vedic seers.In this verse, the worshippers, acknowledging their own insignificance, beseech Saraswati to bestow upon them renown and favor. The invocation of Saraswati as a mother figure also suggests a nurturing and protective aspect, where she is seen as a source of life and sustenance, much like a mother is to her children.

Saraswati's Divine Attributes: The Vedic hymns not only praise Saraswati for her physical presence as a river but also elevate her to the status of a powerful and respected deity. Her attributes as a divine entity are multi-dimensional. She is **nadītamā**—the best among rivers, indicating her unparalleled importance in the geographical and spiritual landscape of the Vedic period.She is **devītamā**—the best among goddesses, signifying her exalted status among the pantheon of Vedic deities. This places her on a pedestal higher than many other deities, reflecting the integral role she played in the religious and cultural life of the Vedic people.

Connection to Rituals and Sacrifices : Saraswati's role as a river-deity is also closely tied to the rituals and sacrifices performed by the Vedic Aryans. Her presence was considered essential for the success of these religious ceremonies. The invocation of Saraswati during yajñas, as seen in **Verse 5.43.11**, illustrates her importance in Vedic rituals:Her divine presence is solicited to sanctify and bless the sacrifices, reflecting the belief that without her favor, the rituals would be incomplete.This connection to rituals further cements her status as a deity who not only presides over the physical and intellectual realms but also plays a crucial role in the spiritual and religious practices of the Vedic society.

Thus, Saraswati's transformation from a river to a revered deity in the Rig-Veda is a testament to the Vedic Aryans' profound reverence for natural forces and their tendency to deify them. Saraswati is celebrated not only for her physical presence as a life-giving river but also for her divine attributes, making her one of the most important deities in the Vedic pantheon. Her worship transcends the mere offering of hymns; it reflects a deep spiritual connection, where she is seen as a nurturing mother, a powerful river, and an exalted goddess, integral to the religious and cultural fabric of the Vedic civilization.

The Saraswati as a Goddess

She has long been revered as the goddess of wisdom and the consort of Brahma. As the bestower of 'vidya' (knowledge) and the patroness of the arts, her influence has permeated centuries. But in the Vedic Age, she was more than a divine figure—she was a living river, the Saraswati, in full flow. Saraswati's significance extends beyond her role as a river and river-deity; she is exalted as a powerful goddess in the Vedic tradition. As a goddess, Saraswati is invoked alongside other major deities, and her presence is integral to the spiritual and intellectual life of the Vedic people. Her divine status is affirmed through her inclusion in the pantheon of Vedic gods and her unique creation narrative, which ties her to the preservation of knowledge and memory.

Invocation with Major Deities : Saraswati's elevation to goddess status is clearly demonstrated in the Vedic hymns, where she is invoked alongside other principal deities. **Verse 5.46.2** serves as a testament to her divine status. The verse calls upon a host of powerful gods—Agni, Indra, Varuna, Mitra, the Marutas, Vishnu, the Nasatyas, and Rudra—to bestow strength upon the worshippers. Saraswati is included in this invocation, highlighting her importance and her role as a divine force.This inclusion among such prominent deities underscores her elevated position in the Vedic pantheon. She is not merely a river or a lesser deity but is recognized as a goddess with significant influence and power.

Creation as the Mother Goddess : A significant aspect of Saraswati's divine narrative is her creation as a Mother Goddess. This creation is deeply connected to a ritualistic context, specifically a yajna (sacrifice) that initially failed to produce the desired results. The yajna, intended to bring forth water and ensure the flow of the Saraswati river, failed when no water emerged from the river. In response to this failure, the Vedic seers created Saraswati as a Mother Goddess.This creation narrative is symbolic, representing the Vedic belief in the transformative power of rituals and the divine. When the physical manifestation of Saraswati as a river did not fulfill the needs of the people, she was reimagined and invoked as a divine presence that transcends the physical realm.

Saraswati and the Preservation of Knowledge : The transformation of Saraswati into a goddess is also tied to the preservation of knowledge and memory in Vedic culture. The creation of Saraswati as a goddess is intertwined with the idea that she would continue to "flow" not in the physical sense but within the minds of the Brahmins:This narrative suggests that Saraswati, as a goddess, took on the role of ensuring the continuity of knowledge, particularly the Vedic hymns, through oral tradition. Since there was no written language at the time, the preservation of these sacred texts relied entirely on memory.Saraswati, therefore, became the embodiment of **samrati** (memory), symbolizing the intellectual and cognitive power that enables the transmission of knowledge across generations. This association with memory and speech positions Saraswati as the goddess of wisdom, learning, and the arts.

Saraswati's Evolution as a Goddess: The evolution of Saraswati from a river to a goddess reflects the broader Vedic worldview, where natural elements were often deified and attributed with deeper spiritual significance:As a goddess, Saraswati is not only a protector of the physical world but also of the intellectual and spiritual realms. Her divine status is linked to the Vedic emphasis on the preservation of sacred knowledge, which was considered vital for the continuation of religious and cultural practices.Saraswati's association with memory and speech also foreshadows her later role in Hinduism as the goddess of learning, music, and the arts, where she is worshiped as the source of all wisdom and creative expression.

Thus, Saraswati's elevation to the status of a goddess in the Vedic tradition is a multifaceted transformation that highlights her integral role in the spiritual, intellectual, and cultural life of the Vedic people. As a goddess, Saraswati is revered not only as a powerful deity alongside other major gods but also as the guardian of knowledge and memory. Her creation as a Mother Goddess in response to the failure of a yajna signifies her enduring presence and influence, ensuring that the sacred hymns and wisdom of the Vedic tradition would continue to flow through the minds of the Brahmins and, by extension, through the generations to come. This divine aspect of Saraswati sets the foundation for her later worship as the goddess of learning and the arts, embodying the eternal quest for knowledge and enlightenment.

The Saraswati as an Apri Deity

Saraswati's role as an Apri deity represents yet another facet of her divine identity within the Vedic tradition. As an Apri deity, she is specifically invoked during sacrifices (yajñas) to take her place among other deities on the sacrificial grass (barhis). This role highlights her integral function within the ritualistic practices of the Vedic people, where she, along with other goddesses, is seen as essential to the success of the sacrificial rites.

The Concept of Apri Deities : In Vedic rituals, **Apri deities** are a group of deities that are invoked together during specific phases of the yajna, particularly during the preparation of the sacrificial space and the offering of oblations. These deities are believed to preside over different aspects of the sacrifice, ensuring its sanctity and effectiveness. The invocation of Apri deities is a critical part of the ritual process, as their presence is thought to bring divine blessings and ensure the proper conduct and success of the sacrifice.Saraswati's inclusion as an Apri deity underscores her importance not only as a goddess of learning and intellect but also as a vital participant in the sacred rituals that form the core of Vedic religious life.

Invocation of Saraswati as an Apri Deity : In the Rig-Veda, Saraswati is invoked alongside other goddesses like **Ila** and **Mahi** during the sacrifices. Two significant verses that illustrate this invocation are **1.13.9** : "May the three goddesses, Ilā, Saraswati, and Mahi, who bring delight and never fail, be seated on the sacrificial grass."In this verse, Saraswati is invoked together with Ilā and Mahi, two other important goddesses in the Vedic pantheon. The phrase "who bring delight and never fail" emphasizes the deities' benevolent and reliable nature, suggesting that their presence at the sacrifice is both auspicious and essential for its success.The act of being "seated on the sacrificial grass" symbolizes the deities' acceptance of the offerings and their active participation in the ritual. This seating is a mark of honor and respect, indicating that the deities are being welcomed to partake in the sacred act. **And Verse 1.142.9:**"Pure and revered amidst the gods and the Maruts, may Bhārati, Ilā, Saraswati, and Mahī be seated on the sacrificial grass."This verse further highlights Saraswati's role in the ritual, positioning her among other revered deities, including Bhārati, Ilā, and Mahi. The invocation of Saraswati as "pure and revered" amidst the gods underscores her sanctity and the high regard in which she is held within the Vedic pantheon.The mention of the **Maruts** (storm gods) alongside the deities adds to the power and significance of the ritual, suggesting that Saraswati's presence, along with the other deities, brings a harmonious and potent energy to the sacrifice.

The Role of Saraswati in Vedic Sacrifices : Saraswati's role as an Apri deity reflects the broader function of deities in Vedic sacrifices. The invocation of these deities is not merely ceremonial but is believed to be essential for the proper conduct of the yajña. Saraswati's presence is thought to sanctify the ritual, ensuring that it is conducted in accordance with divine will and that it achieves its intended purpose.Her role as an Apri deity also reinforces her connection to speech (vāk) and intellect (dhi), as these faculties are crucial in the performance of Vedic rituals. The recitation of hymns, the articulation of mantras, and the offering of oblations all require the precise use of language and thought, domains over which Saraswati presides. Thus, her invocation in this context can be seen as a call for the clear and effective expression of the sacred words that are central to the success of the sacrifice.

Saraswati's Multifaceted Divine Identity : The invocation of Saraswati as an Apri deity is another layer of her multifaceted identity in the Vedic tradition. While she is most commonly associated with her role as a river and a goddess of learning and speech, her role as an Apri deity highlights her importance in the ritualistic and sacrificial practices that were central to Vedic religion.This role also illustrates the fluidity of divine identities in the Vedic tradition, where a single deity could embody multiple aspects and functions. Saraswati's presence in the sacrifice, her connection to the intellect and speech, and her status as a revered goddess all contribute to a rich and complex divine persona that evolves and expands over time.

The Saraswati as Vāk

Saraswati's evolution from a river to a deity and ultimately to a goddess associated with learning and speech is a complex process that finds its early roots in the Rig-Veda. While it remains uncertain whether the full-fledged concept of Saraswati as the goddess of learning had fully emerged during the Rigvedic period, there are significant hints of her connection to intellect (dhi) and speech (vāk), which later became central to her identity.

Saraswati and Intellect (Dhi) : One of the early indications of Saraswati's association with intellect is found in **Verse 2.3.8**, where she is invoked in her role as an **Apri** goddess:The verse praises Saraswati as a deity who **"prompts our intellect"** towards higher thoughts. Here, she is mentioned alongside two other goddesses, **Ila** and **Bhārati**, who, together, are asked to sit on the sacrificial grass and protect the sacrifice.This invocation reflects Saraswati's role in guiding and enhancing the intellect of the Vedic seers, suggesting her emerging association with wisdom and higher knowledge. Although her primary role in this verse is still tied to the ritualistic function as an Apri goddess, her connection to the intellect hints at the nascent development of her later identity as the goddess of learning.

Saraswati as the Illuminator of Intellect : The connection between Saraswati and intellect is further emphasized in **Verse 1.3.12**, where she is described as reigning over thoughts:The verse states that **"Saraswati, with her knowledge, makes one understand this ocean and illumines all intellects."** Here, the metaphor of the ocean represents the vastness and complexity of the world, and Saraswati's role is to illuminate the intellect, enabling a deeper understanding of this worldly existence.This portrayal of Saraswati as a divine force that enlightens the mind and guides understanding further solidifies her association with vāk, or speech, and by extension, the power of knowledge and wisdom.

Saraswati as Vāk (Speech) : The association of Saraswati with vāk, or speech, is a critical aspect of her identity that later becomes central to her role as the goddess of learning, wisdom, and the arts. In the Rigvedic context:Speech (vāk) is not merely the act of verbal communication but is considered a sacred force that embodies the power of the word, knowledge, and truth. The Rig-Veda often extols vāk as the medium through which divine knowledge is expressed and transmitted.Saraswati's connection with vāk positions her as a deity who not only governs over speech but also over the intellectual and cognitive faculties that enable the expression and preservation of knowledge.

Transition to a Goddess of Learning : While the Rig-Veda provides the foundational elements of Saraswati's association with intellect and speech, the full-fledged concept of Saraswati as the goddess of learning and the arts becomes more pronounced in later Vedic and post-Vedic literature:Over time, Saraswati evolves into a central figure in the Hindu pantheon, embodying wisdom, learning, music, and the arts. Her identification with vāk becomes more explicit, as she is worshiped as the source of all knowledge and creative expression.This later development is a natural progression from the early Vedic hints, where Saraswati is already seen as a deity who influences and illuminates the intellect, guiding the thoughts and understanding of the Vedic seers.

Thus, the Rig-Veda offers early glimpses of Saraswati's connection with intellect and speech, which later crystallize into her role as the goddess of learning, wisdom, and the arts. As vāk, Saraswati is not only a river or a deity but a symbol of the sacred power of knowledge and communication, laying the groundwork for her revered status in the broader Hindu tradition.

The Cry for Water

The recurring theme of water in Rig-Veda hymns reflects a profound dependence on this essential resource. As the Saraswati dried up, the inhabitants faced existential threats and displacement. The Rishis of that era endeavored to revive this mighty river by performing a Yagna at Mohenjo-Daro, where the Saraswati met the Sindhu. Water was the central theme of this Yagna, symbolizing their hope for restoration and survival. The hymns dedicated to Saraswati capture the essence of a civilization deeply connected to its natural world, pleading for the divine blessing of water.

Thus, the Rig-Veda's reverence for Saraswati spans multiple dimensions—from a mighty river sustaining life to a revered deity embodying intellect and learning. The hymns dedicated to her highlight the integral role of water in the Vedic civilization and the spiritual significance of this life-giving element. Saraswati enduring legacy continues to inspire reverence and respect for nature's vital resources.

FOUR

RISHI GRITSAMADA (MANDALA 2)

Rishi Gritsamada (Sanskrit: गृत्समद, IAST: Gṛtsamada/Gṛtsamād/ Gṛtsamada śaunohotra.) was a prominent sage in the Rig-Vedic tradition, attributed with composing most of the hymns in Mandala II of the Rigveda. However in an old Rig-Vedic or say family book, he was the first to pray. The second Mandala of the Rig-Veda has 43 hymns, mainly to Agni and Indra. It is one of the "family books" the oldest core of the Rigveda. He was the son of Śunahotra Āṅgirasa and later adopted by Sunaka Bhargava, linking him to the Bhṛgu lineage.

Gritsamada is noted for his deep connection to the Vedic rituals and his ability to align the deeds of the deity Indra with the actions performed in these rituals.

The signature line of his hymns often expressed a wish for strength and heroism during ritualistic offerings.

In Vedic legend, Gritsamada is described as having gained immense strength and size through penance, to the point where the daityas (demons) Dhuni and Cumiri mistook him for Indra. In response to their hostility, Gritsamada praised Indra with hymns, enabling the god to defeat the demons. The sage is also associated with a particular line in the Rigveda: "May we speak loftily at the ritual distribution, in possession of good heroes," reflecting his focus on the importance of ritual and valor.

Gritsamada's contributions to Vedic literature and his legendary stories highlight his significant role in ancient Indian religious and cultural history.

Sukta 1, attributed to Rishi Gritsamada, venerates Agni, the fire god, through sixteen hymns in Jagti Chand. These hymns celebrate Agni's divine attributes and roles, portraying him as the bright and pure presence in Yagyas, born from water, and delighted in nature. Agni is acknowledged as Hota, Prishata Adhvaryu, and Brahma, the guardian of homes, and the fulfiller of wishes, embodying Vishnu and inspiring wisdom. He is also depicted as the steadfast Varun, destroyer of enemies, protector of saints, and giver of wealth and desired results. Agni's power extends to embodying Rudra, Marudgan, and other deities, traveling on blood-colored horses, and protecting humanity. The hymns highlight Agni's role in taking devotees to the divine world, bestowing wealth, protecting homes, and increasing the fruits of Yagyas. Through these praises, Agni's multifaceted nature as a source of light, wisdom, and prosperity is revered.

Sukta 2, attributed to Rishi Gritsamada, offers prayers to Agni, the fire god, in Jagti Chand. He extolled in thirteen hymns for his vital role in Yagyas and his numerous divine attributes. Agni is described as the bright and beautiful power giver, essential in sacrificial fires and worshiped fervently for his significance in Yagyas. He is likened to a cherished calf, sought after day and night, and is praised for his wealth-bearing chariot and his dominion over the sky and earth. Agni's life-giving flames, compared to the moon, spread across the sky and earth for protection, establishing him as the host in Yagya-mandaps. The hymns highlight Agni's role in igniting fire sacrifices, illuminating the heavens, and receiving human offerings on behalf of the gods. He is also celebrated for his ability to bring wealth and children, make the dawn favorable, and grant strength and success comparable to the sun. Agni is invoked to listen to praises, defeat enemies, and provide food, money, and children, and offer happiness and good residence to his devotees. Through these hymns, Agni's importance in Yagyas, his protective nature, and his ability to bestow prosperity and joy are profoundly revered.

Sukta 3, attributed to Rishi Gritsamada offers prayers to Agni, the fire god, in Trishtup Jagti Chand. The hymns praise Agni's pervasive presence in the sacrificial altar, illuminating the entire Yagya place and worshiping the gods. Agni, known as Narashans, is said to pervade all three worlds with his greatness, inviting the gods to the Yagya through offerings of ghee. The hymns call upon the performers to conduct Yagyas with joy and capability, and to honor Indra, who is seated on the sacred Kush grass. Agni is implored to bestow extensive wealth, intelligence, and bravery upon the devotees. The Lord of Light is asked to inaugurate the Yagya, bringing fame, success, and valor. The hymns draw a parallel between Usha (Dawn) and Night, who inspire good deeds and work harmoniously like a weaver, providing water and desired outcomes. Agni, worshiped by scholars, is central to the divine sacrifice, representing the navel of the earth at the altar. Saraswati, Ila, and Bharati are invoked to inspire intellect and protect the Yagya. By Tvashta's grace, the hymns seek fame, food, and brave offspring to sustain the clan. Agni is revered as the knower of deeds, preparing sacrificial food for the gods, with ghee serving as his light and shelter. The prayers conclude by asking Agni to summon the gods and offer them oblations for their happiness.

Sukta 4, attributed to Rishi Somahuti Bhargava extols Agni, the fire god, through nine hymns in Trishutak Chand. Agni is invited as a revered guest, recognized as the knower of all beings and the sustainer of humans and gods. Established by the Bhrigu dynasty in water, space, and humans, Agni is called upon to defeat enemies with the swiftness of horses. The gods, having established Agni as a friend among humans, ensure his presence illuminates the night in the homes of fire sacrificers. The hymns emphasize the importance of nurturing Agni, likening the strengthening of fire to the strengthening of one's body. Agni's flames, bright and vigorous, are described as wagging on the wood like a horse's tail. Agni, ever youthful and equipped with flames to receive oblations, reveals his form through his greatness. He burns forests like a thirsty fire and moves like water, sounding like a horse harnessed to a chariot, and is as beautiful as the sun despite revealing a dark path. The hymns depict Agni as a masterless beast roaming the earth, brightening the world, burning forests, and removing painful thorns. Agni's protection, remembered from the first season to the third, grants bravery, fame, and beautiful forests. The sages, protected by Agni and reciting divine hymns in caves, attain divine wealth, defeat their enemies, and receive chosen wealth from Agni, benefiting their learned devotees with excellent children.

Sukta 5, attributed to Rishi Somahuti Bhargava, Diety Agni, the fire god, is venerated through eight hymns in Anushtup Chand. Agni, appearing as the protector of men like a vigilant father, is acknowledged as a source of wealth and a means of protection. Seven rays are attached to Agni, the hero of the Yagya, who stands as the divine grandson among humans and occupies the eighth place in the Yagya. The hymns highlight Agni's awareness of the offerings and praises made by the Ritvijas. Born of extreme purity, Agni is central to the continuous performance of Yagyas, with the Yajmans considering the Yagya as the desired giver. The ten fingers, symbolizing dedication, serve Neshta Agni by worshiping its forms like Garhapatya. Juhu, filled with ghee, is placed near the altar, signifying nourishment and confirmation of the fire's presence, akin to barley growing due to rain. Agni is likened to Ritvik for good deeds, deserving of Yagyas, hymns, and offerings. The host, recognizing Agni's importance, is urged to perform Yagyas to satisfy all gods, emphasizing that the Yagya is solely for Agni's honor and benefit.

Sukta 6, attributed to Rishi Somahuti Bhargava, Deity- Agni, Chhand-Gayatri. The hymn begins with a heartfelt invocation to Agni, the fire god, requesting him to accept the offerings and listen to the praises being sung. The supplicant expresses a strong desire to please Agni with their offerings, recognizing him as the virtuous son of Bal who enhances the yagya (sacrifice). Agni is praised as a provider of wealth, deserving of reverence, and the supplicant prays for blessings upon his devotees. The hymn acknowledges Agni's power to bestow wealth and seeks his protection from enemies. Further, Agni is lauded for his ability to bring rain from the heavens, which in turn provides the resources needed for significant sacrifices and abundant grains. The young fire is called upon to heed the praises, with the supplicant expressing a desire to worship Agni in the hope of receiving shelter. Agni's deep knowledge of human thoughts and the details of their births is highlighted, portraying him as beneficial to friends and a divine messenger. The hymn concludes with a plea for Agni, who is both knowledgeable and enlightening, to fulfill the wishes of the supplicant and to sit on the sacred grass (Kush) to perform the yagya for the gods.

Sukta 7, attributed to Rishi Somahuti Bhargava, Deity- Agni, Chhand-Gayatri . He begins with an invocation to the young fire god, Agni, who is described as a nurturer, praiseworthy, and luminous. The supplicant requests Agni to bring the wealth desired by many. Agni is asked not to take sides with enemies but to protect the supplicant in every way. With Agni's grace, the supplicant believes they will gain capability and strength. Agni, also referred to as Pavak, is acknowledged as highly worship able and illuminated by the offerings of ghee. The hymn calls for Agni, the nurturer, to be worshiped by their beautiful cows, bulls, and calves. Agni is praised as the most exalted one, intelligent, the son of strength, an organizer of Yagyas, ancient, and desirous of being offered ghee.

Sukta 8, attributed to Rishi Gritsamada, Deity- Agni, Chhand-Anushtup . He opens with a depiction of Agni as having the behavior of a fire horse, possessing delicious food, and being highly desirable. Agni, who is to bring rain, is praised. Agni is lauded as better than a fire hero, and those who are swift are called upon by the Havidaar for the destruction of enemies. Agni, established in houses with noble flames, is worshiped daily, and karma remains intact. Agni, like the radiant sun, is ageless and adorned with rays that shine with flames. Agni, the destroyer of enemies, is very bright and decorated with amazing beauty. Agni has obtained the shelter of Indra, Soma, and other gods. The hymn concludes with a proclamation that, under Agni's protection, no harm can come to them, and they are able to defeat their enemies.

Sukta 9, attributed to Rishi Gritsamada Bhargava, Shonak, Diety- Agni, Chhand- Trishutak .He praises Agni as brilliant, bright, strong, divine, nourishing, truthful, and full of fire, deserving the best seat in the Yagyashala. Agni, who brings desired rain, is called upon to fulfill duties and protect the supplicant and their sons. Agni is to be worshiped at his birthplace, where offerings are made upon lighting the fire. As the best Yagya performer, Agni is asked to procure necessary food from the gods and be the master of wealth, recognizing the praise given. Agni is described as a sight to behold and a destroyer of sorrows, whose divine and earthly wealth remains undestroyed. He is requested to provide food to the supplicant and make them a ruler of wealth. Finally, Agni, along with his companions, is asked to have mercy, protect, and nurture with opulence and non-violence, shining everywhere.

Sukta 10 attributed to Rishi Gritsamada Bhargava, Shonak, Diety- Agni, Chhand- Trishutak .They venerates Agni as both fire and a paternal figure, kindled by humans in the sacrificial place. Agni is described as luminous, immortal, full of intelligent food and strength, and capable of being served by everyone. The wise, indestructible fire of wonderful light is called upon to listen to the supplicant's call, with his red horses transporting him to various places. The Ardhavas created fire from two forests, with Agni present in various vines and filled with immense light at night, protecting all worlds. The fire is spread by the offerings received by intellect. The hymn highlights the ritual of watering the fire of the omnipresent yagya with ghee, requesting it to be consumed peacefully. Once fully lit, the fire is untouchable. The supplicant asks Agni to understand their praises, defeat enemies with his brilliance, and provide shelter and wealth, calling upon him with hymns like Manu.

Sukta 11 attributed to Rishi Gritsamada Bhargava, Shonak, Diety- Indra, Chhand- Viratstana Trishutak .This a hymn is dedicated to Indra, seeking his favor and protection. The supplicant begins by asking Indra to listen to their praise and not to disrespect them, as they seek wealth and blessings from him. Indra is praised for his bravery in defeating Vritra, who attacked the waters sent by Indra. Despite Vritra considering himself immortal, Indra destroyed him through increased praise and strength. Indra is honored for his role in the illuminated Yagya, where auspicious hymns are revealed for him. The supplicant boosts Indra's strength with praises and presents him with thunderbolts to defeat enemies with brilliance like the sun. Indra is acknowledged for killing Vritra, who hid in a cave and amazed the space and sky with his power.

The hymn continues to praise Indra's great deeds, his shining thunderbolt, flag, and horses, which are likened to the sound of water-spewing clouds. The flat land and clouds are pleased with Indra's thunder and rain. The Marudgan spread Indra's word everywhere, and Indra's thunderbolt killed Vritra hidden in the clouds, causing the sky and earth to tremble. Indra is praised for his role as a well-wisher of humans, drinking Soma to disintegrate the demon's illusion. The supplicant requests Indra to drink the Soma and be satisfied, hoping to find a place in his heart for the fruits of their actions. They seek Indra's shelter and desire wealth and a brave son from him. The hymn concludes by asking Indra to grant residence, friends, and great men, and to share the Soma with his helpers, the Marudgan. Indra is praised for preventing evil and granting greatness to his servants. The supplicant highlights Indra's strength in defeating Vritra and driving away bandits, wishing for Indra's continued friendly nature and protection. The hymn ends with a plea for Indra's blessings, wealth, and children, and the promise to praise him in their yajna.

Sukta 12, Second Anuvak, Rishi Gritsamada Bhargava, Shonak, Diety-Indra, Chhand- Trishutak .He extols the power and heroic deeds of Indra, highlighting his supreme status among humans and gods. Indra is revered for his strength that frightened the sky and earth, stabilized the trembling earth, calmed the mountains, and supported the sky by creating space. By killing Vritra, Indra caused the seven rivers to flow and freed the cows restrained by the demon. He is the creator of the world, subduer of the wicked, and conqueror of enemies' wealth. Indra is praised as the giver of immense wealth to the poor and the guardian of decorated hosts. He commands horses, cows, and chariots, controls the sun and dawn, and inspires water. In battle, Indra's presence ensures victory, and he is capable of destroying the strongest mountains and defeating sinners and indolent individuals. He is recognized for killing the demons 'Shambar' and 'Ahi' and is described as luminous and powerful, capable of making rivers flow and holding the thunderbolt. Indra's might makes mountains tremble and the sky and earth bow down. He is the protector of those who filter soma and the keeper of fulfilling hymns. The hymns dedicated to him are as nourishing as food. The Sukta concludes with a plea to Indra to accept the filtered soma and provide sustenance to the host, embodying truth. The supplicant promises to sing his praises along with their beloved children.

Sukta 13, Rishi Gritsamada Bhargava, Shonak, Diety- Indra, Chhand-Trishutak, Jagti Soma, originating from rain and growing in water, gains its essential softness, becoming capable of being squeezed. This nectar-like Soma is the drink of Rudra. Rivers carrying water flow everywhere, reaching the sea and moving along lower paths. Indra, having orchestrated this, is worthy of praise. Donations and praises are given, with water both destroying and being praised for its role. Indra, like a householder spreading wealth among subjects, chews this creation at doomsday. His deeds alone make him praiseworthy.

Indra beautified the sky and earth, charted river courses, and killed Vritra. Just as he gives water to a horse, devotees offer him praises. Indra is the giver of food and money, producing dry fruits from wet trees and dry food from rain, unparalleled and deserving of praise. His actions protect vegetation, illuminate the sun, and reveal all living beings, establishing his worthiness of praise. He opens the mouth of the thunderbolt to accept sacrifices and destroy demons, surrounds and kills demons for the sages without a rope, showcasing his immense wealth and power. All rivers flow with Indra's power, and devotees offer sacrifices to him. He has established the sky, earth, day, night, water, and medicine, affirming his praise-worthiness. Indra's efforts are respected, as he acquires enemy wealth through action and provides food to the born. His destruction of 'Turgiti' and 'Vayya' and saving the blind and crippled Paravraj with water highlight his worthiness of praise. Indra is prayed to daily for his divine donations, blessings of children, and consumption money, affirming his praiseworthy nature.

Sukta 14 attributed to Rishi Gritsamada Bhargava, Shonak, Diety-Indra, Chhand- Trishutak .He calls for the preparation and offering of Soma to Indra. It begins by urging the bringers of Soma to offer it to Indra, the destroyer of Vritra, who desires to drink it. Indra is praised for saving cows and killing demons, and it is suggested to cover him with Soma as one would with a cloth. Indra, who destroyed 'Uran' and 'tumor' with his ninety-nine arms, is to be offered Soma. The hymn continues by honoring Indra for killing various demons such as 'Swashna,' 'Shushana,' 'Pipru,' 'Namuchi,' and 'Tudhikra,' and for his feat of razing the stone cities of 'Shambar' and defeating 'Varcha's' followers. Indra is described as the destroyer of enemies, including those who brought down one lakh demons and 'kuts.' The bringers of Soma are encouraged to offer it to Indra, assuring them that their wishes will be fulfilled.Indra is to be filled with Soma, likened to cows filled with milk, making the host happy. Indra's connection to the luxuries of sky, earth, and space is highlighted, and he is to be filled with Soma just as a vessel is filled. The hymn concludes by asking Indra, the giver of the best abode, to provide wealth and bless the supplicants with great children, praising him in the yagya.

Sukta 15 attributed to Rishi Gritsamada Bhargava, Shonak, Diety-Indra, Chhand- Trishutak. Indra's powerful deeds and the influence of Soma are celebrated. Indra's strength, derived from drinking Soma, enabled him to kill the demon 'Ahi' and stabilize the solar system, bringing light to earth and space. Indra turned the world's face towards the east and used his thunderbolt to open river gates, ensuring their long flow. He protected sages by defeating demons, burning their weapons, and giving wealth to Dabhiti. Indra helped people cross rivers safely and made the Indus River flow northwards. He even restored the sight and mobility of Paravruk, who praised him. Indra, pleased by the Angiravanshis' praise, removed obstacles by opening a mountain door. He killed demons Chumiri and Dhuni, protecting sage Dabhiti. The hymn concludes by asking Indra for blessings, wealth, and children, promising to praise him in the yajna.

Sukta 16 attributed to Rishi Gritsamada Bhargava, Shonak, Diety-Indra, Chhand- Jagti, Trishutak, The hymn praises Indra, the great lord, and offers oblations in his honor through bright fire and beautiful chants. Indra, immortal and a consumer of Soma, is recognized for making the world age and his unparalleled strength and knowledge. His power is so vast that neither the sky, earth, sea, nor mountains can withstand him. Indra is celebrated in Yagyas for his enemy-slaying capabilities, and Soma rituals are performed to honor him, using Adhvaryu stone to crush and filter Soma.

Indra's thunderbolt, chariot, horse, and weapons are described as symbols of his might. He is a protector in battles, likened to a boat saving those at sea. The hymn requests Indra to protect and return the devotees safely from harm, just as a cow returns to its calf. The supplicants promise to please Indra with their stotra (praise), seeking his lavish dakshina (reward) to fulfill their wishes. They ask for his exclusive blessings and vow to praise him in their Yagya, hoping for the gift of children.

Sukta17 attributed to Rishi Gritsamada Bhargava, Shonak, Diety-Indra, Chhand- Jagti, Trishutak .Hepraises Indra and urges men to worship him with new hymns, drawing inspiration from the Angiras. Indra, joyous from Soma, opened clouds blocked by Vritra and increased his glory in battle by drinking Soma to destroy enemies. He is depicted wearing Surya Lok on his head, showing his effort and power. Indra's chariot horses caused wicked people to scatter. He is the lord of the world, covering the sky and earth, inducing darkness to protect.Indra immobilized moving mountains, released water from clouds, supported the earth, and established the sky. As the protector of the world, he is asked for wealth, similar to a dependent seeking support from parents. The hymn calls for Indra to manifest wealth, satisfy those who praise him, and make the supplicant rich. Indra's donations fulfill all wishes, making him worthy of yajna. The supplicant requests exclusive blessings and children, promising to praise Indra in the Yagya.

Sukta 18, Attributed to Rishi Gritsamada Bhargava, Shonak, Diety-Indra, Chhand- Trishutak .He describes a sacred and praiseworthy sacrifice that begins at dawn, featuring four stones, three notes, seven verses, and ten types of characters. This Yagya, performed with delightful hymns and offerings, aims to provide divinity to humans and satisfy Indra in all three realms. Horses are attached to Indra's chariot, and intelligent Stotas (praise singers) participate in this auspicious event. Indra is invited by his guardian horses to drink Soma, which is specially presented for him. He is urged to join the chariot with a varying number of speedy horses and come to partake in the Soma. Indra's companionship and strength are sought, and the supplicants desire his continuous friendship, hoping for victory in all wars. They ask that the blessings of Indra's wealth, which fulfill desires, be given exclusively to them. The supplicants, blessed with children, promise to continue praising Indra in their Yagya.

Sukta 19, Attributed to Rishi Gritsamada Bhargava, Shonak, Diety-Indra, Chhand- Trishutak praises Indra for consuming the joyful offerings filtered by the priests. Delighted by the Soma, Indra used his thunderbolt to pierce the water-holding 'Ahi,' sending streams to the sea, obtaining cows, and illuminating the sun with his radiance. He provided the best wealth to those offering sacrifices and protected his devotees from opposition while killing Vritra.

Indra brought the sun for 'Etash,' who filtered Soma and presented it to him in the Yagya, akin to a son giving wealth to his father. Indra subdued 'Sushna,' 'Ashush,' and 'Kuyava' for his charioteer 'Kutsa' and destroyed ninety-nine cities of 'Shambar' for 'Divodas.'The hymn seeks to strengthen Indra with praises, desiring the benefits of Saptapadi friendship and requesting Indra to use his thunderbolt against 'Piyu.' The supplicants compose beautiful hymns for Indra, hoping to gain food, strength, residence, and happiness through their prayers. They ask that Indra's monetary donations fulfill their wishes exclusively, promising to praise him in the Yagya, blessed with children.

Sukta 20, Attributed to Rishi Gritsamada Bhargava, Shonak, Diety-Indra, Chhand- Trishutak, Viradrupa , the hymn addresses Indra, the creator of the world, likening the act of building a chariot to presenting food to him. The supplicants illuminate Indra with praise, praying for happiness. Indra is called to be their worshiper and protector, driving away enemies and supporting those who serve the sacrificial fire. The Yagya rituals performed aim to shelter and aid those who offer prayers and do good deeds.The hymn celebrates Indra's devotees, who achieved growth and defeated enemies through their devotion. Indra, pleased with the hymns of the Angira dynasty, helped them find cows and destroyed enemy cities. Indra is praised for his readiness for penance and for cutting off sources of pain for living beings.As the slayer of Vritra and destroyer of Puras, Indra defeated the Dasyus who created darkness, and he created earth and water for humanity. The hymn requests Indra to fulfill the beautiful wishes of the host. When seeking water, the stotas increased Indra's power, and he used his thunderbolt to kill demons and break their iron fort. The supplicants ask Indra to grant them the wealth they desire, promising to praise him in the Yagya and be blessed with children.

Sukta 21, Attributed to Rishi Gritsamada Shonak, Diety- Indra, Chhand- Trishutak, Jagti . He celebrates Indra's invincibility and his role as the conqueror of the world, wealth, humans, land, horses, cows, and water. The hymn begins by urging the offering of Soma to Indra, praising him as the creator and conqueror of all. Indra's efforts and victories in defeating many enemies, performing sacrifices, and taking care of his subjects are lauded. Indra is recognized for his incomparable charity, his ability to destroy the violent, provide desired rain, and inspire action. He is attributed with revealing the sun through Usha and guiding the Angiras in recovering kidnapped cows and inspiring water through Yagya. The hymn concludes with a plea for Indra to grant great wealth, fame, good fortune, and protection, filling the supplicants' days with happiness and their speech with sweetness.

Sukta 22, Attributed to Rishi Gritsamada Bhargava, Shonak, Diety- Indra, Chhand- Ashti, Atishkavri .He praises Lord Indra for his immense power and his role in adding 'Trikadru' to the Yagya. Soma, in its true and bright form, pleased Indra, helping him accomplish great tasks. Indra used his strength to conquer 'Krivi,' completing the sky and earth with his glory. He consumed a part of Soma, sharing the rest with the gods, thereby gaining strength. Indra emerged victorious over evildoers through increased virility from Soma, showcasing his knowledge of truth.Indra's past beneficial deeds are praised, particularly his strength in killing Vritra and releasing the waters, highlighting his Shatkarma (virtuous actions). The hymn concludes by acknowledging Indra's knowledge of food and strength, asking him to grant desired opulence and perfection to the supplicants.

Sukta 23, Attributed to Rishi Gritsamada Bhargava, Diety- Brahaspati, Brahminspati, Chhand- Jagti Trishutak is dedicated to Brahminspati (Brahaspati), praising his divine attributes and actions. The hymn starts by equating the creation of rays to the creation of stotras (hymns). Brahminspati is lauded for eliminating detractors and darkness, riding a divine chariot that destroys enemies and clouds. He guides sacrificers on the right path, protects them from sin, and destroys those who do not praise him. Brahminspati ensures that those under his protection remain unharmed and unaffected by sin or enemies. He drives away those who commit violence against his devotees and follows a noble path of wonderful deeds. The hymn calls for the deterioration of the intellect of evildoers and the protection of devotees. Brahminspati is asked to remove obstacles, nurture children, and destroy blasphemers.

The hymn highlights Brahminspati's role in granting wealth, destroying enemies, and ensuring that evil enemies do not become masters. His unique donations and inexhaustible strength are praised, as well as his ability to protect and provide opulence during war. Brahminspati's ancient bravery and role in destroying detractors are acknowledged. Brahminspati is called upon to grant resplendent wealth and not to hand the devotees over to enemies. He is praised for clearing debts and killing rebels through Yagya-karma. The hymn recounts his role in revealing hidden cows, releasing water blocked by Vritra with Indra's help, and ensuring prosperity for his devotees. The hymn concludes with a request for happiness and prosperity, promising to sing stotras along with their descendants in the Yagya.

Sukta 24, Attributed to Rishi Gritsamada Bhargava, along with Shonak, offers profound prayers and teachings directed towards the deity Brahminaspati (Brihaspati) Chand- Trishutak. Through these hymns, the Rishi extols Brahminspati as the supreme god of wisdom and eloquence, the master of praises, and the protector of all beings. He recounts Brahminaspati heroic deeds, such as vanquishing the demon Shambar, liberating the stagnant waters, and uncovering the hidden cows, thereby emphasizing the deity's power to remove obstacles and bestow prosperity. The hymns also highlight Brahminaspati role in bringing rain, revealing the sun, and ensuring the earth's fertility. Through these prayers, Gritsamada Bhargava seeks the deity's blessings for wealth, protection, and happiness, requesting that Brahminspati accept their offerings and continue to guide and protect them. The Rishi's preaching reflects deep devotion and reverence, showcasing the significant role of divine favor in Vedic rituals and daily life.

Sukta 25, Attributed to Rishi Gritsamada Bhargava, along with Shonak, directs his prayers towards Brahminaspati (Brihaspati) with the intent of invoking his divine favor and protection in Jagti Chand. The hymn begins by emphasizing the power of the priest who ignites the sacrificial fire, wishing him the ability to defeat enemies and attain prosperity through righteous means. The Rishi speaks of the intimate relationship (Sakhya Bhava) between the host and Brahminspati, which ensures longevity and prosperity for the host, extending even to his grandchildren. The hymn further describes how the host, blessed by Brahminspati, achieves victory over his enemies, gains abundant cattle, and becomes renowned and knowledgeable. The strength of Brahminaspati devotee is likened to the unstoppable force of a river and the relentless flame of fire, illustrating the invincibility granted by the deity's favor. Those whom Brahminspati considers friends are blessed with the first milk of the cow, symbolizing abundance and nourishment, and they gain the strength to vanquish their foes. This friendship also ensures that all good things, symbolized by flowing juices and various divine tastes, come to the devotee, leading to prosperity and the enjoyment of diverse pleasures.

Sukta 26, Attributed to Rishi Gritsamada Bhargava and Shonak offer a hymn dedicated to Brahminaspati (Brihaspati) in Jagti Chand. The hymn emphasizes the power and blessings bestowed upon those who praise and worship Brahminaspati. It begins by stating that one who praises Brahminaspati can destroy enemies and that a devout worshiper of the gods will triumph over the godless. The hymn further highlights that those who satisfy Brahminaspati will defeat fierce enemies in battle and that the Yagya (sacrificial ritual) will receive wealth from those who oppose it. Devotees are encouraged to praise Brahminaspati, confront the arrogant, and maintain strength and restraint, assuring that by preparing offerings (havi) for Brahminaspati, they will receive abundant wealth. The hymn also assures that the host who faithfully serves Brahminaspati will be blessed with food and wealth from their relatives and children. Additionally, those who offer ghee-laden offerings to Brahminaspati are guided on an easy path, protected from sin, poverty, and enemies, and their endeavors are accomplished successfully.

Sukta 27, Attributed to Rishi Kumro, Gritsamada, and Gritsamada offer reverent hymns to the Adityas, focusing on the deities Mitra, Varuna, Aryama, Bhaga, Daksha, and Ansha in Trishtup Chand . The Rishi begins by praising these divine figures, asking for their attention and highlighting their attributes of compassion, glory, non-violence, and friendliness. The hymn portrays the sun as a great and vigilant entity, knowing the hearts of all beings and protecting all worlds, both movable and immovable. The sun is acknowledged as a vital force in many deeds, repaying debts with truth and life force. The Rishi seeks refuge and protection from these deities, requesting guidance on an easy path and the provision of divine happiness through sweet words. The hymn also asks for protection from Mother Aditi and Aryama, wishing for a non-violent life filled with happiness and bravery.

The Adityas are further praised as the sustainers of the worlds, involved in rituals and Yagyas, and known for their bright complexion, vigilance, and non-violence. They are depicted as taking forms of fire, wind, and sun for the world's sake. Varuna is acknowledged as the master of all, capable of granting long life and prosperity. The hymn includes a plea for forgiveness for any wrongs committed and requests for safety, brilliance, and protection from the darkness. The Rishi expresses gratitude for the divine support that ensures fortune, defeat of enemies, and fulfillment of duties on earth. The hymn concludes by seeking the magical protection of the Adityas, allowing them to live in supreme happiness, free from violence, and enriched with children and prosperity.

Sukta 28, Attributed to Rishi Kumro, Gritsamada, and Gritsamada offer their hymns to the deity Varuna, emphasizing his glory and benevolence in Trishtup Chand. They describe Varuna as self-illuminated and the creator of all living beings, whose brightness brings happiness to those who host sacrifices in his honor. The Rishi expresses a desire for fortune through constant praise, meditation, and service to Varuna, hoping to become radiant with each dawn. Varuna is lauded as the lord of the brave, worshipped by many, and capable of granting a divine abode to his devotees. The hymn implores Varuna, and the Adityas, to be friendly and remove any faults from the worshippers, acknowledging their role in sustaining the world and creating water and rivers.

The Rishi seeks liberation from sins, likening the entanglement of sin to being bound by a rope, and asks Varuna to ensure that their prosperity remains unbroken. They call upon Varuna to eliminate their fears and have mercy, freeing them from sins as one would free a cow from a rope. The hymn also requests that Varuna not punish them for any transgressions in their Yagyas, instead taking away their violent tendencies. Indra, another powerful deity, is also saluted for his valiant deeds. Additionally, the hymn addresses ancestral debts, asking Varuna to free the Rishi from these burdens and ensure they do not have to seek financial help from others. Varuna is asked to protect them from terrifying dreams and potential dangers, including bandits. Finally, the Rishi expresses a desire to never have to speak of their poverty to wealthy patrons and prays for the necessary resources to live a prosperous life with their children, continually praising Varuna in their Yagyas.

Sukta 29, Attributed to Rishi Kumro, Gritsamada, and Gritsamada Va offer their hymns to the Vishwadevas, the collective deities representing all the gods in Trishtup Chand. The hymn begins with a plea to the swift-moving and universally revered gods to discard the worshipper's guilt and protect them, appealing to Varuna for his benevolent protection. The Rishi prays for strength, asking the gods to remove violent enemies and grant happiness both now and in the future. Acknowledging the gods as friends, the hymn seeks their favor and assistance, including from Varuna, Aditi, Indra, and the Maruts.

The Rishi praises the gods' unwavering friendship and requests their swift arrival at the Yagya, expressing a deep appreciation for their divine companionship. The hymn reflects on the many sins erased through reliance on the gods, likening their guidance to a father's advice to a wayward son. It seeks the removal of all sins and bondages, pleading that the gods do not treat the worshipper like a hunter would a bird. The Rishi seeks refuge from the terror of bandits, requesting protection from those who cause harm.Finally, Varuna is specifically addressed, with a prayer that the worshipper never has to beg for resources in front of the wealthy, and that they are never lacking in necessary funds. Blessed with children, the worshipper promises to continue praising the gods in the Yagya, expressing gratitude for the protection and blessings received.

Sukta 30, Attributed to Rishi Gritsamada, Bhargava, and Shonak direct their hymns to the powerful deity Indra, invoking his attributes and heroic deeds in Jagti, Trishtup Chand. They praise Indra as the rain-stirring, brilliant, inspiring destroyer of diseases whose hymns are perpetually in motion. The hymn recounts how Aditi informed Indra about the one who empowers Vritra, the obstruction to prosperity. It describes the daily journey of rivers to the sea, guided by Indra's will. When Vritra, shrouded in rain clouds, confronted Indra, the deity used his sharp weapon to defeat him, firing a thunderbolt that shattered Vritra's power.The Rishis implore Indra to destroy the malicious sons of Vritra with his thunderbolt, just as he had vanquished enemies in ancient times. They request Indra to hurl his stone thunderbolt from the sky to grant prosperity and secure wealth for their descendants. They call upon Indra and Soma to completely annihilate any enemies and to inspire seekers against adversaries, seeking protection and freedom from fear. They ask Indra to alleviate troubles, fatigue, and laziness, to support the Yagya, and to bring forth prosperity through the desired results of their rituals.The hymn also invokes Saraswati for protection, urging her to join forces with the Maruts to conquer enemies, recalling how Indra had defeated the boastful Shandamarka. They appeal to Indra to locate and strike down any secret foes with deadly precision. Finally, they urge Indra to perform heroic deeds, vanquishing enemies who raise their heads, and granting the spoils of victory to his devotees. The Rishis praise Indra's divine power, expressing their desire for recognition as brave warriors and the enjoyment of opulence through their devout salutations and praises.

Sukta 31, Attributed to Rishi Gritsamada, Bhargava, and Shonak offer their hymns to the Vishvadevas, the collective deities representing all gods in Jagti , Trishtup Chand . The hymn begins by metaphorically describing the human body as a chariot, likening its journey to birds searching for food in the forest. The Rishi calls upon Varuna, along with Aditya, Rudra, and the Vasus, to protect this chariot. The gods are requested to safeguard the chariot as it seeks sustenance, with the horses representing the human spirit's ability to traverse even the highest grounds.

The Rishi prays for divine assistance from Indra and the Maruts, seeking a refuge free from violence that enables the chariot to attain ultimate opulence and nourishment. The hymn envisions the gods and goddesses, capable of serving the world, hastening the chariot's progress. It calls upon Ila, Tejasvi, Bhaga, Pusha, and the twin Ashvins, the lords of the sun, to drive the chariot, along with the dawn and night, which inspire and illuminate each other. The Rishi praises the sky and earth with new hymns, offering food, medicine, Soma, and animals as wealth.The gods of space, Ahi, Surya, Trit, Indra, and Savita, are invoked to provide space and joy through the hymn. The fast-moving fire is also asked to derive happiness from the praise. The hymn concludes by acknowledging the Vishvadevas' worthiness of Yajna (sacrifice) and expressing the devotees' eagerness to praise them. The Rishi prays for strength and sustenance, hoping to gain the gods' strength and support, just as a horse powers a chariot.

Sukta 32, Attributed to Rishi Gritsamada, Bhargava, and Shonak direct their hymns to the deities Dhavaprithvi and Perbrati, invoking the protection and blessings of heaven and earth in Jagti , Trishtup Chand. They pray for shelter and favor for the praisers and sacrificer, acknowledging the supreme quality of their divine sustenance. The Rishi asks Indra to prevent the enemy's illusions from becoming fatal, both by day and night, and to keep them safe from terrorizing armies, stressing the importance of maintaining divine friendship. They seek Indra's joy and request a healthy, milk-giving cow as a blessing, offering praise continuously.

The hymn calls upon the goddess of the night, asking her to heed their invocations, fulfill their wishes, and bestow a brave, wealthy son. The night goddess is praised for her grace, protection, and ability to grant excellent wealth. The Rishi appeals to the deep, dark night, referred to as the sister of the gods, to accept their divine offerings and bless them with children. The night is depicted as possessing beautiful, protective arms and fingers, and the Rishi requests her to safeguard the worlds. Further, the hymn invokes various divine figures including Gungu, Kuhu, the god's wife, the dark night, and Goddess Saraswati. They also call upon Indrani for the best shelter and Varunani with wishes for happiness, seeking comprehensive divine protection and blessings for prosperity and well-being.

Sukta 33, Fourth Anuvak, Attributed to the Rishis Gritsamada, Bhargava, and Shonak pray to the deity Rudra, following the Trishutak Chhand . Their prayer is a fervent plea for blessings, protection, and prosperity: "O Rudra, the father of the desert! May we receive your blessings of happiness. May we never be deprived of seeing the sun, and may our brave sons always triumph over their enemies. Let us have many sons and grandchildren. Hey Rudra! Grant us the enjoyment of a life spanning a hundred years with the happiness-giving medicine provided by your enemies. Destroy our foes and erase our sins completely, removing all diseases from our bodies.

You, Rudra, are the best among the wealthy, with a thunderbolt in your arm. May you attain immense growth and save us from sin, ensuring that sin always stays away from us. Shower us with the desired blessings without being angered by false praises or improper salutations. You are a great benefactor; make our children strong with your medicine. I will calm the anger of Rudra, who is invoked by the name Havyukta, through praise. May the beautiful Rudra with a soft belly, yellow complexion, and beautiful nose do no harm to us. Rudra, the desired one, I pray to you for good food and relief from sin, much like a man troubled by the sun finds solace in the shade. Your arm, which bestows happiness, brings joy through its medicine, providing desired rain and removing our sins. We praise Rudra with a yellow complexion and a white aura, singing his praises in a resonant voice. Praise the bright Rudra with Namaskar, the handsome one with a strong body, illuminated with bright light, master and sustainer of all universes.

O venerable Rudra with Vasudhari! You protect us in many forms, unmatched in power. Praise the famous, chariot-riding, monstrous-looking young Rudra, the destroyer of enemies, who brings happiness when praised. May your army destroy our enemy. Bless us as a father blesses his son. You are the giver of many riches and the protector of noble people. Your charity flows when praised. Your pure medicine, discovered by our ancestor Manu, was meant to destroy fear, and we wish for the same medicine. May Rudra's weapon not fall upon us, and may the fierce wrath of Tejaswi Rudra not be directed at us. Loosen the string of your bow towards your host, providing happiness to our sons and grandchildren. O Rudra with the power to shower desires, listen to our call. We, along with our sons and grandchildren, will recite your praises in this Yagya."

Sukta 34, Attributed to the Rishis Gritsamada, Bhargava, and Shonak offer their prayers to the deity Marut, following the Jagti and Trishutak Chhand . Their invocation is a heartfelt plea for strength, protection, and prosperity: "These deserts cover the sky with water streams. Their strength defeats the enemy. They are as fierce as animals, and the world is pervaded by their power. They are luminous and watery like fire, inspiring moving clouds and causing rain. O desert people with bright hearts! You are born from Rudra. Just as the sky is adorned with stars, you too are adorned with your qualities. You are the destroyer of enemies and the one who inspires water. May you receive beauty in the same way as lightning gets beauty from the trees.

Like horses, the desert irrigates vast areas. They move fast near the cloud while shouting the word 'horseman'. O desert! You are crowned and equally angry. You make the trees tremble. You reach the dotted deer for the sake of food. These deserts are like water carriers for the offering host. They, with generous minds, move like a horse with an easy gait, mated with a dotted deer, fed with food. Hey Marut! You are equally angry. Your weapons are shining. Just as a swan goes to its abode, in the same way, you also come with the clouds full of water on a path free from obstacles, along with the cows for the joy born of Soma.O desert! Come towards our filtered Soma like you come towards the Stotra. Strengthen the lower part of the cow like horses. The sacrifice of the host should be full of food. O desert! You give us food and sons. He will praise you when you arrive. You give food to those who praise you. Provide the stota with generosity, battle skills, and intact strength. The heart of the desert is bright. His charity benefits everyone. When he attaches horses to his chariot, he provides the desired food to the sacrificer, just like a cow gives milk to a calf. O desert! Protect us from the violent enemy who is like a vritra. Drive him away with your heat.

Hey Rudra! When you were milking the lower part of 'Prishni', you killed the one who insulted the Stota. You also killed the enemies of 'Trit'; at that time, your power became known to everyone. O Marudgan of good deeds! You always go to yagya. You are called when Soma is accomplished. The devotees take Suk in their hands and ask for the best wealth from the desert people. The Maruts in the form of Angira, who attained the divine world, carried the first yagya. May they engage us in yajna-karma in the morning. Just as the dawn dispels the night, the deserts dispel the darkness with their light that irrigates water.

Those sons of Rudra, Marut, grow in the basic cloud of water having special sound and Arun color. He is always brilliant and brings water with his devotion and is very beautiful. We pray for our protection while asking for wealth from those desert people. In order to achieve the desired, these five elements, namely Prana, Apana, Samana, Dhyana, and Udana, are controlled by Trit. O desert! May we receive the same means by which you protect the host from sin and the one who praises you from the enemy."

Sukta 35, Attributed to, Rishis Gritsamada, Bhargava, and Shonak offer their prayers to the deity Apanpat, following the Trishutak Chhand. Their supplication is filled with a yearning for sustenance, beauty, and divine favor:

"With the desire for food, I recite this hymn. Fast-moving and wordy, may the water-grandson Agni give us abundant food and beautiful looks. They desire praise, so I praise them. We will sing this praise composed with heartfelt emotion for him. May they know our praise well. He has created the entire world by the beneficial force of the living beings. Waters mix with water, and they all increase the volume of water in the sea. Clear and sacred water surrounds the deity named Apanpat.

The girl, devoid of ego and adorned with make-up, meets her handsome husband. Similarly, fire fed with fuel-free ghee burns brightly in the midst of water to obtain rich food. These three goddesses, Ila, Saraswati, and Bharati, eat food for the sake of Apanpat without any trouble. It increases the substance produced in water. We drink the essence of Apanpat (the first manifested water). Uchaishrava horse was born in the ocean filled with water. Hey scholar! You save the devotees from treacherous and violent people. Disloyal and deceitful people do not attain this deity. Exploitation of the gods who reside in their home is done easily. Those gods increase water for rain and consume good food. They are adorned well to donate wealth to the host who is strengthened in the water. All the living beings are just a part of the true form of Apanpat, who is revealed to be vast, pure, and brilliant, and who always resides equally in the waters. He has produced medicines containing fruits.

They move in a crooked manner, stand high in the middle of the clouds, and hold the lightning. Rivers flow following his fame. Their form, shape, and color are like gold. His place is also blessed with deer. Those who donate gold offer perfume to him. The ray form body of Apanpat has a beautiful name. These grow despite being serious. Electricity, along with water, makes them glow in space. Their food is water only. We will worship our friend Apanpat with yagya, havidata, and namaskar. I will decorate their upper part. I hold them with wood and food and chant stotras.

Those fertile Apanpats manifested their womb in the water. He takes refreshments sonically. Sometimes water wants them, and they shine. The divine fire called Apanpat resides on earth in the form of food. Apanpat is the best place. They are bright and luminous. The water masses carry them and cover them while they are moving. Oh fire! you are beautiful. I have appeared before you to get a son. I am a beautiful hymn for the benefit of the host. May we receive all the welfare of the gods. We, having sons and grandsons, will praise you in this yagya."

Sukta 36, Attributed to, Rishis Gritsamada, Bhargava, and Shonak offer their prayers to the deities Indra and Madhva, following the Jagti Chand . Their hymn is a devoted invocation for divine presence, satisfaction, and strength: "Hey Indra! Soma is full of milk and juice for you. Scholars prove it by crushing it with a stone. You are the master of the world. Hey Marut! You are the charioteer, decorated with weapons, the son of Rudra and the leader of space. You sit on Kush and accept Soma from Hota. O best-called scholars! Be happy by coming and sitting on Kush with us. Oh fire! You are a scholar. In this Yagya, be satisfied by consuming Soma along with the Gods.

Oh fire! You are a scholar. In this yajna, perform yajna to invoke the gods. You are the one who calls the gods. May you attain all the three places like Garhapatya, etc. through our Haavi Kamana. Accept the honey of Soma obtained from the best altar. Be satisfied by drinking your portion from the place where fire is kept. Hey Dhanesh Indra! You are ancient. The same from which you get the strength and power to conquer the enemy has been sifted and brought for you. May you be satisfied by drinking Soma from Ritvija. Hey friend Varuna, enjoy our yagya. The gathering recites stotras. Listen to our call. Food prepared by the Ritvijas is present, you beautiful one, accept these Soma near Prashasta."

Sukta 37, Attributed to, Rishis Gritsamada, Bhargava, and Shonak offer their prayers to the deity Dravingodha, following the Jagti Chhand . Their invocation is a heartfelt plea for strength, fulfillment, and divine favor: "O fire, giver of wealth! Become strong by taking food from the yagya performed by Hota. Hey halflings! Those who wish for Agni Purnahuti, offer Soma to them. This giver of money fulfills the wishes of Agni. Oh fire! Drink Soma along with the seasons in the Hota Yagya. Those whom we invoked in the past, we invoke the same people even now. He is worthy of being invoked as the giver and master of all. The Adhvaryus have proved sweet Soma for them. O fire, giver of liquid! Drink Soma along with the seasons in Hota Yagya.

O fire, giver of liquid! Your vehicle should be equipped with a horse. Hey plants! You are strong and non-violent. Drink Soma along with the seasons in the Yagya of Neshta. O fire, giver of wealth! Those who drank Soma in Hota's Yagya, became healthy in their father's Yagya, and ate food in Neshta's Yagya, should drink the death-preventing Somras of Ritwik, the giver of gold. Hey Ashvidvaya! Today, add your chariot, which is a vehicle that moves fast and takes you to your desired destination. Make our havi delicious. You are a food person. Drink our Somras. Oh fire! You receive praise through Samidha offering and stotra. You are the protector of all those who wish for our sacrifices. Drink Sompaan with those who wish for our Havi and with the Gods, Lords, and Universal Gods."

Sukta 38, Attributed to, Rishis Gritsamada, Bhargava, and Shonak offer their prayers to the deity Savita, following the Trishutak and Pankti Chhand . Their hymn is a reverent plea for light, wealth, and divine protection: "Savitadev, the light who supports the world, appears every day for the purpose of delivery. This is his daily rule. They give wealth like gems to those who praise them and make the host a part of welfare. Savitadev, with long arms and light, extends his hands to bring joy to the world. For their sake, extremely sacred water flows and air circulates in space. When Savitadev is released by the fast-moving rays, even the travelers who keep walking stop. The desire of those who go to attack the enemy also disappears at that time. When Savita completes her duty, the night hides the light. For the wise, the work done stops midway. When the sun that divides the seasons rises again, people abandon the expanses.

The light generated in the fire house spreads in the food grains of the host. Usha Mata has given the best part of the Yagya inspired by Savita to Agni. At the end of Savita's divine fast, Nrip returns from the chariot wishing for victory. All movable objects desire their abode and people engaged in work move towards home even if their work remains incomplete. Hey Savita Dev! The explorers find the part of water located through you in space. You divided the trees for the birds to live in. No one can stop your work. At sunset, the moving Neptune, which gives happiness to all movable objects, attains its necessary and easy abode. We salute the bright Sun whose fast even Indra, Varuna, friends, Aryama, Rudra, and enemies cannot stop. May the Sun, whom all human beings praise, who protects the wives of Gods, protect us. We please the extremely brilliant Sun, worthy of worship and meditation. We seek the goodwill of Savita Dev by desiring to be safe, having wealth and animals. Hey Bhaskar! The famous and beautiful wealth that you have given us, may we get it from the heavenly world, earth, and space. Give me the same wealth which is beneficial for the descendants of those who praise. I praise you very much for your good qualities."

Sukta 39, Attributed to, Rishis Gritsamada, Bhargava, and Shonak offer their prayers to the deity Ashwini Kumars, following the Trishutak Chhand . Their hymn is a devoted plea for protection, strength, and divine favor: "Hey Ashwini Kumaro! Bind your enemies like two stones. Like two birds coming and sitting on a tree, both of you should also sit near the host. You are worthy of being invoked like the mantra chanter Ritvija of Brahma status and the two ambassadors. Hey horses! You are as excellent as the two chariots that move in the morning, as good as a twin of the common-born, as famous as two beauties, as cooperative as a couple, and the knower of all deeds. May both of you attain your worshipper.

Hey Ashvidvaya! You are the first among the gods. You come as fast as the two horns of an animal, as fast as the hooves of Vashishtha and Ashwadi. You are the killer of enemies and have the power of your actions. Come before us just like the chakwa chakvi come during the day. Hey Ashwinikumars. Just as the boat sails across, let us sail across. Carry us across like the two wheels of a chariot. Protect us from violence and save us from old age. Hey Ashwinikumars! You are as inexhaustible as the winds, as swift as the rivers, and as visible as the mantras. Come visit us. You are the one who gives pleasure to the body like both the hands and both the legs. You provide us with good wealth. Hey Ashvidvaya! Just as sweet words come out from both lips, speak sweet words. Just as milk comes out from both breasts, make life sweet. Protect us like the two notes of the nose. Hear our praises like both ears.

Hey horses! Give us strength like both hands. Provide water like sky and earth. These praises wish you. Just as a sharpening tool sharpens a sword, sharpen your praises in the same way. Hey Ashvidvaya! These stotras attributed to sage Gritsamada are going to enhance your growth. You are everyone's master and lover. May you receive these praises. We will praise him immensely in the yajna along with our sons and grandsons."

Sukta 40, Attributed to,, Rishis Gritsamada, Bhargava, and Shonak offer their prayers to the deities Somapushno and Aditi, following the Trishutak Chhand . Their hymn is a reverent plea for protection, prosperity, and divine favor: "You are the father of wealth, sky, and earth. As soon as you were born, you became the protector of the world. The gods made you the one who gives immortality. As soon as Tejaswi Som and Pusha were born, the gods served them. Both of them destroyed the darkness by doing harm. With their help, Indra produces milk in the lower parts of young cows. Desired year Som and Pusha! You divided the world. You are filled with five rays for the world, which is free from impurities and the seven seasons. As soon as we wish, you bring your moving chariot in front of us.

Som Pusha resides on the earth in the form of medicine and resides in the elevated sky in the form of the moon. Both of you should provide wealth in the form of a praiseworthy, desirable, and beautiful animal. Hey Som and Pushan! You revealed all the ghosts. Pusha sees the whole world. You both are the protectors of our deeds. With your strength, we can conquer the enemy army. May Pusha, who makes the world happy, be satisfied with our work. Som, who is rich in wealth, give us wealth. May Tejaswini Aditi protect us from enemies. We will recite a lot of stotras in the yajna with our sons and grandsons."

Sukta 41, Attributed to, Rishis Gritsamada, Bhargava, and Shonak offer their prayers to the deities Indra, Vayu, Mitra, Varuna, and Parbharti, following the Chhand Gayatri, Anushtup, Urrik, Barhati, and Trishutak .Their invocation is a plea for strength, prosperity, and divine favor: "Hey Vayo! Come with your Sahasra-chariot, equipped with Niyudgan, for the sake of drinking Soma. Come with your appointment, you have drunk Soma full of energy. May you attain the house of the one who proves Soma. Hey Indra and Vayo! You come here for Soma filled with Niyudgana and drink wax mixed with milk. Hey friend Varun! This Soma has been proved for your sake. You are a promoter of truth. Listen to our call. May Mitra and Varun, the lord of all without malice, reside in this best stable and pillared place.

The emperor of all, the one in the form of ghee, the one who eats food, the charitable Aditi, the son of Mitra and Varuna, the simple-natured host. Both Ashwinikumars are free from falsehood! The Soma juice obtained by the leader of Rudradvath Yagya should be brought here on a chariot drawn by horses. May the two Ashwini Kumars, who shower wealth, grant us that wealth, far or near, which cannot be snatched away by the enemy of humans. Hey Ashwinikumars! You come for us with the best wealth of various types. That Indra is very intelligent. He frees us from the humiliating and defeating fear of the world.

If Indra wishes to give us happiness, then sin will not come to us, and we will get welfare. Indra has the ability to conquer intelligent enemies. It is he who should make us fearless. Oh world gods! come here, listen to our call, and sit on this Kush. Hey world gods! A very joyful juicy confirmation enhancer possessed by the Gritsamad descendants is for you. Drink the strong beautiful somras. Indra is the best among Marudgana, let those desert people listen to our call to whom Pusha is going to donate.

May Saraswati, who is supreme among mothers and rivers, make us wealthless rich. Hey Saraswati! You are radiant. Food resides in your shelter. Attain satisfaction by drinking Soma in Yagya. Hey Saraswati, you give us descendants in the form of five sons. May Goddess Saraswati, the supreme goddess of food and water, accept this offering. This havi is beautiful, and the gods love it. Gritsamadavanshi gives this havi to you. O sky and earth! You are the successful director of the Yagya. Come to this yagya. We praise you and also praise the fire carrier Agnidev. O sky and earth! You are going to make the sadhana of heaven etc. successful and move towards the gods. Be the one to take this Yagya of ours to the gods. O sky and earth! You are free from hatred and enmity. May the gods who come for this Yagya come and sit near you today to drink Soma."

Sukta 42, Attributed to,, Rishis Gritsamada, Bhargava, and Shonak offer their prayers to the deities Kapijjal and Indra, following the Trishutak Chhand . Their hymn is a plea for guidance, protection, and welfare: "Kapijjal, who utters words repeatedly and directs the future, inspires speech just as he steers a boat. Hey Shakuni! May you be blessed. No kind of defeat should come to you out of nowhere. Hey Shakuni! The eagle bird should not do violence to you. Even Garuda may not kill you. That brave man could not reach you even with a bow and arrow in his hand. You speak in the south direction repeatedly and speak loving words indicating welfare for us. Hey Shakuni! You should pronounce words giving information about welfare in a sweet voice in the south direction of the house. Evil thieves or demons should not become our masters and rulers. Along with our sons and grandsons, we will recite stotras in this yagya."

Sukta 43 attributed to the revered Rishi Gritsamada, Bhargava, and Shonak, the divine deity Kapijjal and Indra are honored through the majestic chhanda—Jagti and Atishakvari. These ancient hymns speak of the natural harmony between the divine and the earthly. The birds, searching for sustenance, utter melodious words as they circle above like praisers, akin to the Som singers reciting the Gayatri chhanda and Trishtup chhanda. Kapinjal, too, enchants the listeners with his recitations of these divine words.

"Hey Shakuni! Just as the singers of Soma drink Soma, you too sing beautiful songs. You should also utter the same words as the Ritviggans utter in the Yagya. You receive information of welfare that increases virtue for us from all sides. When you sit in silence, you seem not happy with us. When you fly, you make sounds as sweet as a karkari. We, the sons and grandsons, will sing the praises composed in this yagya." Thus, through these verses, the bond between the celestial and the mortal is celebrated, echoing through the ages.

The second Mandala of Rig-Veda concludes with this Sukta, emphasizing the unity of divine power and the importance of praise and worship in seeking divine blessings and protection.

FIVE
RISHI VISHVAMITRA (MANDALA 3)

Vishvamitra (Sanskrit: विश्वामित्र, IAST: Viśvāmitra) *is one of the most revered rishis or sages in ancient Indian tradition. He is one of the seven Brahmarshi, the highest order of sages. Vishvamitra is credited with composing most of the Mandala 3 , including the Gayatri Mantra (3.62.10), one of Hinduism's most sacred and powerful mantras.*

The *full meaning and power of the Gayatri Mantra have been comprehended by only 24 rishis throughout history. Vishvamitra is believed to be the first sage to have understood and wielded this power, with Yajnavalkya being the last. The mantra, which Vishvamitra composed, is central to Vedic rituals and is considered a source of spiritual enlightenment and wisdom.*

Before renouncing his royal status to pursue spiritual wisdom, Vishvamitra was a king. Because of his royal origins, he retained the title of Rajarshi, meaning 'royal sage,' even after becoming a Brahmarishi. His journey from a king to a sage symbolizes his transcendence from worldly power to spiritual greatness. Historically, Vishvamitra Gāthina was a Rigvedic rishi and the chief author of Mandala 3. He was a disciple of Jamadagni Bhargava and served as the purohita (royal priest) of the Bharata king Sudās. In texts composed after the Rigveda, Vishvamitra's persona evolves from a historical figure into a more mythical sage, embodying spiritual strength, wisdom, and determination. His legacy continues to inspire through his association with the Gayatri Mantra and his exemplary journey from royalty to sage hood.

Sutak 1, First Anuvak, is attributed to the Rishi Gathino Vishwamitra, with Agni as the deity and Trishtuk as the meter. This section is a hymn of praise and an invocation to Agni, the fire god, seeking his protection, strength, and blessings for the devotees.The hymn begins with a call to Agni, who has asked for Soma to be offered during the Yagya. The devotee requests strength from Agni, acknowledging his protection over the body. The hymn continues with praises for Agni, describing the successful performance of the Yagya and the offerings made. The gods in the sky recognize and praise Agni, who is intelligent, strong, and a friend by nature, bringing happiness and performing Yagya in the waters of rivers.

As Agni manifests, the seven rivers enhance his brightness, similar to how a mare reaches a newborn. The hymn poetically describes the relationship between fire and water, where neither extinguishes the other, symbolizing harmony. Agni is depicted as the son of earth and sky, who, when invoked through stotra (hymn of praise), brings rain and nourishes the earth. The hymn also emphasizes Agni's power and presence, noting that he alone fills the lap of his parents (earth and sky) and consumes the offerings of fire medicine. The relationship between Agni, the sky, and the earth is likened to that of a husband and wife, where both nurture and protect the fire.

Agni, residing in space and the waters of rivers, is portrayed as the father of the world and the protector of humans. He is also the defender in battles, the bringer of nutrition, and the one who shines brightly. The hymn concludes with a request for Agni to bestow wealth, protect the devotees, and grant them prosperity, including sons and land. Vishwamitra's invocation seeks Agni's grace, strength, and the fulfillment of all sacrificial rites, ensuring that the Yagya reaches the gods and that the devotees receive the blessings of food, wealth, and progeny. The hymn is a plea for Agni's mercy and benevolence, asking for protection and the fulfillment of desires.

Sukta 2, attributed to Rishi Vishwamitra, the deity being praised is Agnivashvanar and the meter is Jagti. The hymn extols Agni, the fire god, in verses 1 to 15, as well as in verses 17 and 19. The hymn begins by praising Lord Vaishvanar, who enhances the Yagya and brings happiness akin to the purity of ghee. Just as a chariot is perfected with meticulous intellect, those who invoke the Yajman and Ritvik deities purify the fire with Garhapatya and invocation forms. The fire, upon its appearance, illuminates the sky and earth, acting as a loving son to its parents, an immortal carrier of offerings, non-violent, a giver of food, and radiant like a revered guest among humans. The intelligent ones manifest the fire in the Yagya, possessing the power to avert calamity, akin to praising a draft horse. The radiant fire is praised with the desire for food, fulfilling the wishes of the Bhrigu, capable of granting desires, and adorned with brilliant divine radiance. The Ritviggans, seeking happiness, spread Kusha and pick up the Khuk, praising Agni, who is brilliant, beneficent, a remover of sorrows, and a seeker of fame. The priests, wishing to serve, decorate the sacrificial ground with Kusha. Fire fills the heavens and earth, and the priests immediately hold the manifest fire. The omnipresent, food-giving fire-god is kindled to receive offerings like a horse. The master of the sacrifice, the visible fire gods are attained, as offerers endowed with beautiful sacrifices and doing good to the host. These fires are served with salutations. The immortal gods, by the will of fire, gave cosmic forms to earthly lightning and the sun. The doer placed earthly fire on the earth and the rest in the sky. Men desiring wealth ritualized their lord Agnideva, sharpening him like a sword, pervading high and low places, holding all living beings in all worlds. The newly born Vaishvanara fire enhances desires, roaring like lions, indestructible, extremely fast, providing consumables to the host. Praised by singers, the seat of space, the sun ascends to the world. Like ancient sages, he becomes conscious and rotates as the sun, giving wealth to the priest. Mighty, gifted, praiseworthy. New wealth is sought from the yellowish, bright fire of various movements, brought by the wind from the sky and established on earth. The fire is worshipped by stotra, inspiring in sacrifice, causing knowledge, illuminated, in the form of a flag, situated as the sun, and conscious at dawn. Holy, upright, excellent, invoking gods worthy of praise, Agni Dev is asked for wealth, being omniscient, visible, and beneficial to people of different castes.

Sukta 3, attributed to Rishi Vishwamitra, the deity being praised is Vashvanaragni and the meter is Jagti. The hymn extols Agni in verses. The intelligent stotas sing beautiful praises to the extremely powerful Vaishvanar in the Yagya to attain the right path. The immortal Agnidev serves the gods by carrying the sacrificial fire, ensuring that no one can defile this ancient Yagya. The luminous fire acts as the messenger of the Gods, traveling between the sky and the earth. Inspired by the gods, the wise fire stota beautifies the sacrificial fire established in front of the temple. Scholars worship Agni through their actions, which increases the means for performing Yagya. The wishes of the host find shelter in the fire where devotees offer their deeds. Agni, the father of Yagya, grants strength to those who praise him and fulfills desires, embodying strength on earth and in the heavens. The Gods established Agni, the joy-bringer with a golden chariot, yellow complexion, residing in water, omnipresent, fast-moving, sacrificial, nourishing, and bright Vaishvanar Agni.

The diverse association of gods and priests performing the Yagya rituals praises the fast-moving, charitable fire, which leads and destroys enemies, moving between the sky and the earth. Oh fire! Please the gods with Havi, give us a beautiful son and long life, ask for rain for food, and always remain conscious. Provide food to this host and be the best friend of the gods. The Lord of humans, in guest form with great intelligence, the swift fire, the affectionate vessel of the inspiring priests, and the signifier of sacrifice, is worshipped by great men with salutations. Luminescent and beautiful, Agnidev fills his subjects with power, enlightening all deeds with the best mantras. Brilliant Vaishvanar Agni is saluted for his glory, becoming omniscient and pervading all worlds. Great wealth is obtained by the action of Vaishvanar Agni, which destroys sorrows and grants money to the host for good deeds like Yagya. Agni appears in the form of fire, sky, and earth, full of virility, praising their parents.

Sukta 4, attributed to Rishi Vishwamitra, the deity being praised is Apriya and the meter is Trishtuk. It begins with an invocation to Agni: "Oh fire! May you attain prosperity and consciousness with a favorable mind. You are fast-paced. Shower us with wealth through your glory. Bring the gods to this Yajna, for you are friends of the gods." The hymn urges Agni to perform the Yajna for the friendly deities wholeheartedly.

Varuna, Mitra, and Agni, who perform Yagya three times every day, may the thinned Agni grant the fruit of our Yajna in the form of rain to fulfill our wish for water. May everyone receive the beloved praise of the fire that invokes the gods. To generate happiness, Ila should approach the desired, supplement-worshiped fire. The Yagya-skilled Agnidev is asked to perform the Yajna for us. The path of progress for fire in Yajna is certain, as the bright flame rises up, with the light emanating from the navel of the Yajna. We spread Kush on the earth for the gods. Yagya is achieved through water, the deity that pleases the world, and those with a pure heart, when requested, appear in our Yajna through the door in the form of fire.

May the bright day and night develop, smiling at each other. Mitra, Varuna, and Indra are gracious to us in their brilliant forms, which they wear for us. The hymn praises both the divine and the main form of fire. Ritvik, desiring food with the desire of Yagya, praises Agni in the form of Yagya. May you receive Bharti in the form of fire along with the radiance of the sun. May humans attain Ila along with the gods, and Saraswati should also come here along with brilliant scholars. These three goddesses should be seated on the seat of Kush.Hey Tvashta! Please be happy and provide us with such strong semen from which a son capable of doing good, fulfilling Soma, and being a worshiper of gods can be born. Hey plants! Bring the gods here. The one who sanctifies the living being should perform the Yagya to the fire god Devahvan, for he is the knower of the gods. Oh fire! May you, Aditi, become enlightened and sit on the seat of our Kush along with Indra and the gods. May the gods be satisfied with the form of fire.

Sukta 5 , attributed to Rishi Vishwamitra extols Agni, the deity of fire, under the Trishtup meter. He is the knower of Agni Usha and possesses the consciousness to emulate scholars, illuminating with exceptional brightness. Those who seek favor from the gods ignite Agni, thus opening the door to knowledge. The hymns of those who praise the revered fire are enhanced by words and mantras. They light up at dawn, desiring to be illuminated as messengers of the fire gods. The Sakha forms of the hosts reside among humans to provide the desired results of the Agni Yagya, making them worthy of sacred fire sacrifice and deserving of the praise from intelligent praisers. As Agni increases, he embodies companionship, becoming a friend and a knowledgeable medium spirit with a charitable and inspiring Vayu form. Agni is friendly towards rivers and festivals, and as the omnipresent protector of the earth, he maintains the place of rotation of the Sun, preserves deserts in space, and performs yagyas that please the gods. The great fire, the knower of all, produces beautiful waters worthy of praise, shining even when dormant. Praised Agnidev, who loves his place full of light, provides innovation to the luminous, brilliant, sacred fire, sky, and earth. Agni, born of medicines, grows and becomes fruitful like water flowing on the road, rising from earth to sky as our protector. The fire lit and praised by us should become the messenger of the gods, inviting them to the yagya. When Matarishva activated the Havivahaka fire for Bhrigu, the brilliant fire stunned even the Surya Lok with its brilliance. Oh fire, may you always grant your devotee a land rich in wealth and a lineage capable of producing offspring, all through your grace.

Sukta 6 , attributed to Rishi Vishwamitra praises Agni, the deity of fire, under the Trishtup meter. He addresses those performing yagya, urging them to seek Soma and draw inspiration from the mantra, using Sruk as a means to worship the Goddess. The fire, invoked to the south with its front face to the east, consumes offerings to bring wealth. As Agni appears, he completes the sky and earth, exalted in glory and worthy of worship. The tongues of fire that are part of Agni should be revered. When humans offer sacrifices and praise Agni's glory, the sky, earth, and gods worship him to ensure the success of the sacrificial work. The great fire, a friend of the hosts, mediates between the sky and earth, equally loving and immortal. The sky and earth nourish the moving fire like a cow giving milk. Agni, of great deeds, expands the sky and earth through yajna-karma and is an expert in diplomatic work. Those who fulfill wishes become worshipers of the host by birth.

O brilliant fire, you tie the beautiful horses in front of everyone and call all the gods to make them sacrificial. Agni dries the water in the forest, shining brighter than the sun, illuminating the dawn. Worshipers praise Agni as an object of reverence. The gods who reside in the vast space and bright sky, and the ancestors who respond to the call of 'Om', all are forms of fire with chariots. Agni is invited to come with all the gods in chariots, his horses bringing him here to be strengthened with Soma. The fire god, praised by the vast earth for prosperity, belongs to the gods. Agni is asked to grant a cow-filled land, the cause of various deeds, to the one with beauty and strength, and to bless us with a son capable of increasing our lineage and producing offspring, all through his grace.

Sukta 7, attributed to Rishi Vishwamitra and dedicated to Agni, the deity of fire, in the Trishtup meter, the flames of Agni, with their bright backs, advance in excellence and spread in all directions, akin to the parents of heaven and earth who provide long life to Agni for the sake of the yagya. The cows in the sky are likened to the horses of fire, and Agni's name is among the bright rivers that flow with sweet water. Agni desires to live in truth, ensuring the earth remains firm on correct behavior. Residing in the Badwanals, Agni, the lord of supreme wealth, keeps records and frees the Badvanlas to live. The flowing rivers follow the fire, with Agni, the great son of Tvashta, desiring to possess the entire world. Like a young man approaching his wife, the fire lit near water spreads across the sky and earth.

Worshipers, who know the fulfillment of desires and happiness from the non-violent fire's shelter, remain under Agni's command. Those whose words of praise are worthy of mention illuminate the sky and are luminous themselves. Agni receives welfare feelings expressed by praising the parents, heaven and earth. Agni Dev, capable of irrigating water, inspires those who praise his glory that shines in the night. The Sapta Hota, consisting of five Adhvaryus, water the protection of Yagya, and those who do not give up in hard work, attain happiness as the gods come to perform the yagya of the stotas.

Agni is adorned in two forms as the Sapta Hota Soma is proven, leading to the formation of Prasatra while praising, protecting the Yagya, and speaking truth to Agni. The God-invoker and the luminous fire, great and giver of blessings, ensure that the flames become omnipresent, joyful, and knowledgeable, calling the gods and the sky and earth to the yagya. The dawn in which the Yagya is performed with offerings to the ever-moving fire is a beautiful, wealth-filled dawn. Agni, capable of destroying the host's sins with his great grace, is invoked to grant the praiser a land rich in wealth and a son capable of increasing the lineage and producing children. This is the grace sought from Agni.

Sukta 8, attributed to Rishi Vishwamitra, the deities Vishvodeva, Yupa, and Vrishchan are praised in the Trishtup and Anushtup meters. The Adhvaryu waters the plants with divine Somras, seeking the favor of the gods. Whether these plants lie dormant as seeds or rise high, they are implored to grant wealth. Yupa, residing in the eastern direction of the fire, is asked to remove sins by bestowing beautiful, age-free children and great wealth. The plants are urged to move to the best water-filled places on earth and become measurable, providing food to the host.

Yupa is described with a beautiful tongue and strong limbs, the best among plants. Knowledgeable and intelligent people enhance it with unperturbed hearts. Evolved from a tree, Yupa adorns itself with humans in the sacrificial place, making the days auspicious. The hardworking Adhvaryugan purify Yupa with water and chant Toma Stotra for the Yagya.

The Adhvaryugans, wishing for the gods, protectors of desires, and plants cut with axes, are thrown into the pit to grant wealth and children.

Aditya, Rudra, and Vasu, spreading across the Sun, Earth, and Space, perform the Yagya, increasing the flag-like fire of Yagya. Yupa, arrayed like swans and covered with a beautiful flag, leads the learned on the path of the bright Yupa gods rising east through the Adhvaryus. After removing thorns, the beautiful Yupa trees resemble the horns of horned animals, becoming protectors in war. Plants, separated from their origin by the sharp-edged ax, are wished to be reborn in excellent form with a thousand branches, symbolizing prosperity and growth for all.

Sukta 9, attributed to Rishi Vishwamitra and dedicated to the deity Agni, composed in the meter of Brahti and Trishtuk, the verses extol the virtues and significance of the fire god. "Oh fire! You are going to attain the supremely opulent, indestructible, luminous, trouble-free world. We humans are like your friends. Choose you as my protector." Agni is acknowledged as the protector of forests, a calm presence within sheltered waters, and yet a formidable force when called upon. He is praised for fulfilling the wishes of his devotees and providing satisfaction to the sixteen Ritvijas who offer sacrifices. Agni's power, which once defeated enemies in their caves, is recognized by the world gods, who revere him. The maternal figure churning the willing fire symbolizes the nurturing and summoning of Agni for divine purposes. As the protector of Yagya, Agni bears the offerings chosen by humans for the gods. In the evening, the fire's noble deeds bring comfort and fulfill desires even for the naive. The sacrificial fire, pure and fast-moving, is praised and worshiped by thirty-three hundred and forty-nine gods, establishing Agni as the revered Hota on the sacred Kush.

Sukta 10, attributed to Rishi Vishwamitra and dedicated to the deity Agni, composed in the Ushshrink meter, the verses celebrate the luminous Prajaswami Agni Dev. "O Prajaswami Agni Dev! You are luminous. We offer Medavijan Chaitanya to you." Agni is praised as the eternal priest, protector, and illuminator of the sacrificial fire. He is acknowledged for bestowing vigorous sons, cattle, and riches upon his devotees. Anointed by the seven hotas, Agni illuminates the yajna and associates with the gods, composing ancient and great hymns.

"Agnidev is worth visiting for food and wealth. The same speech which praises them should increase that fire in the form of praise." Agni is revered as the best among the yajna performers, bringing happiness and beauty to the hosts by defeating enemies. He is divine and grants blessings to his devotees, providing them with beautiful, shining, and opulent features. Agni, married and indestructible, grows in strength through churning and is praised by learned speakers.

Sukta 11, attributed to Rishi Vishwamitra and dedicated to the deity Agni, composed in the Gayatri meter, the verses extol the virtues and wisdom of Agni. "Agni is the priest and special overseer of the Yagya. He has complete knowledge of the Yagya." Agni is recognized as the performer of the sacrificial fire, the messenger of the immortal gods, and the one who desires sacrifices in the form of fire, showcasing his immense intelligence.

As the ancient fire, Agni is the knower of all deeds through his intelligence, his brightness capable of destroying darkness. The gods made Agnidev, the son of Bal, famous since ancient times, intelligent since birth, and the accepter of sacrifices. He is likened to chariots by the heroes of man, acting quickly and remaining eternally young, with no one capable of harming him.Agnidev, invincible to enemies and a conqueror of entire armies, strengthens the gods and is associated with food signs. Those who offer sacrifices receive all food from the fire, and the purifying, luminous Agni grants the host a beautiful abode. By praising the learned Lord Agnidev, devotees attain all desired wealth. "Oh fire! May we attain all the desired wealth, all the gods reside in you."

Sukta 12, attributed to Rishi Vishwamitra and dedicated to the deities Indragni, composed in the Gayatri meter, the verses are an invocation to Indra and Agni. "Hey Indragni! Called by the stotras, you come here for the sake of divine, worthy of selection Soma. Pleased with our sadhana, drink this soma juice." Indragni is invited to partake in the soma, which strengthens the senses and aids in performing Yagya.

"I worship Indra and Agni, who make happy those who praise Him by getting inspiration from Soma, who performs the means of Yagya. In this Yagya, both of them should attain satisfaction by drinking soma juice." Indragni, the destroyer of enemies and all evils, victorious and undefeated, is invoked to bestow abundant food. Worshipers use mantras to honor Indragni, seeking their blessings for food and sustenance. "Hey Indragni! The scholars who praise us expand our actions while walking on the path of sacrifice." Indragni's combined strength and their role in inducing rain are highlighted. They are credited with beautifying the divine world and ensuring victory in war through their strength. Indragni's power is further emphasized by their feat of shaking ninety cities of demons together on their first attempt, showcasing their divine prowess and influence.

Sukta 13 , attributed to Rishi Rishvo Vishwamitra and dedicated to the deity Agni, composed in the Anushtuk meter, the verses extol the virtues and significance of Agnidev. "Hey Advayuryas! Praise for Agnidev. These fire gods come here with the seat of fire god Kush, supreme among those who perform yajna. Be seated on it." Agni, under whose control lies the sky and the gods, inspires and blesses the hosts repeatedly, rewarding their deeds with wealth.

"May that fire god give us the best wealth and house that we can enjoy. The sky, the earth, and the space are contained in the great fire, and we attain it." The intelligent ones who praise Agnidev with captivating hymns enlighten him, acknowledging him as the new fire that calls the gods and obeys the people. "Oh fire! Be our protector in times of praise. You are the one with thousands of wealth; the deserts increase you, and you increase our happiness." Agnidev is entreated to grant wealth, fame, and prosperity, providing for both son and household, bestowing wealth that never decays, in abundance or in thousands.

Sukta 14 , attributed to Rishi Rishvo Vishwamitra and dedicated to the deity Agni, composed in the Trishtuk meter, the verses honor Agnidev, the lord of the world. "The one who invokes the Gods, the one who increases the happiness of those who praise him, the one who performs the Yagya with truthfulness, the extremely intelligent one, the lord of the world, Agnidev, comes to our Yagya. His chariot is bright. His crest itself is in the form of hair. Those sons of force produce their glory on the earth."

"O sacrificial fire! I salute you. You are powerful and manifest your deeds. Please accept the greetings offered to you. O fire god worthy of sacrifice! You are brilliant. You get the dawn and the night who come along with the scholars and give us shelter. You reach them by air. The Ritviggans water that ancient fire well with Havi. May dawn and night come repeatedly and reside in our homes like a couple." "O mighty fire god! Friend, all the gods like Varun etc sing hymns towards you because you are the son of Bala and the Sun in person. You remain situated in the light by expanding your guiding rays. Oh fire! Today we will give you the best offering with our own hands. You, the brilliant ones, pleased with our greetings, wish for a yagya. Worship the gods through us."

"Oh mighty fire! The host receives your protective power. He gets food from you only. Pleased with our favorite hymns, please grant us wealth worth thousands. Oh fire! You are powerful, omnipresent, and luminous. Make the sacrifice that we human beings offer for you in the Yagya tasty and become conscious to protect all the hosts."

Sukta 15 , attributed to Rishi Utkol Katya and dedicated to the deity Agni, composed in the Trishtuk meter, the verses extol Agnidev's luminous power and protective abilities. "O fire! You are extremely luminous with wide radiance. You destroy enemies and evil demons. May the best be great, give happiness and be filled with the best invocation. I wish to seek your shelter.""Oh fire! After the appearance of dawn, you should light up for our protection at sunrise. You yourself are about to appear. You too receive our praise just as you receive your son from your father. Hey Agnidev, you are a desired person. You are the one who sees humans. You shine more in dark nights. You have a lot of flames. You give us the fruits of our deeds in your ancestral form. Remove our sins and make us those who desire wealth."

"O fire, enemies cannot defeat you. You are the one who showers wishes. You become famous by conquering enemy cities along with their wealth. You are brilliant, great, and a giver of refuge since birth. Be the one who performs our Yagya. Oh fire! You make the world old every day. You are very intelligent and bright. For the sake of the gods, please make all our actions flawless. You stop here like a chariot and deliver our offerings to the gods. Pervade the sky and the earth with our Yagya.""Oh fire! You are the one who showers wishes, please increase us. Give us food. You, adorned with excellent light, together with the gods, make the sky and the earth suitable for harvesting food. May evil spirits never come near us. Oh fire! You are the one who praises the earth which is the cause of many shortcomings and which gives wealth. May we be blessed with a son capable of enhancing the lineage and producing children. This kindness of yours should be on us."

Sukta 16,attributed to Rishi Utkol Katya, and dedicated to the deity Agni, composed in the Trishtuk meter Oh Agni, the powerful deity of fire, you are the lord of good fortune, blessed with wealth and opulence, and the hero who defeats Vritra. You bring prosperity and happiness, and in battles, you lead us to victory against our enemies. O Agnidev, rich in blessings, grant us prosperity, wealth, children, health, strength, and power. Your presence in the world completes all activities, and you bear the weight of sacrifices offered to the gods. You honor those who worship you and come to their aid in times of war. Mighty Agni, protect us from suffering and ensure we are never devoid of heroes. May we be free from criticism and unworthy of anger. You, the owner of progeny-like opulences manifested in the Yagya, grant us wealth that brings happiness and increases the sacrificial offerings.

Sukta 17, attributed to Rishi Utkol Katya, and dedicated to the deity Agni, composed in the Trishtuk meter. Agnidev, the deity of fire, practices righteousness and shines with hair like flames. You are extremely bright, pure, and a performer of good deeds. At the beginning of the yagya, you ignite and nourish the growing deity of the yagya with offerings containing ghritā and other substances. O fire! You are intelligent and omniscient since birth. Just as you offered oblations to the earth and sky, perform our yajna to the gods by offering our oblations, just like Manu did. Wise Agni, your food encompasses Ajya, Aushadhi, and Soma. O brilliant one! You offer sacrifices to the gods with these offerings and provide happiness and well-being to your guests. Radiant and praiseworthy Agni, we salute you. The gods have appointed you to deliver sacrifices free from attachment, and you are the navel form of nectar. The one who performs the Yagya is happy, sitting in the best places, and fulfills his duties. Perform this Yagya of ours to please the gods.

Sukta 18 , attributed to Rishi Kato Vishwamitra and dedicated to the deity Agni, composed in the Trishtuk meter, the verses implore Agnidev to be a well-wisher like a friend or parent and to be happy with us. Agni is asked to burn to ashes those who are enemies of humans and act against others. The fire god is requested to become an obstacle in the path of enemies and ensure that the wishes of those who do not offer sacrifices go in vain. Agni, being omniscient, is invoked to give pain to those with unstable minds and to hinder them with his ageless rays. Offerings containing samidha and ghee are made to the fast and powerful Agni with the desire for wealth, seeking continuous blessings and wealth as long as praises are offered. Agni, praised by the descendants of Vishwamitra, is asked to shine with brilliance, provide food, health, and fearlessness, and grant the best of wealth when full of samidhas, spreading luminous arms towards the house of the one who praises for wealth.

Sukta 19, attributed to Rishi Kushikputri Gathi and dedicated to the deity Agni, composed in the Trishtuk meter, the verses honor Agnidev, the praiser of the gods, who is omniscient and wise. Agni is accepted as the hota (priest) in the yagya, performing fire sacrifices to worship the gods. He is asked to grant wealth and food and accept the offerings made. The verses present Juhu, the means of offering haviyukt havi, complete with a circle, to Agni, inviting the gods to participate in the yagya and bless the participants with wealth. Agni's protection is sought to strengthen the seeker's heart, grant wealth and children, and bestow great wealth without fear. Agni is praised as luminous and is called upon to worship the world light in the yagya, invoking the gods. The intelligent sages present in the yagya call Agni Hota, seeking his protection and provision of food for their sons. This marks the end of the first chapter.

Sukta 20 , attributed to Rishi Kushiki Gathi and dedicated to the deities Agni and Vishvadeva, composed in the Trishtuk meter, the verses describe the Havivahaka fire gods who dispel darkness at dawn and invoke the gods Usha, Ashvins, and Dadhika with their hymns. The gods are encouraged to listen to these verses and attend the yagya. Agni, you possess three types of food and residences, and you perform the yagya with three tongues that satisfy the gods. Your body has three forms desired by the gods, and you, freed from laziness, protect our hymn in all your forms. You are knowledgeable, luminous, immortal, and full of food, endowed with radiance by the gods, and you provide the desired results that satisfy the world. The powers bestowed upon you by the gods are ever-present. Like Aditya, you reveal the seasons, control the world, destroy vows, engage in righteous deeds, and overcome all sins with your praise. I invoke Dadhika, Agni, Usha, Brihaspati, Tejaswi, Surya, both Ashwini Kumaras, Bhava, Vasu, Rudra, and all the Adityas in this yagya ritual.

Sukta 21 , attributed to Rishi Kushiki Gathi and dedicated to the deity Agni, composed in the Trishtuk and Vadina meters, the verses implore Agni to deliver the yagya to the gods and partake in the sacrifices. Agni is the divine form that sits in the yagya, consuming the life-giving butter. The drops of ghee dripping in the yagya are meant for Agni and the gods, and the supplicant requests Agni to provide them with the best wealth. Agni, intelligent and worthy of study, is honored with the dripping ghee, being the best among sages and shining brightly. The verses ask Agni to protect the yagya. Agnidev, omnipotent and always in motion, is irrigated by the drops of Havi in the form of affection, praised by intelligent people for his brightness and intelligence. The verses express utmost love for Agni, requesting him to accept the sacrifices and distribute the drops of Havi to the gods.

Sukta 22 , attributed to Rishi Kushiki Gathi and dedicated to the deities Purushya and Agni, composed in the Trishtuk and Anushtuk meters, the verses honor Agni. They recall the time when Indra, desiring Soma, kept the discarded Soma in his stomach. Agnidev, you are omniscient and should consume the Veegvati Havi like that horse. All the creatures of the world praise you. Agni, you are worthy of worship. Your light pervades the earth, medicine, and water, and your radiance fills space, as deep as the ocean and as bright as the sun, wonderful for humans. You flow like celestial water and organize the life-ghost gods. To inspire the water in the world above the Sun or in space, you are the one. Reach the battlefield accompanied by weapons and provide us with food that will help us suppress our enemies and remain healthy. To those who praise you, you give a land full of inspiring and virtuous wealth. Grant us a son who will increase our lineage and is capable of procreating children. This favor should be towards us.

Sukta 23 , attributed to Rishi Devshraya Devvasichat Bharto and dedicated to the deity Agni, composed in the Trishtuk and Satovrahati meters, the verses honor Agni, born from friction and established in the house of the host. Agni is omniscient, the complete performer of the yagya, the wise god, and the destroyer of dense forests, ageless and wearing nectar in the yagya. The sons of Bharat manifested this rich Agnidev through Arani-Manthan. Agni, you look towards us with abundant wealth and provide us with food every day. This ancient, beautiful fire god is born from ten fingers. Devashrava praises the divine Agnidev, born from Arani and appearing from the air, influenced by those who worship fire. For the sake of attaining the best day, we establish you in the holy place of this earth. May you illuminate with wealth the homes of those living near the three rivers Drishdwati, Apaya, and Saraswati. Agni, you give the earth full of deeds and wealth to those who praise you. Grant us a son who will increase our lineage and is capable of procreating children. Please bestow this favor upon us.

Sukta 24 , attributed to Rishi Vishwamitra and dedicated to the deity Agni, composed in the Anushtuk and Gayatri meters, the verses call upon Agnidev to defeat the enemy leader and troublemakers. Agni is described as invincible, defeating enemies and providing food to his hosts. Agni, who loves the Yagya and is deathless, is lit on the best altar, performing the Yagya well alongside the supplicant. Agni, with bright consciousness, is called upon as the son of strength to sit on the throne. Agni protects the dignity of praises along with all the bright fires in the yagya of those who worship him. He is requested to provide wealth to the person giving the sacrifice, bless them with children, and increase their lineage.

Sukta 25 , attributed to Rishi Vishwamitra and dedicated to the deities Agni and Indragni, composed in the Virat meter, the verses praise Agni as a wonderful, omniscient entity, the son of heaven and earth, endowed with consciousness. Agni performs separate sacrificial rituals in the deva-yajna, being intelligent, empowering, and equipped to offer sacrifices to the gods with food of various kinds. Agni is called upon to bring the gods to the sacrifice. As the omniscient lord of the world, endowed with radiant power and food, Agnideva illuminates the heavens and the earth, protecting the sacrifice alongside Indra. Agni is invited to the house of the one who filters and offers the moon for the sake of the moon. The water-born fire-god is all-knowing and eternal, reputed in space, a shelter of water, and adorns the creatures in his care.

Sukta 26 , attributed to Rishi Vishwamitra Atma and dedicated to the deities Vasharnar and Marut, composed in the Jagti and Trishtuk meters, the verses describe the Kaushik-jana invoking Vaishvanar Agni while collecting havi with the desire for wealth. Agni, who follows the path of truth and knows about heaven, is the giver of yagya results and reaches the place of sacrifice in his chariot. The bright-complexioned Vaishvanar is invoked in the form of electricity for shelter. Agni, compared to a high-pitched foal raised under its mother's shelter, is called the living being among the gods, asked to bestow the best horses, men, and great wealth. Agni, the learned, omniscient, and inviolable, joins the desert and earth vehicles, making the desert full of water and vibrating clouds like mountains. The dependents of Agni attract the Marut Sagar, and excellent shelter of the Maruts is wished for. Like a lion in the form of rain, Agni roars and provides water to the famous desert.

The glory of Agni and the strength of the desert are prayed for. Horse-drawn deserts with dot symbols are obtained for the yagya for the sake of havi along with indestructible wealth. Agni, brilliant by birth, expresses his form vocally, with light as his eye, containing nectar. Full of various life forms and measuring space, Agni's strings do not decay, symbolizing the real sacrifice. Agnidev, who knew the beautiful light by heart, made himself powerful by taking the forms of fire, air, and sun, seeing the sky and the earth. The sky and earth are asked to complete the fire, intact like a sharp cloud, flowing, intelligent, nurturing, capable of communication, and placed in the lap of parents, embodying the form of truth.

Sukta 27 , attributed to Rishi Vishwamitra and dedicated to the deities Ritvo and Agni, composed in the Gayatri meter, the verses address Ritvijo, the gods blessed with happiness who accept offerings and make the host happy for various durations. The host gods bestow their blessings. The hymn worships Agnidev, the wise and wealthy one who completes the yagya. Agni, being luminous, prepares Havya, serving and saving worshippers from sin. With flaming hair appearing during the yagya, Agni, the purifier, asks for desired results. Worshipped mentally with purifying ghee, Agni carries the sacrificial offering.

The Ritvijas destroy obstacles in the yagya, extending a hook while worshipping Agnidev with stotras for shelter. The deathless, light-filled Agnidev inspires everyone in the yagya ritual and leads the yagya with cooperation. Powerful in war and established at the time of yagya, Agni performs and guides yagya works. Carried by Daksha-putri (Earth) like a father, Agnidev is worthy of being chosen, and Daksha's daughter Ila bears him. Agni, the regulator of the world and inspirer of water, is properly lit by knowledgeable people through havi for performing the yagya. Praised for not letting man go without food, Agni is worthy of worship, destroying darkness upon ignition. Agnidev, who carries offerings like a horse and showers wishes, is ignited and worshipped. Agni showers wishes, irrigates with ghrit, and enlightens the worshippers, being bright and great.

Sukta 28 , attributed to Rishi Vishwamitra and dedicated to the deity Agni, composed in the Gayatri, Ushnik, Trishtuk, and Jagat meters, the verses honor Agni, who is bright since birth. The hymn expresses that strength is derived from Agni's hymn as he consumes the Purodash and Havya in the morning. Agni, though very young, consumes the matured and perfected Purodash offered for his sake. At the end of the day, Agni is called upon to consume the Purodash in the best manner, being the son of strength and engaged in sacrificial work. Agni, the scientist, accepts Purodash in the middle of the month, ensuring the Adhvaryugans do not destroy his sacrificial offerings. The mighty fire god wishes for the Purodash to be given in the third Sawan, presenting the glorious Chetanya Soma before the gods with praise. Scientist Agnidev accepts the offering in the form of Purodash at the end of the day.

Sukta 29 , attributed to Rishi Vishwamitra and dedicated to the deity Agni, composed in the Anushtuk, Trishtuk, and Jagati meters, the verses celebrate Agni, born in the fire for the sacrifice of the Bolahava, who protects the ritual. Agni is manifested through staging, established at the top like the womb of Syo, always ready in his work, worshipped every day. The knowledgeable Ani and Arani manifest Agni, showering wishes of getting pregnant, with carrier properties. Ilaputra, of the best light, is born from Agni Arani. Agnidev is worshipped for sisterning the Viyas in Nabhisya Uttar Yedi, leading mankind in deeds of fame, and representing the side of fire. Agni is the first worshipper, revealed in the beginning, victorious in work, knowledgeable, and praised by the knowledgeable.

Agni, produced by two pieces of wood, is graceful and powerful, unstoppable like the chariots of Adhani Kumars. As soon as Agni is generated, one becomes victorious in their work, beautified by the fruits of deeds. The omniscient Agnidev is appointed by the gods to carry the oblation in the yajna ceremony, sitting in his place as the performer of the yagya, the vehicle to know everyone, and the protector of the gods. Agni is worshipped through Havi, giving permission to sacrifices, expressing desires, becoming stronger in battle, conquering enemy armies. The gods conquered demons with Agni's help. Agni is manifest in the wood bud, adorned and praised.

Tanunpat is the fire which never becomes widespread, visible as Asuras and Narashans, spreading radiance in space as Matarishwas, like air when they appear. Agni is born from knowledge and churning, honored in the best place, completing the yagya without hindrance. Worshipped for those who wish for the gods, Maranadharma Ritvijas revealed Agni, inexhaustible, indestructible, steadfast, liberating from sin, with joyful sounds from ten sisterly fingers. Ancient Agni, decorated in the yagya performed by Sapta Hotas, plays in the forests, always conscious, born from the midst of Asura. Kaushik Rishis, first born by Brahma, fought against enemies like Marudgan, knowing the entire world, lighting the fire in their planet, offering oblations, and praising Agni. Agni, the intelligent and omniscient, completes the yagya, offering sacrifices to the gods, praised daily, and considering Soma as accomplished.

Sukta 30 , attributed to Rishi Vishwamitra and dedicated to the deity Indra, composed in the Trishtuk metre, Hey Indra! The devotees of Yoga Charan wish to praise you, scrutinizing every aspect of your being, and offering sacrifices while bearing the pain of enemies. You hold the highest status in the world. O green-complexioned one, come quickly to our havan, where stones crush Soma, and milk thoughts or showering desires are prepared for you. O wish-granting Indra, your crest is worth seeing, victorious and fearsome in battle, performing various deeds with the help of Guru and Bharti. You destroyed otherworldly evil single-handedly, making the sky, earth, and mountains immovable. Despite being hurt by many, you bravely defeated Sutra and stabilized the gods, making the sky and earth suffer in your glory.

Hey Indra! May your chariot come quickly against the enemy, and may your thunderbolt work to kill them. Destroy the enemies who confront you and those who flee. Make the world a place of sacrifice, for only you possess such power. You bring prosperity to those you bless, providing household animals, gold, and happiness. Your grace brings immense power to donate food, and you are praised by many. You disintegrate the roaring circles that hinder you and paralyze Vritra with your might. You established the earth and held the sky and space firm, ensuring the earth receives water through your inspiration. Even before your thunderbolt struck, the cloud of water broke apart, simplifying the way to extract the cow from the water form.

Indra separated the sky and earth, filling them with food and wealth. As a charioteer, you present horses yoked to the chariot, supporting us. Surya moves in luminous directions, inspired by you, and at dawn, the world eagerly awaits the brilliant sun. The dawn period ends with people performing yagya rituals, attributing many good deeds to you, Indra. You used quality water in rivers, putting tasty food like curd and ghee in cows, which roam like pregnant cows with milk. Despite enemy obstacles, you grant desired results to Yajna performers, dealing with slow-moving, weapon-wielding enemies.

Hey Indra! Destroy the enemy weapons causing severe pain and punch holes in their defenses. Engage in yajna-karma after defeating the demons, root out their dynasty, and clear away their remnants. Use painful weapons on those who hate Yagya. As the nourisher of the world, make us full of horses, grant us immortality, and ensure our growth with great food and wealth. Bring us wealth, fulfilling our wishes for cows, horses, and delicious fruits, and may we gain fame and heaven. Indra, you are praised among the best ministers for your good deeds and prosperity. Provide us with consumable perfume, and you live pervading the sky, a Guru from the hair of truth. You are enthusiastic in battle, rich, opulent, and brave, killing formidable enemies and conquering the rich. We seek your shelter and blessings.

Sukta 31, attributed to Rishi Kushik, Vishwamitra and dedicated to the deity Indra, composed in the Trishtuk metre,

Hey Indra! The devotees of Yoga Charan wish to praise you, scrutinizing every aspect of your being and offering sacrifices while bearing the pain of enemies. You hold the highest status in the world. O green-complexioned one, come quickly to our havan, where stones crush Soma, and milk thoughts or showering desires are prepared for you. O wish-granting Indra, your crest is worth seeing, victorious and fearsome in battle, performing various deeds with the help of Guru and Bharti. You destroyed otherworldly evil single-handedly, making the sky, earth, and mountains immovable.

Despite being hurt by many, you bravely defeated Sutra and stabilized the gods, making the sky and earth suffer in your glory.

The person without a son marries his daughter to a suitable man, attaining Daihitra and surviving on the faith of conceiving a daughter. However, the daughter does not bring wealth like a son, who performs the last rites while the daughter commands respect. Indra, you are brilliant, manifesting powerful rays of trembling fire for our yagya, with their wombs in the form of water and their great birth as medicine. These Soma-inspired rays have great importance. During the battle with Vritra, Marudgayan met Indra. Desert people understood that the great brightness of the sun guides even under darkness. The dawns considered Indra to be the sun, reaching before him, making Indra the master of all rays. Strengthened by the seven wise Angiras, Indra found the cows stopped on the mountain and retrieved them through the path of sacrifice. Impressed by Angiras' worship, Indra reached the mountain.

When Sarma reached the broken gate of the mountain, Indra provided her with abundant food and wealth, recognizing the sound of well-footed cows. Endowed with great wisdom, Indra reached there with a friendly disposition toward the Ogras. The mountain revealed its hidden wealth for the great warrior Indra, who, with the help of young Maruts, destroyed the enemy. The Angiras worshiped Indra, who, foremost among the opulent, knowledgeable about rich things, killed Shushna, desired Godhan, and bestowed respect while protecting from sin.

Intelligent people should engage in performing Yagya, striving for immortality through stotras, as Yagya is a great shelter. The Angira dynasty acquired cow wealth, made the body strong, and spread joyous sound across the sky and earth. Indra, the king of heaven, gave birth to men and sang with the sun in the morning, killing Vritra with the deserters. He alone is worshipped, donating cows for the Yagya and providing delicious milk. The Angiras made a clean, bright place for Indra, who, through good deeds, established Indra in heaven with a pillar between sky and earth. Even if combined speech cannot describe the sky and earth, it coherently praises Indra, whose powers are powerful.

Hey Indra! We appeal to your great friendship and power. We will offer you heartfelt friendship, hymns, and oblations. Make us wise and protect us. Indra kindly gave land and wealth to his friends, manifesting the desert, sun, dawn, earth, and fire. Indra's calm nature revealed fast, consistent water, purifying Soma, and fighting with fire, sun, and wind. He engages the world in his works, providing happiness. The desert people, friendly like Riju, take shelter of Indra's power. Indra, the destroyer of trees, showering desires, providing food and drink, is praised, great, and eager to go to the Yagya. He reaches us with welfare-bearing friendship and great shelter.

Hey Indra! Ancient and worshipped like Angiras, you are praised for destroying the enemies of the gods and providing usable money. Your brightness fills our great shore with water. Equipped with a chariot, you protect us from enemies and give strength to conquer cows. Those who destroy Vritra give cows and kill demons disrupting the Yagya, stopping untruths with your light. Hey Indra! Provider of food benefits, increasing joy in war, rich in wealth, the best among the wealthy, listening to praises, formidable, killing enemies in battle, and conquering wealth, we seek your shelter.

Sukta 32, attributed to Rishi Vishwamitra and dedicated to the deity Indra, composed in the Trishtuk metre,

O Indra! Master of Soma, drink this Soma in the middle season, which is very dear to you. Full of wealth and Soma, separate your horses from the chariot, fill their faces with the best grass, and make them happy in this yagya. Hey Indra! Drink the new Soma fortified with milk, presented for your happiness. Drink Soma with Marudgan and Rudras until satisfied. Those Marudganas who dry up the enemy and increase your strength also enhance your fighting power by praising you. Wearing the Vajra and adorned with a headgear, drink Soma along with the Rudras in the main Svana. Vritra believed no one knew his secret, but with the Maruts' help and inspiration, you learned Vritra's secret. Encouraged by the Marudganas, you, like Manu Yagya, become permanent by accepting my Yagya. Drink Soma for strength, come with Marudgan, the vessel of Yagya, and release the water from the space.

Hey Indra! You cover the bright waters and killed the sleeping Vritra in battle, releasing water like a horse in battle. We worship Indra, blessed with growth through sacrifice, indestructible, great, eternally young, and worthy of praise. Even the mighty sky and earth cannot limit Indra's glory. All the gods together could not hinder Indra's great deeds. He is the sustainer of sky, earth, and space, revealing the Sun and the Dawn. Your wish and glory are paramount. Drink Soma and be powerful, for no one in the heavenly world can stop your shine. Born in the highest world, you drank Soma for happiness, spreading across the sky and earth, becoming the creator of the Rampurna creation.

Indra, you have created many arrogant people who stop the water and destroyed their ego. When you walk with the earth hidden in your waist, even heaven cannot match your glory. Our sacrifice increases you, and the work in which Soma Sanskar is performed is dear to you. You are worthy of yagya, protecting your host for the sacrificial fire, making your 'Vajra' powerful for killing ego. The Lord inspired by ancient, medieval, and new stotras is invoked by the host for new wealth. Whenever I wish to praise Indra, I start praising him, asking Indra to spare us from sorrow. Just as people on both banks of a river call the boatman, our maternal family calls Indra. The sound of Swahaakar is made for the paan, and I water Soma to please Indra. Beautifully flavored Soma goes before Indra, pleasing him. Indra, called upon by many, cannot be stopped by the rough sea. Even the sub-sea around the ocean cannot save you, for you removed Mahabali Vritra at your friends' request. Indra, who benefits from food, is full of enthusiasm, blessed with wealth and opulence, best among heroes, who listens to praise, destroys the enemy in fierce battles, and conquers wealth, I call upon you for shelter.

Sukta 33 , attributed to Rishi Vishwamitra and dedicated to the deity Nadhya (River) , Indra, composed in the Anushtuk andTrishtuk meters, the verses celebrate the Vipasha and Shutudri rivers. These rivers, flowing with water and emerging from the eastern part, desire to meet the sea, becoming competitive like horses and adorned with the speed of two cows moving towards the ocean. Indra inspires these rivers, guiding them like two charioteers, as they move with flowing waves towards each other. The Sindhu river is likened to a mother, while the Vipasha river is described as fortunate, moving towards shelter like cows yearning for their calves. These rivers, filled with water, irrigate the regions created by God and their movement never stops, achieving harmony with the land they nourish.

O rivers full of water, pause for a moment to listen to my invocation as I, the son of Kushik, Vishwamitra, praise you to attain happiness and fulfill my desires. Indra, the King of Heaven, wielding the thunderbolt, struck the horse and drove Vṛtrāsura away from the river, clearing the path for both rivers. Indra's brilliant arms inspire the world and his heroic act of killing Vritra is celebrated. Indra searched out those creating obstacles and killed them with thunderbolts, allowing the waters to flow freely. The rivers, addressed with great reverence, are asked to remember their promise and continue to be worshipped with stotras. As sisters, the rivers are praised by Vishwamitra, who has come from afar with a winning horse. The rivers are asked to lower their levels to allow passage, flowing only up to half of the chariot wheel. The rivers listen and bow down like a mother to her son or a wife to her husband, showing their respect and granting passage.

The Indians of the Bharata lineage, desiring to cross the rivers, are permitted to do so, inspired by Indra. Vishwamitra praises the rivers, acknowledging their importance in performing yajnas. Scholars praised the rivers well, recognizing their role in providing food and wealth. The rivers, full of abundance, move swiftly, filling even the small rivers with water. Vipasha and Shutudri, who do good without sin, are described as flowing in such a way that their waves remain in control, not going too high, and allowing for safe passage.

Sukta 34 , attributed to Rishi Vishwamitra and dedicated to the deity Indra, composed in the Trishtuk meter, the verses celebrate Indra's conquests and his power. Indra, worshipable and powerful, is adorned and praised for the sake of food and prosperity. He is foremost among both gods and humans. Indra, famous for his deeds, cured Vritra and stopped enemy attacks, killing the illusionists and revealing beautiful cows. Indra supports the Angiras, reveals the day, and defeats armies, illuminating the sun like a flag for humanity, achieving immense glory in fierce battles. He enters obstacles and enemy forces, increasing wealth and consciousness for those who praise him, bringing light to Usha.

Devotees chant the great deeds of Indra, who crushes the powerful with his might and cunning. Indra, the lord of gods and giver of strength to humans, obtains wealth in great battles and distributes it to his praisers. Learned praisers sing Indra's praises through mantras in the host's house, bringing happiness when Indra, the all-conqueror, rejoices. Indra, the holder of earth, sky, and space, grants gifts like horses, the sun, cows, gems, and gold, always protecting the Aryans by defeating sinners. Indra creates the day, provides medicines, space, and plants, and destroys enemies by clearing clouds. He kills any opponent appearing before him. Hey Indra! You are capable of securing food, advancing in battle with enthusiasm, rich in wealth, the best among heroes, and attentive to praises. You win wealth by destroying enemies in battle through your aggressive deeds. We appeal to you for shelter and wealth.

Sukta 35 , Rishi Vishwamitra praises Indra, the deity associated with this hymn, composed in the Trishtuk meter. The hymn vividly describes Indra's chariot adorned with green horses, likening Indra's anticipation for his horses to that of Vayu, who eagerly awaits his steeds. The worshippers invoke Indra to arrive swiftly, tying two horses to his chariot to expedite his journey, and seek his protection from enemies, acknowledging him as the bestower of desires and lord of food grains. They chant mantras to summon Indra's renowned hundred horses, asking him to approach the Soma offering with his brilliance. They promise joy to Indra's mighty horses, ensuring him of a perfectly prepared Soma. The hymn emphasizes the importance of Soma, urging Indra to drink it with a joyful heart, and highlights the ritual preparations, including the spreading of flowers and presenting grains for Indra's horses. Scholars praise Indra, the lord of wishes, and offer detailed havis. Indra is asked to consume the Soma, sweetened by Adhvaryu, stone, and water, and to drink it with delight, accompanied by the Marudgans. The worshippers call upon Indra, the embodiment of wealth and valor, the destroyer of enemies, and the conqueror of wealth, seeking his shelter and blessings.

Sukta 36 , attributed to Rishi Vishwamitra and Gor Angiras in the Trishtuk meter, the hymns are dedicated to Indra. The hymn begins by inviting Indra to accept the Soma, renowned for its potency and ability to enhance divine works through offerings. Indra, celebrated for his mighty deeds, is called to partake in the Soma, which has been meticulously prepared and sanctified, invoking his strength and luminescence. The worshippers remind Indra of the ancient times when Soma was offered to him, emphasizing its divine efficacy. They urge Indra to drink this Soma, prepared anew, and become powerful once more.

Indra's prowess in battle, his capability to challenge and defeat enemies, and his universal glory are extolled. When strengthened by Soma, Indra's power is unparalleled, and even the heavens and the earth cannot contain him. Known for his generosity and valor, Indra's association with the hymn enhances the success of the yajna, bringing forth the milk-giving cows. The hymn further illustrates the flow of rivers towards the ocean, likening it to Indra's journey towards the well-prepared Soma. The Adhvaryugan purify and sweeten the Soma, symbolizing the meticulous preparation for Indra. Indra's consumption of Soma is linked to his victorious feats, such as vanquishing Vritra and expelling demons. The worshippers seek Indra's blessings for wealth, strength, long life, and brave progeny, acknowledging him as the master of wealth and the provider of good fortune. They invoke Indra's enthusiasm and valor in battles for food gain, recognizing him as a formidable hero, the destroyer of enemies, and the conqueror of wealth.

Sukta 37 , attributed to Rishis Vishwamitra and Gor Angiras in the Trishtuk meter, the hymns are dedicated to Indra, the deity renowned for his heroic deeds. The worshippers invoke Indra, seeking his assistance in acquiring wealth and defeating enemies, specifically referencing his triumph over Vritra. They call upon Indra, the one who performs a hundred deeds, to appear before them, bringing joy and inspiration.

Indra is celebrated for his virtuous actions, and the worshippers sing his praises in the battlefield, confident in his ability to vanquish arrogant foes. Indra's boundless brilliance and mastery over humans are extolled, and many have invoked him to destroy enemies and gain wealth. The hymn continues to praise Indra's capability in defeating adversaries in battle, particularly those who challenge in wealth and bravery. The worshippers urge Indra, the performer of many deeds, to drink the powerful, illuminating Soma that dispels nightmares and enhances his strength in all senses. They beseech Indra to come to them, whether near or far, carrying his thunderbolt, and accept their yajna from his divine abode.

Sukta 38, attributed to the sages Prajapati and Vishwamitra in the Trishtup meter, the hymns are dedicated to Indra. The worshippers, likening themselves to Tvashta, chant praises for Indra, comparing their dedication to the might and action of a powerful horse. They seek to increase their intelligence and desire to witness the scholars who have ascended to heaven.

Indra is asked to inquire about these scholars who, through self-control and pious activities, earned their place in heaven. The praises for Indra in this yajna grow with the speed of the mind. The wise men, while performing noble deeds, decorated the earth and sky to obtain water, establishing a balance between them and creating space.

Indra, seated in his chariot, is adorned by all intelligent beings. Known for his good nature and strange fame, Indra assumes the form of the world and is immersed in immortality. The hymn celebrates the ancient and supreme Indra, the shower of desires, who created the waters to quench his thirst. Indra and Varuna, the grandsons of heaven, are praised for their auspicious deeds. The worshippers call upon Indra and Varuna to beautify the three broad forests in the yajna. They recall seeing the Gandharvas with distinct hair like the wind during a previous yajna attended by Indra. Those who drink the sacred juice from cows for Indra's sake and perform noble deeds dedicate their works to him.

The hymn also acknowledges the golden light of the sun, limitless and embracing the sky and earth like a mother. Indra and Varuna are implored to protect those who recite ancient hymns and to guard them from all sides. Indra's speech, pure and stable-minded, is praised by all intelligent people. Finally, Indra is invoked to grow enthusiastically in battles for food and profit. Full of wealth and opulence, best among leaders, fierce, and a conqueror of enemies in the battlefield, Indra is called upon for shelter and protection.

Sukta 39 , attributed to the sage Vishvamitra in the Trishtup meter, the hymns are dedicated to Indra. The worshippers acknowledge Indra as the master of the world, invoking him with hymns that arise from the heart and are crafted by praisers, beseeching him to accept their offerings made during the yajna. Indra is celebrated for the eternal and bright praise that originates even before sunrise, a tradition handed down from ancestors and believed to bring welfare.

The hymn references Ashvidvaya, with his praises sung joyously at the break of day to dispel darkness. It is noted that no one criticizes their ancestors who fought valiantly for cattle, and it was Indra, glorious and illustrious, who provided the Angiras with rich cattle. When Angiras' friend Indra climbed the mountain on his knees in search of cattle, he revealed the sun hidden in the darkness. Indra is credited with first sprinkling sweet juice on the milk-giving cows, then bringing forth a cow complete with feet and hoofs. He captured the deceptive demon hidden in the space of the cave with his right hand. Born from the womb of night, Indra assumed light, and the worshippers express their desire to live in a sin-free and fearless place. They implore self-reliant Indra to accept their praise.

The hymn further calls for the sun to illuminate the sky and earth for the yajna, emphasizing a desire to stay away from sin. The Basu-gods are also praised, and there is a plea for Indra to grant wealth to the donor. The worshippers extol Indra for his enthusiastic pursuit in the war for food gain, his wealth and opulence, his leadership, his receptiveness to praise, his prowess in killing enemies in fierce battles, and his ability to conquer wealth. They appeal to Indra for shelter and protection.

Sukta 40 , attributed to the sage Vishvamitra in the Gayatri meter, the hymns are dedicated to Indra. The worshippers invoke Indra, known for fulfilling wishes, to partake in the sanctified Soma. They invite him to drink the sweet Soma mixed with pleasant food. Praised by many, Indra is asked to irrigate his stomach with the filtered Soma, which enhances the intellect and satisfies desires. Indra, as the lord of the Maruts, is implored to increase the sacrifice along with all the worthy deities. The emancipated Soma, filled with radiance and offered with a happy heart, is entering Indra's stomach, and he is encouraged to wear it. The accomplished Soma is described as suitable for everyone and extremely bright, residing with Indra in heaven.

The hymn continues to praise Indra, highlighting how he becomes happy with the stream of Soma worthy of invocation. The well-known Soma is offered to Indra, and the food obtained for growth is attributed to his benevolence. Indra grows by drinking the Soma, which is rich in soma and havis, presented by those performing sacrifices to the gods. Indra is reminded of a vow he once violated, and the worshippers call him to come, whether near or far, and accept their praise. They request Indra, brought from far, near, and in Madhya Pradesh, to come to the yajna to drink Soma, emphasizing his vital role in their rituals and offerings.

Sukta 41, attributed to the sage Vishvamitra in the Gayatri meter, the hymns are dedicated to Indra, also known as Vajrin. The worshippers call upon Indra, asking him to come to their yajna with his horse to drink Soma. Indra is summoned by Ritwik Hota, who is present in the yajna, with flowers spread and stones prepared for Soma Siddhi during the morning Sawan. Indra is urged to come and consume the purodash offered by the worshippers. Known as the slayer of Vritra and worthy of praise, Indra is asked to immerse himself in the praises chanted during the Savan-Traya. The hymn poetically compares the praises to cows licking their calves, emphasizing the devotion and reverence of the worshippers.

Indra is also called upon to strengthen his body with Soma for the sake of giving wealth, ensuring that those who praise him are never criticized. The worshippers express their fervent wishes and praises, seeking Indra's protection so they can accept the sacrifice. Indra, who loves his horses, is requested to unleash them and come to the yajna, deriving pleasure from the Soma. The hymn concludes with a vivid image of Indra's large-haired, sweat-laden horses bringing him to the seat of Kush, which brings him happiness, in a chariot that also gives joy. The worshippers' devotion and admiration for Indra are evident throughout the hymn, highlighting his strength, valor, and generosity.

Sukta 42, attributed to the sage Vishvamitra in the Gayatri meter, the hymns are dedicated to Indra. The worshippers invite Indra to partake in their Soma, which is mixed with milk and renowned for its quality. They call upon Indra to come near with his chariot and horse. The Soma, crushed and filtered from stones, is placed on Kush for Indra to drink in sufficient quantity and attain satisfaction.

The hymns are filled with praises for Indra, invoking him for Soma Paan and urging their speech to reach the yajna's place to attain Indra's proximity. Through laudatory hymns, they repeatedly invoke Indra to come to their yajna and accept the Soma offering. Indra, known for his numerous deeds, is asked to carry the yajna sanskar Soma in his stomach and provide food and wealth for the worshippers.

Indra is recognized as a scholar and a formidable warrior in the battlefield, capable of defeating enemies and conquering their wealth, prompting the worshippers to seek prosperity from him. They ask Indra to come to their yajna and drink the Soma prepared by mixing it with milk and other ingredients. The well-cultured Soma is placed in Indra's stomach to satisfy his mind and affirm their devotion.Indra, being ancient, is revered by the sages of the Kaushikvanshi lineage. They seek protection and appeal to Indra with beautiful praises, desiring him to drink the well-cultured Soma and bestow his blessings upon them.

Sukta 43 , attributed to the sage Vishvamitra in the Trishtup meter, the hymns are dedicated to Indra. The worshippers call upon Indra to approach them with his yoked chariot, specifically prepared for him to partake in the ancient Soma. They invite Indra to release his beloved horse near the wells and join the Ritwikgan for Soma Paan. Indra, the luminous lord, is urged to cross the ancient humans and come to the yajna with his horse to drink the nectar, paying heed to their prayers. The praises of friendship, uttered by the stothas, are meant to summon him. Indra is called to the yajna that promises to increase their food supply, accompanied by Vritta and Havi containing food, and to drink the Soma.

The worshippers highlight the beauty and capability of Indra's horses, which assist in reaching the place of the yajna, akin to friends. They praise Indra while he enjoys the Soma mixed with roasted rice, asking for his strength to protect humans, control over all things, and the ability to drink Soma and gain ever-lasting wealth. Indra's great horse, harnessed to the chariot, is expected to bring him before the worshippers. The horses, guided by Indra, are known for destroying enemies and moving efficiently in the directions of battle. Indra is recognized as the giver of desired fruits and the drinker of perfectly nourished Soma. The worshippers mention Shyena bringing Soma to Indra, whose joy from the Soma helps him destroy hostile forces.

Finally, Indra is asked to grow enthusiastically in the intellect benefiting from food, to be blessed with wealth and opulence, to be the best among heroes, and to listen to praises. The hymn concludes with a plea for Indra to win wealth by defeating enemies in fierce battles and to offer them shelter and protection.

Sukta 44 , attributed to the sage Vishvamitra in the Vrahati meter, the hymns are dedicated to Indra. The worshippers offer Indra Soma, which has been prepared by crushing it with stones, noting its pleasant and invigorating properties. They invite Indra to come before them on a chariot with horses to partake in this Soma.

Indra is praised for making the sun shine and fulfilling the desires associated with Soma. Known for his intelligence and awareness of their wishes, Indra is acknowledged for increasing their wealth by providing the desired results. Indra's influence is described as holding the sun world with green rays and the earth made green with medicinal plants. He roams between the green-colored sky and earth, feeding his horses and traversing the realms.Indra, the granter of desired results, is said to illuminate all worlds upon his birth. Riding green horses and wielding green weapons, Indra raises his thunderbolt to destroy enemies. The hymn recounts how Indra revealed Soma mixed with bright milk and produced by stones. He took his horses and retrieved the cows stolen by the Panis, showcasing his strength and benevolence.

Sukta 45 , attributed to the sage Vishvamitra in the Vrahati meter, the hymns are dedicated to Indra. The worshippers invoke Indra, comparing his hairy, peacock-like horses to those arriving at the place of sacrifice. They ask Indra to avoid being ensnared by any obstacles, like a hunter traps birds, and to overcome all barriers to reach their yajna swiftly, akin to a traveler crossing a desert.

Indra, renowned for killing Vritra and releasing the waters by tearing the clouds, is celebrated for destroying enemy cities and positioning his chariot before the worshippers. He is also praised for defeating powerful foes. The hymn likens Indra's nourishing of the yajna rituals to sages and cowherds feeding their cows with barley, and to the filling of the deep ocean with water. The cultivated Soma in the yajna is seen as attaining Indra, just as cows attain grass and small rivers merge into larger bodies of water. The worshippers beseech Indra to provide them with wealth, likening his generosity to a father bestowing riches upon his son. They ask Indra to grant them the fruit of their desires, similar to how bamboo hooks sweep ripe fruits. Indra is acknowledged as the master of the divine world, renowned for his good words and beautiful fame, praised by many. The hymn concludes with a plea for Indra to bestow them with bountiful and beautiful food, emphasizing his own strength and generosity.

Sukta 46 , attributed to the sage Vishvamitra in the Trishtup meter, the hymns are dedicated to Indra. The worshippers extol Indra as the lord of wealth, the giver of desired results, the one excelling in battle, full of strength, and the defeater of immortal enemies. Indra is described as eternally youthful, the wielder of the thunderbolt, eternally famous among people, and of great courage.

Indra is celebrated for his fierce actions, worthiness of worship, and his ability to consume wealth. He intimidates enemies with his strength and is recognized as the sole master of the entire universe. Indra, full of Soma, is described as limitless in every way and stronger than mountains, surpassing even the gods of light. His greatness exceeds the sky, the earth, and the vast space. The hymn continues to praise Indra's seriousness and greatness, noting his fierce nature towards enemies and his all-pervasive presence as a protector of those who praise him. Just as rivers flow towards the sea, the anciently troubled Soma is destined to be transformed and reach Indra. Finally, Indra is likened to a mother conceiving, with the sky and earth bearing Soma in longing for him. Indra, the fulfiller of wishes, is celebrated as the Adhvaryugans drink the same Soma, completing the sacred ritual.

Sukta 47 , attributed to the sage Vishvamitra in the Trishtup meter, the hymns are dedicated to Indra. The worshippers invoke Indra, the companion of the desert and the bestower of fruits, to drink the Soma, which is offered as food to increase happiness and prepare for war. Indra is acknowledged as the ancient Lord of Somas, who waters the Soma in his stomach.

Indra is praised for his bravery, companionship with the gods, and his alliance with the Maruts. As the destroyer of Vritra and knower of all actions, Indra is called upon to drink Soma, vanquish enemies, destroy violent creatures, and provide fearlessness from all sides. Indra, along with his friends, the gods, and the desert people, is asked to drink the consecrated Soma. The Maruts, who aided Indra in battle and accepted him as their lord, are credited with increasing his strength in war, leading to the defeat of enemies.

Indra, full of horses and supported by the Maruts, is recognized for his prowess in slaying demons and combating adversaries for the sake of cows.

The Maruts, wise and ever-pleasing to Indra, are invoked to accompany him in drinking Soma. Indra, full of Maruts, is acknowledged as the one who brings rain, controls, and rules the world. The worshippers praise his tremendous deeds, divinity, and wonder, appealing to him with love to seek his new shelter and protection.

Sukta 48 , attributed to the sage Vishvamitra in the Trishtup meter, the hymns are dedicated to Indra. The worshippers invoke Indra, the protector and collector of Soma offered by Sadya Jaat, desiring him to drink Soma mixed with milk. They recount how, as soon as Indra was born, he quenched his thirst with Soma juice on the mountain. His mother, Aditi, gave him Soma juice before breastfeeding him in the house of his father, Kasyap.

Indra asked his mother for food and saw the milky form of bright Soma in everyone's breast. Desired by the gods for his prowess in defeating enemies, Indra began moving around, displacing and dismembering his foes. He killed Vritra and performed many great deeds of valor. The enemies of Indra found him terrible, as he quickly defeated them with his bravery, taking various forms and controlling evil spirits with his power, drinking Soma from the Chamas.Indra, referred to as Maghavan, is acknowledged for his growth through enthusiasm in the battle for food. Blessed with wealth, opulence, and excellent leadership, he listens to praises and is monstrous in appearance, destroying enemies in fierce battles and winning wealth. The worshippers call upon Indra for shelter and protection, praising his strength and heroic deeds.

Sukta 49 , attributed to the sage Vishvamitra in the Trishtup meter, the hymns are dedicated to Indra. The worshippers call upon those who praise to extol the greatness of Indra. Indra, who saves people and helps them achieve their desires by drinking Soma in the yajna, is revealed by the gods, the sky, and the earth. He is made the master of the world by Brahma, recognized for his good deeds and his ability to destroy sins.

Indra, adorned with brilliance in battle, sits on a chariot with horses, a hero dividing the fighting armies. He is invincible, ruling the armies and, along with the Maruts, weakening the strength of enemies in battle. Indra is extremely powerful, capable of ending the lives of enemies, and is compared to a swift, powerful horse in competitive battle.

Indra enriches the sky and earth with excellent wealth and is likened to a father of praises offered in yajna. He provides aid when called upon and moves as advanced as a chariot moving upward, aided by the desert people. Indra causes darkness at night and makes the sun rise, dividing the results of actions like a rich man divides his wealth.The hymn concludes by praising Indra for his enthusiasm in battle, wealth, opulence, leadership, and ability to listen to praises. Indra is called upon for shelter, recognized as capable of destroying enemies in battle and winning wealth, and invoked for protection and support.

Sukta 50 , attributed to the sage Vishvamitra in the Trishtup meter, the hymns are dedicated to Indra. The worshippers invite Indra to their sacrifice to drink the prepared Soma, which is meant for him and is capable of vanquishing those who cause trouble. Accompanied by the Maruts, Indra is showered with flowers during the yajna, and he is satisfied with the food and offerings presented to him.

To bring Indra to the yajna, the worshippers add horses to the chariot, calling upon him to partake in the perfectly prepared Soma Rasa. Indra, praised and pleased with the offerings, consumes the Soma mixed with milk to attain the best element. The worshippers ask Indra, full of Soma, to drink it happily and provide cows to those who praise him for the success of the yajna.The hymn expresses a desire for fulfillment through cows, horses, and excellent wealth, seeking fame through prosperity. Indra is praised by Kaushiko, a man of action desiring heavenly happiness, through mantras. Indra, obtaining food and increasing wealth and opulence through enthusiasm in war, is recognized for his excellent leadership and as a listener of praises. The worshippers call upon Indra, a budding figure who destroys enemies and accumulates wealth with restraint, to seek his shelter and protection.

Sukta 51 , attributed to the sage Vishvamitra in the Trishtup, Gayatri, and Jagti meters, the hymns are dedicated to Indra. The worshippers chant hymns to Indra, the protector of human beings, who grants them their desires and is constantly increasing in wealth, clothes, and opulence. Indra is often called upon by those who praise him and is noted for his extreme beauty and admirable qualities.

Indra is celebrated for performing hundreds of deeds, destroying deserts, pioneering oceans, giving food, and demolishing enemy cities. He travels quickly for war, splits clouds to make water fall, and defeats enemies to attain heaven. The worshippers hope that Indra will receive their words of praise.In the battlefield, everyone praises Indra, who destroys enemy armies and wholeheartedly respects praises. Those performing the yajna attain ecstasy by drinking Soma in the host's house. Vishvamitra calls upon others to praise Indra, who destroys enemies and brings the desert with him.

Indra, mighty and a hero of humans, is praised by Ritvik with good mantras, tormented by demons. Indra goes with force to kill Vritra and is the ancient owner of food. The worshippers bow only to Indra.Indra's discipline is widespread among humans, and because of him, the earth bears great opulence. By Indra's order, Surya protects medicines, food for humans, and trees for consumption. The hymn concludes by acknowledging Indra's widespread influence and his role in maintaining the world's prosperity.

Sukta 51 , attributed to the sage Vishvamitra in the Trishtup, Gayatri, and Jagti meters, the hymns are dedicated to Indra. The worshippers chant hymns to Indra, the protector of human beings, who grants their desires and is continually increasing in praiseworthy wealth, clothes, and opulence. Indra often called upon by those who praise him, is known for his beauty and admirable qualities.

Indra is celebrated for performing hundreds of deeds, destroying deserts, controlling water, pioneering oceans, giving food, destroying enemy cities, traveling swiftly for war, splitting clouds to bring rain, and donating wealth to defeat enemies and attain heaven. The worshippers hope that Indra will receive their words of praise.

Everyone praises Indra in the battlefield for destroying enemy armies and respecting praises wholeheartedly. Those performing the yajna attain ecstasy by drinking Soma in the host's house. Vishvamitra calls upon others to praise Indra, who destroys enemies and brings the desert with him. Indra, mighty and a hero of humans, is praised by Ritvik with good mantras, tormented by demons. Indra goes with force to kill Vritra and is the ancient owner of food. The worshippers bow only to Indra. Indra's discipline is widespread among humans, leading to the earth's great opulence. By Indra's order, Surya protects medicines, food for humans, and trees. Indra, the horseman, accepts the hymns from priests and provides food to those who salute and praise this new offering.

Indra, accompanied by the Maruts, drank Soma in the Yagya of Sharyat and is called to do the same in this yajna. Talented yajna performers serve him through Havi. Indra, with the wish for Soma, is called by ancestors and consecrated for great war by all gods at birth. The worshippers highlight Indra's friendship with the desert, inspired by water, and invite those pleased by Indra to sit and drink Soma in Indra's house. Indra, the God of wealth, is encouraged to drink Soma quickly with his strength and to concentrate on the Annayukta Soma consecrated for him. The Soma is meant to bring joy to Indra, permeate both his kitchens, reside in his body, and strengthen his arms for the sake of wealth.

Sukta 52 , attributed to the sage Vishvamitra in the Trishtup, Gayatri, and Jagti meters, the hymns are dedicated to Indra. The worshippers call upon Indra in the morning to consume their Soma, which is presented with mixed curd, sattu, and purodash. Indra, being mature and adult, is offered purodash worthy of the yajna.

They beseech Indra to accept their offering, comparing it to a loving husband listening to his wife. Indra, renowned since ancient times, is invited to eat their morning purodash and gain prominence in his work. During the middle of the month of Sawan, Indra is called to consume the best purodash containing Gavadi. His servants eagerly praise him, and the stotas, who travel to serve him, worship him with great mantras and accept the offerings.

Indra, blessed with the deity Pusha, is offered milk-mixed sattu and roasted barley for the sake of the horse. The worshippers request him to come with the Maruts and accept the purodash. They recall how Indra killed Vritra and praise his brilliance, asking him to drink the Soma. The Adhvaryus are instructed to present roasted barley for Indra, acknowledging him as great among heroes and the remover of enemies. The daily praises offered for Indra are meant to encourage him in the act of consuming Soma.

Sukta 53 , attributed to the sage Vishvamitra in the Trishtup and Anustup meters, the hymns are dedicated to the deities Parvati and others. The worshippers call upon Indra, asking him to bring food containing good children in his best chariot. They praise his luminosity and invite him to their yajna to consume the offerings, strengthen through sacrifices, and grow through their excellent praises.Indra is requested to live happily at the yajna place for some time, to partake in the blissful Somras, and to be strengthened by the virtues of the yajna. The worshippers liken their devotion to children holding onto their father's elders while feeding them. The Adhyayus are also called to praise Indra and give good advice, with faith in Indra's virtues, and to sit on the Kush-up seat of the host, making their praises attractive to him.

The hymn invokes Indra's journey to the yajna place, asking him to be brought by horses in his chariot. They pray for Indra's blessings as the messenger of fire anointed by them, even from afar. Indra is requested to drink Soma with demigods, brahmanas, sages, men, and eyes, staying to enjoy the offerings before returning home. He is reminded of the fortunate and beautiful woman in his house and to free the horses when he arrives.The hymn acknowledges the Yagya performed by Sudas on behalf of the king, with Medhatithi and other Angiras. Indra is praised as the giver of great wealth and the one who increases food, especially in the Ashwamedha Yagya. Indra's ability to take various forms through Maya and inspire all seasons is celebrated. Despite his influence, he is praised for his consistency in drinking Soma throughout the monsoons.

The hymn concludes with praises for Vishwamitra, who, through his brilliance and advice to Adhvaryu and others, brought about the rays of light and controlled the ocean's speed. Indra's good behavior towards Kaushik during the sacred ritual with Pijvanputra Sudas is highlighted. Scholars and great sages are called to praise the gods during the yajna ceremony, reciting verses like swans and drinking sweet Soma with the gods.

Sukta 54 , attributed to the sages Prajapati, Vishvamitra, and Vachyo, the hymns are dedicated to the Visvedevas and other deities, and chanted in the Trishtup meter. The hymn, praised as a study form of Manthana, is recited repeatedly in the great yajna, with Agnidev (the fire god) filling his house with glory and listening to the stotra, always remaining full of divine splendor and meditating on the praises.

The worshippers address the sky and earth, explaining their ultimate power and expressing a desire for complete enjoyment, invoking the gods to attend human yagyas and attain happiness. They salute the sky and earth, wishing for their actions to be true and capable of completing the great yajna, enjoying the best wealth by serving food. The ancient sages received beneficial wishes from the sky and earth, and the warriors, acknowledging their glory, also salute them.The hymn questions the nature of truth and the paths to the gods, observing the constellations in the celestial world and the sun, the seer of humans, seeing the sky and earth from all sides. The sky and earth, bound in mutual attraction, live together despite being separate, never destroyed, and capable of creation. They manifest all material things, holding the sun, moon, river, sea, mountains, and more, with all life existing within them.

The worshippers praise the sky and earth as the givers of life and caretakers of all, contemplating their antiquity, evolution, and production. They call upon Mitra and other gods with fire-like tongues to listen to their praises, and the sun, the seer of humans, to inspire wealth and accept hymns.Ribhugan, the creator of the beautiful world and the truth-taker, is asked to provide resources for protection, while the powerful Maruts, destroyers of enemies, are called to provide wealth. The hymn acknowledges Vishnu, who covered the world with his power, and Indra, who fills the sky and earth with his might and bestows wealth.

Ashvidhya and Ashwini are invoked for brotherhood and wealth, with the scholars serving Indra and attaining opulence. Indra, invited by many, is asked to accept the hymn for wealth and gain. The ever-moving Sun, Mother Goddess Aditi, and non-violent Varun are called to drive away harmful thoughts and make the house rich with animals and children.Agni, the messenger of the Gods, is asked to equip the worshippers with the means of action and free them from the inclination to commit crimes, with the sky, earth, reservoir, sun, and stars listening to the hymns. The deserts, pleasing the mountain Havi, and Aditi with her sons and gods, are called to provide auspicious wealth. Agni is asked to make the path simple, achieve success in the journey, fill the medicines with sweet juice, and provide wealth-producing food. The hymn concludes with Agni tasting the sacrificial offering, lighting the atra, overcoming hindering enemies, and brightening the days with a determined heart.

Sukta 55 , attributed to the sage Prajapati Vishvamitra in the Trishtup meter, the hymns are dedicated to the Visvedevas and other deities. The hymn begins with a description of the early morning, illuminated by the rising dawn, as the immortal Adityas appear in the sky. As the sun rises, the host attains the proximity of the gods through the performance of yajna, where all the great gods possess the same power.

The worshippers pray to Agnidev, asking him not to destroy them, and recalling the divine powers of their ancestors who should not harm them. They describe how the sun, inspiring the yajna, rises in the sky and the unified great power of all the gods. The hymn continues with the worshippers remembering their ancient hymn to the fire, expressing their desires and the power of fire to grant them.The Prata-Swami Agnidevs are established at all places for the purpose of yajna, rejoicing at the altar and appearing from Araniriya, with their parents being earth and sky. These gods nourish the earth with rain and provide residence, representing the same divine power. Agnidev, associated with ancient medicines, resides within all medicines and produces fruits and flowers without the need for semen donation, demonstrating the equal power of all gods.

The hymn describes how both parents sleep in the west as the sun sets, moving alone in the sky during sunrise with the inspiration of Varun, their equal strength being emphasized. The gods, traveling with the sun, rejoice greatly in the yajna and are the cause of all shortcomings while living on earth. Agnidev, omniscient and present everywhere, appears undefeatable, showcasing the unity of divine power.The hymn further explains how the immense power of the gods is spread between the sun, sky, and earth. The gods, present in fire medicines, show great kindness and care for every living being. The night and bright morning, both emanating from the outer sun, represent the rule of caste and sleep, with the fire-like sun having the greatest power among the gods.

The hymn continues to praise the sky and earth, likening them to mother and daughter, nurturing and sustaining all life with rain and water. The clouds, resembling calves, lick the earth and produce rain, demonstrating the unity of divine power. The hymn concludes by describing day and night, spread between the sky and earth, with the virtuous attaining their paths.The hymn highlights the power of rain, the roaring cloud inspired by Indra, and the significance of seasons in the horse form of Indra, offering sacrifices to the sun. The Tevatas, represented by Tvashta Dev, create and nurture all people, demonstrating their equal power. Indra, bringing together the sky and earth, making animals and birds appear, and being famous for defeating enemies, is celebrated along with his fellow gods for their strength.

The worshippers pray to Indra, the sustainer of the world and master of earth and sky, accompanied by well-wishing friends, to care for bright creatures and provide strength through disease-killing medicines. The hymn emphasizes the unity of divine power, with all gods possessing the same great power.

Sukta 56 , attributed to the sage Prajāpati Veśvāmitra or Vāchya in the Trishtup meter, the hymns are dedicated to Vishvadeva, the deity of the universe. The worshippers pray that the illusory demons arising from the affirmation of the deities should not impede noble deeds and that scholars should persist in their good actions. They invoke the sky and earth to remain obstacle-free along with the people, emphasizing that even the immovable mountains cannot be bent.

The hymn describes the Samvatsara, the bearer of six seasons such as spring, and its rays, which are received by the three stable worlds. Heaven and space are hidden in the cave, with only the earth visible. The

Samvatsara is depicted as providing water through heat, rain, and autumn, nourishing the three worlds like a breast, and holding the qualities of people, heat, rain, and cold. It is full of life force and capable of sustaining the earth by holding water.The Samvatsar Jaitanya is mentioned in relation to all medicines in their form, and the beautiful names of the Adityas are known. The Samvatsara ensures the free-flowing waters of the ocean remain consistent for four months and fixed for eight months. The deities reside in the rivers through triple locks, and Surya, the creator of Lok-Traya, is also the lord of the yajna. The rivers Ila, Saraswati, and Bharti, running from space, should remain in the three savanas of the yajna.

The hymn calls upon the Sun to give strength to everyone, to rise in the sky every day in all three seasons, and to provide beautiful, consumable wealth, animals, heavenly gems, and Gaavadi wealth. The Sun is praised for his brilliance and ability to guide actions that lead to wealth. They pray for blessings from Savita Dev Sawan three times, asking for an increase in wealth from Savitadev, King Mitra, and Varun, the gods of sky, earth, and space. The hymn concludes by acknowledging the three best places, adorned with fire, air, and the sun, and the fast-moving deity blessed with yajna. This deity, who cannot be despised, is called to come to the yajna usthana in all three monsoons, emphasizing the unity and power of the divine.

Sukta 57 , attributed to the sage Vishvāmitra in the Trishtup meter, the hymns are dedicated to the demigods Viśvedevas. The worshippers invoke wise Indra to protect and guide them, much like a cow without a protector. They seek the blessings of both Indra and Agni to receive praise that yields desired fruits.

The hymn praises Indra and the auspicious Mitravarun, who worship and provide desired rain by milking the clouds in space. The gods of the world are called upon to enjoy the sacrificial altar and bestow happiness upon the worshippers. Those who desire Indra's power and knowledge become humble and seek wisdom, while those who crave fruits are drawn towards animals and cattle.In the yajna, the worshippers praise the sky and the earth with sweet words while wearing the stone that gives Soma Abhishav. Agnidev's lovable, worshipable, and delightful radiance rises before mankind. Agni's flame is used to invoke the gods, who are extremely juicy, sweet, and enlightened. The flame calls the deities capable of performing yajna for the protection of the worshippers, offering them Soma-paan.

The hymn concludes with a plea to stunning Agnidev. The worshippers ask for his merciful mind, full of blessings, to help them grow by giving the desired fruits, much like nectar nourishes plants through water. Agni is praised for his intelligence and ability to provide residence, and the worshippers seek wisdom that benefits everyone.

Sukta 58 , attributed to the sage Vishvamitra in the Trishtup meter, the hymns are dedicated to the deity Ashvana. The hymn begins with a depiction of drops of juice in the form of dew at the end of the dawn night, roaming among the ancient fire and Bhaskar, the sun. The day, full of bright light, revolves around the sun, illuminating all. People are eager to praise Ashwini Kumar even before sunrise.

The worshippers call upon Ashwini Kumars, the charioteers of the best and true form, to come to the yajna with their two horses. They seek protection from evildoers and offer havya for Ashwini Kumars, urging them to come. Decorated horses and a beautiful chariot with special wheels are prepared, and the hymn is recited for the Ashwini Kumars, inviting them to listen and follow the praises of ancient wise men.The worshippers respectfully call Ashwini Kumars to the yajna, likening their offering of happiness to a friend. As Aditya-Dev rises after dawn, the worshippers ask Ashwini Kumars to come soon. They express that Ashwini Kumars' words can remove troubles and that they should come through the paths of scholars to kill enemies. The sweet juice-filled Soma is prepared for their sake.

The hymn praises the ancient and necessary friendship of Ashwini Kumars, acknowledging their leadership and beneficial wealth for their family. By drinking the happiness-giving Soma, both the worshippers and Ashwini Kumars find satisfaction. Ashwini Kumars are described as endowed with all appropriate abilities, eternally young, and givers of handsome wealth. They are urged to come, equipped with air and horses, and drink Soma in the light of day. The hymn concludes with a call for Ashwini Kumars to receive the sufficient oblation. Their praiseworthy chariot moves between the sky and the earth, attracted by worshippers. The very sweet juice and Soma mixed with milk are presented for Ashwini Kumars to drink. Their best chariot, which brings wealth, repeatedly reaches the beautified house of the host who fulfills Soma.

Sukta 59 , attributed to the sage Vishvamitra in the Trishtup and Gayatri meters, the hymns are dedicated to Mitra. The worshippers describe how the gods, when worshipped, inspire the entire world to engage in agriculture and other activities. Mitra, the god who creates eternal life through rain, earth, and sky, holds both realms together. These friendly deities look favorably upon those who do good deeds. Worshippers offer ghee-laden oblations to honor Mitra and seek his favor.

Aditya is invoked, with the worshippers asking that those who offer him sacrifices alongside their friends become masters of food grains. They affirm that no violence can touch those under Aditya's protection, and sin will not approach those who sacrifice for him. The worshippers pray to be saved from diseases and strengthened by food, observing the fast of Aditya on the vast earth. They ask for Aditya's blessings and favor. Aditya, lying in beautiful light and being the master of all, is worthy of salutation. Yajna rituals are performed upon his appearance, and the worshippers seek his blessings and auspicious affection. Aditya, the originator of great worlds, is to be worshipped with salutations. The friendly gods, pleased with praises, are to be offered pleasing oblations in the fire.

The hymn continues to describe the influence of the friendly deity who sustains human beings through rain, ensuring the land is full of food, wealth, fame, and knowledge. Mitra Devta is praised for subjugating the sky and making the earth prosperous and full of edible food. All five varnas—Brahmin, Kshatriya, Vaishya, Shudra, and Nishad—are called to show respect to the friendly deity capable of conquering enemies. These friends nourish all the gods through their form. Finally, it is stated that if a person offers the flowers of scholars, gods, and other human beings, the friendly gods provide auspicious essence for him. The hymn concludes with a reminder of the importance of honoring and respecting Mitra and the friendly deities.

Sukta 60 , attributed to the sage Vishvamitra in the Jagati meter, the hymns are dedicated to the deities Ribhava and Indra. The worshippers acknowledge the wealth, deeds, and power of Rituyon, a descendant of Sudhanva, and praise him for his brilliance in defeating enemies through yaksh karma. They recognize his ability to understand all actions as soon as he wishes.

The hymn recalls the power with which Rituyon divided the chamas, the intelligence with which he won the skin from the cow's body, and the knowledge with which he created Indra's two horses. Through these deeds, Rituyon has become entitled to a share of the yajna and attained divinity. The descendants of humans, the Ribhus, have imbued the body with life through their friendship with Indra and sacrificial acts. This son of

Sudhanva, who performs virtuous deeds, has attained an imperishable position by the power of his actions.

The worshippers call upon the Lord to board the chariot with Indra and go to the place where Soma is accomplished, accepting the hymns of human beings. The sons of Sudhanva, who carry the power of nectar, are unstoppable in their great deeds. No one can withstand the power of the Ribhus. Indra is praised for strengthening the earth with strong and knowledgeable people, much like the sun strengthens its rays. Indra, along with the Lords, drinks Soma and derives happiness from the praises in the house of the host. Indra, along with Indrani and the Ribhus, is invited to enjoy the third season and the certain monsoon for Soma drinking. All days are best for worshiping Indra, and he is called upon to distribute food to those who praise him, coming to the yajna with powerful devotees. With the help of a hundred skilled horses, even deserters are defeated, and the yajna proceeds without violence.

Sukta 61, attributed to the sage Vishvamitra in the Trishtup meter, the hymns are dedicated to the deity Usha. The worshippers praise Usha as the giver of wealth and food, urging her to unite with the best knowledge and accept the hymn of the one who praises her. Usha, being beautiful like the ancient maiden and loved by many, is called to come quickly for the yajna, armed with hymns.

Usha is described as free from the bondage of death, with a chariot laden with gold, embodying the true form of words. Her beauty is adorned with the radiance of rays, and the strong people of various castes easily join her chariot. Usha, moving along the same path, comes before the creatures of the entire world, floating in the high sky and following the path like the chariot of the Sun.

The hymn further describes Usha as one who covers like a cloth and destroys darkness, full of wealth, and devoted to the Sun as his wife. She illuminates the sky and earth in Soma, being a devotee of great good fortune, decency, and good deeds. The beautiful dawn, appearing before the worshippers, is praised with salutations, confirming those praises and carrying the exalted glory of the sky. Usha is described as very beautiful, graceful, and radiant.

Everyone knows that the morning full of truth appears brightly in the sky, filled with wealth and pervading the sky and the earth in many ways. The hymn calls upon Agni to receive Usha, bringing pleasant wealth through prayer. Usha, as Aditya, sheds water through rain and enters between the sky and the earth, appearing as the radiance of Mitravarun and spreading her brightness like gold.

Sukta 62 , attributed to the sages Vishvamitra and Jamadagni in the Trishtup and Gayatri meters, the hymns are dedicated to Indra, Varuna, Brahaspati, Pūṣā, Sun, Moon, and Mitra-Varuna. The worshippers call upon Indra and Varuna, likening them to the darkness that covers and subjugates everything, recognizing their wandering activities that benefit the seekers. They ask where their fame and glory lie, through which they increase food and strength for their friends.Indra and Varuna are invoked by those seeking wealth and strength. The worshippers also call upon Marut, blessed with heaven and earth, to listen to their hymns. They seek strength and supernatural opulence, asking Indra and Varuna's defense forces to protect them and nurture them with all-loving, all-giving promises and generous words.

Brahaspati is asked to accept the advice offered by the worshippers, providing excellent and beautiful wealth to the host offering the sacrifice. Ritvijo are urged to worship Brahaspati with the best hymns and salutations during yajna and auspicious deeds, praying for valor that cannot be bowed down by enemies. Brahaspati, who showers happiness on all human beings, is strong, kind, and inspires the best path, deserving of all respect and greetings.Pushan, luminous and capable of showering happiness, is praised with new hymns. The worshippers chant great praise towards Pushan, asking him to accept their words of wisdom and truth with loving feelings. They pray for Pushan to be their nurturer and protector in every way.

Savita Dev, who inspires intellects on the right path, is meditated upon for his brilliance, all-illuminating, all-giving, and sin-destroying power. The worshippers seek his guidance and blessings. They pray for praise of Savitadev, the giver of all light, brightness, luxuries, and wisdom, who inspires and creates good deeds.Soma is praised for his resourceful deeds and for providing shelter. The worshippers pray for Soma to produce disease-free, health-giving grains for humans and animals, increasing lifespan and destroying diseases. They seek Soma's presence in their yajna place.

Varuna, addressed as a friend, is asked to irrigate the worlds with sweet words full of knowledge and moisten the earth with sweet juice. The worshippers acknowledge Varuna's pure conduct, seeking his growth through praise and salutations, adorned with strength, and knowledge. They ask Varuna to sit like a full house, preached by a knowledgeable person, and to drink Somras for daily consumption.

The third Mandala of Rig-Veda concludes with this Sukta, emphasizing the unity of divine power and the importance of praise and worship in seeking divine blessings and protection.

SIX

RISHI VAMADEVA (MANDALA 4)

Rishi Vamadeva (Sanskrit: वामदेव, Romanized: Vāmadeva) is a highly regarded sage in, known for his profound contributions to the Rigveda and other sacred texts. He is credited as the author of **Mandala 4 of the Rigveda**, which contains hymns that are revered for their spiritual depth and insight.He is described as the son of the sage Gotama and the brother of Nodhasa, who also contributed hymns to the Rigveda. This lineage is rooted in the tradition of sages who were known for their wisdom and spiritual practices. Vamadeva is the father of Brihaduktha and belongs to the distinguished lineage of Sage Angiras, a group of ancient seers and poets associated with the Rigveda.

*Vamadeva's influence extends beyond the Rigveda into the Upanishads, particularly the **Brihadaranyaka** and **Aitareya Upanishads**. These texts highlight his spiritual insights and teachings, further cementing his reputation as a sage of profound wisdom. In these scriptures, Vamadeva is often depicted as a sage who has realized the nature of the self and the ultimate reality, making him a significant figure in the philosophical discussions of the Upanishads.His hymns in the Rigveda reflect a deep understanding of the divine and the natural world, while his presence in the Upanishads showcases his role in exploring and articulating the nature of the self and the cosmos.*

Sukta 1 (First Anuvaka) attributed to Rishi Vamadeva with Gautama, Agni and Varuna as the deities, and the chant in Trishup meter, extols the virtues and powers of fire. "Oh fire! You are luminous and swift. The gods, filled with competition and the desire to conquer enemies, receive you for war. The hosts attract you with praise, for you are indestructible, luminous, and extremely knowledgeable. The gods revealed you to humans for performing yajna, for you are the knower of deeds and are present in all yagyas. Varuna is your brother, a vessel for sacrifices, the bearer of water, and a supporter of human growth. You, equipped with a boat of friends, deliver Varuna to us, granting us happiness and welfare. You protect us from sins and become close through protective actions, especially at the end of Usha. At the morning's end, destroy water-borne diseases and bring desired results to the hosts. Agni, in your supreme opulence, you are the giver of all deeds, desired like the sacred cow's milk, and are as nourishing as a cow. May our Yagya receive the purifying fire, full of light, spreading its brilliance in the infinite sky. Those with golden chariots, auspicious flames, and glowing fires are as pleasant as a house full of food. Adhvaryugan regularly install them in Uttarvedi, fulfilling their hosts' wishes. May Agni's majesty, worshipped by those who praise it, appear before us, created by the immortal Gods for Yajna. The fire, best among men, resides within everyone, spreading glory in clouds. Sapta Hota sings praises for Agnidev, loved by all. Our ancestors, invoking Usha, brought out cows from mountain caves with the power of Agni's worship. Angira Rishis, with knowledge of praise, praised Usha and saw Aditya's radiance. The darkness of night, inspired by dawn, illuminated the space, revealing Aditya. Angira Rishis saw the stolen cows, making the places eligible for Yagya. Agnidev, filled with friendship, calms Varuna's anger. Worshippers of Agni receive beautiful results, for he is the one who invokes the gods, extremely luminous, and performs more yagyas than all. Agnidev, who eats offerings, makes devotees happy."

Sukta 2 attributed to, attributed to Rishi Vāmadeva, the deity is Agni, and the chant is Triṣṭup. This Sukta extols the virtues of Agni, emphasizing his essential role in the lives of humans and gods. "Agni resides among humans as eternal fire, defeating enemies with his luminous presence. He calls upon the Agnidevtas and performs the majority of yajna rituals, illuminating the altar with his glory. 'O mighty fire god! Today, you have proved helpful in our work. You are a sight to behold, received as a messenger by connecting your strong horses to the chariot, carrying offerings between gods and humans.' Agni is the form of truth, praised for his powerful horses that shower food and water. 'Oh fire! Your horses, chariots, and opulence are the best, calling Aryama, Varuna, Mitra, Indra, Vishnu, Marudgana, and the two Ashwini Kumaras for the sake of Havyukta Yajamanas.' Agni should make our yagya beneficial for cows, bulls, and horses, filled with offerings, children, wealth, and teachings. The one who carries wood for Agni sweats, but Agni fills him with wealth and protects him from ill-wishers.

'O fire! The person who honors you on the northern altar with the desire for food, and who installs you in his home for divinity, may his son be righteous, firm, and generous.' Agni protects those who praise him at night and in the morning, moving like a golden swinging horse. 'Oh fire! You never perish. Hosts offering you havi, correcting the sruk for you, and worshipping you should never be poor. The violence of the violent should never touch them.' Agni remains happy and bright, favoring those who provide well-arranged, violence-free offerings. Just as one removes the harness from a horse, Agni should separate sins and virtues, granting wealth and following closely. Among the gods in human homes, Agni appoints Hota as the most knowledgeable, making gods visible with his radiance.

Agni is bright and fulfills human desires, deserving to be enshrined on the northern altar. For hosts consecrating Soma and serving Agni, he grants happiness, fortune, and wealth. Agni creates paths for sculptures with his hands, like Rishis engaged in yagya work. 'We seven vipra, initially brilliant, were created by Agni as sons of the luminous Aditya, destined to become radiant and break water-filled clouds.' Our ancestors achieved fame through noble, traditional yagyas, destroying darkness and rescuing cows kidnapped by the Panis. Like purified iron, they illuminated the fire, increased Indra, and defeated a huge herd of cows, nourishing people with the power of growth.'O fire! We worship you, becoming people of good deeds. The dawn that destroys darkness carries fire giving happiness with all its radiance. We worship your delightful glory.' Agni is a scholar, accepting hymns, providing wealth, and granting the best residence among families."

Sukta 3, attributed to attributed to Rishi Vāmadeva, the deities are Agni and Rudra, and the chant is Triṣṭup. This Sukta emphasizes the power and importance of Agni in yajna and human life. "Hey men! Worship Agnidev, the one who invokes the gods, the master of yajna, the one who fills the sky and the earth with food, who has the luster of gold and performs fierce actions capable of making enemies cry, to gain protection before death. 'Oh fire! Just as a mother adorned in beautiful clothes gives a place for her husband, we also give you a place in the Uttara Vedi. Hey Agnidev! You perform great deeds, come before us adorned with your glory. May this praise reach your worship.' Agni, the seer who listens to hymns, is disinterested and prays for indestructible fire. Just as the stone anoints Soma, the host praises the fire.

'Oh fire! Become a god in this sacrificial fire of ours! You are a knower of truth and doer of noble deeds. You know our hymn and create joy. When will your joyful hymns be sung? When will you fill our house with a spirit of friendship?' Agni questions our sins in front of Varuna and Surya, asking what crime we have committed against Prithvi, Aryama, and Bhaga. 'Oh fire! Why do you question our deeds in Yagya, the age of great sacrifice, auspicious and leading in truth?' Agni questions the great and guardian Pusha, Rudra, Vishnu, and in the presence of the great Samvatsara for the sake of truth.'Oh fire! We give the cows milk related to the Yagya performed for truth. Among them, black cows nourish humans with life-giving white milk. Great Agnidev, who showers desired fruits, is watered with nutritious milk, gathering all his glory. Aditya showers water and crosses mountains with the righteousness of cows, breaking through mountains.' Medhathithi and others found cows after breaking the mountain. Angiras, busy in their work, received Usha happily. The sun rose after the appearance of fire from Arani Manthan. 'Oh fire! Rivers of imperishable, sweet water inspired by Yagya flow uninterrupted like a horse ready to move.'

'Oh fire! Never attend the yagya of someone who does violence to us or an evil neighbor. Do not make anyone else a friend except us. Do not desire sacrifices of a crooked-minded brother. We do not consume food given by the enemy. Enjoy only the money given by you.' Agni, the performer of the best yajna, protects us and provides shelter. 'Destroy increased ignorance by destroying our grave sins. Show affection through worshipable hymns, accept our offerings filled with praises, and may praises to the gods increase you. Oh fire! You are the lawgiver, the knower of deeds, and the creator of humans. With your wish, we recite this profound and fruitful hymn composed by us.'"

Sukta 4 attributed to, attributed to Rishi Vāmadeva, the deity is Rakshoagni, and the chant is Triṣṭup. This Sukta focuses on the powerful and protective nature of fire in the form of Rakshoagni, who destroys enemies and protects devotees. "Oh fire! You expand your radiance like a hunter expanding his net. Just like a king traveling with his minister, you move with fearless glory, destroying the enemy's army swiftly. Your sharp brilliance disintegrates demons. 'Oh fire! Your dynamic, fast-moving rays reach the entire world, burning enemies with your overwhelming power. Enemies cannot hinder you, and your radiance moves as fast as falling stars.'

'Oh fire! Use your power to stop enemies. No one can do violence to you. Protect our children from those who think ill of us, ensuring no enemy subjugates us, for we are your devotees.' Agni with sharp flames, get ready to kill the wicked, covering enemies with your flames and burning them like dry wood. You are ready to kill the wicked, defeating enemies stronger than us, manifesting your divine radiance, and tormenting evil beings. 'First, destroy all enemies, known and unknown."O young, dynamic fire! A man who praises you attains your grace. Lord of sacrifices, you shine before those who seek your favor, granting them wealth and a long, prosperous life. May those who desire your love for daily offerings and praises enjoy one hundred years of good fortune, blessed by your presence every day.' 'O God of Fire! We praise your wisdom, echoing the words uttered for you. May you grant us sons, grandchildren, and excellent chariots and horses. For our sake, you should receive nourishing food daily.'

'Oh fire! You shine day and night. People serve you daily, adopting the wealth of enemies and enjoying life with their children while serving you with a happy heart.' Agni protects those who approach him with wealth and beautiful horses for yajna, treating him as a guest. 'Oh fire! You are young, intelligent, and well-groomed. Let us destroy demonic enemies through the brotherhood inspired by your praises. This speech has been received by Gautama, and you are the destroyer of enemies. Pay full attention to our words of praise."Oh fire! You are omniscient, with ever-conscious rays. These protective rays, rejoicing in yajna, protected Mamata's blind son Dirghaman from a curse. Your enemies fail in their attempts to destroy you.' 'Oh fire, may we who praise you become rich and seek your shelter.

May we get food and benefits from your inspiration. You expand the truth and destroy sin, eliminating enemies near and far. Let us serve you with our praises, and incinerate those who offer false praise. Protect us from slanderous enemies.' Thus concludes the fourth chapter."

Sukta 5 attributed to attributed to Rishi Vāmadeva, the deity is Vaishvanar Agni, and the chant is Triṣṭup. This Sukta emphasizes the worship and reverence for Vaishvanar Agni, who sustains the cosmos and bestows wealth and protection upon devotees. "Let us all, seekers and priests of equal love, strive to please the extremely bright Vaishvanar Agni through our sacrifices. Just as a pillar supports a roof, Agni Dev holds the sky with his entire form. 'Hey Hotas! By being dedicated to death, we, the fire gods, give wealth to the hosts with mature intellect. Do not disrespect them.' The indestructible Agnidev, full of sharp brilliance, prevails in both the middle and the best places.

He showers wishes, is full of essence and rich in wealth, yet remains mysterious like a cow hidden in a mountain. Scholars should strive to understand his nature through great stotras. 'The person who wants to do violence to Varun's brilliant friend and beloved, may the sharp-toothed, beautiful, and wealthy Agni Dev burn him to ashes with his extremely painful fire.' Just as a hateful woman or midwife falls into sorrow, a person who despises fire and truth falls into disgrace.'O Pavak! We do not give up our vow to obtain from you. Just as someone loads a weak person with a heavy burden, please grant us beautiful wealth that repels enemies, is full of food, nourishes knowledge, and contains great seven metals.' Through all appropriate and purifying methods, let us attain Vaishvanar Agni. 'Vaishvanar has appeared in the east, moving from the bright earth to the immovable sky, increasing the fire.' Scholars say that the milk cows provide like water is kept secret by Vaishvanar in the fire cave. He is the protector of the vast earth's beloved place, his power and wonder highly praised.

The fire god, to whom the milk-giving cows serve in auspicious yajna, is luminous and resides in the cave, moving swiftly. Highly worshipable, Vaishvanar fire is prevalent in the solar system. Like father and mother, there should be consciousness for drinking the best milk from the bright Vaishvanar cow spreading between the sky and earth. The motherly cow, the goddess of luminous Vaishvanar Agni, desires to drink and drink in the upward space.'O fire, what do they say here that you are unarmed and offering sacrifices to the goddess of fortune?' If someone asks me with the utmost respect, O learned one, tell the truth. If we get beautiful wealth by praising you, then you become the lord of wealth. You are the owner of all wealth on earth and in the sky. 'What is the means to acquire this wealth?' Hey Agnidev, tell us the best solution to achieve it without running from criticism. What are the duties to be performed? Just like a fast horse goes to war, we shall move forward to attain eternal life. The bright and imperishable Usha, filled with the sun's light, will be published for this reason.

What does a man deprived of truth and unsatisfied with contrary knowledge say in this world? An unarmed man finds inner suffering due to false knowledge. 'The bright amount of this resplendent fire illuminates the yagya place, giving happiness to the host and shining brightly like a horse full of wealth.' Worshipped by praises of Agnidev Yagya, it shines beautifully, concluding this Sukta."

Sukta 6 attributed to attributed to Rishi Vāmadeva, the deity is Agni, and the chant is Triṣṭup. This Sukta emphasizes the greatness and omnipresence of Agni, his role in yajnas, and his ability to bestow wealth and protection upon his devotees. "Hey Hota Agni! You are the best among the Yajniks, situated in the highest position and conqueror of all enemies. Spread the praises of those who honor you. 'Agnidev performs Yajna, creates happiness, and is very knowledgeable and intelligent. He sits among guests in the Yajna Mandap, rising high like the sun and holding sunlight like a pillar.'

The ancient and Samvat Juhu is filled with ghee, and Adhvaryu, who increases fame, achieves his wish by doing circumambulation. The rising bud is pleasant, and the well-wisher receives the host of cattle. 'When Kush is spread and Agni is enriched, both the Adhvaryugan are taken inside for this reason. The ancient Agnidev, who performs the Yajna, also abounds in killing with a horse, like guardians, increasing their opulence and extending blessings to all three categories of living beings - the best, the middle, and the lowest.' 'Agnidev, who bestows happiness, has the form of sweet-spoken Yajna, moves everywhere with finite speed, and his beam of light runs everywhere like a horse. When they shine, all the living beings in the world get scared.' 'Oh fire! Your sparkle is beautiful. You are omnipresent and terrifying to the wicked, your beautiful and beneficial form clearly visible. Even the darkness of the night cannot stop your light, and evil beings like demons cannot succeed in their sinful experiments on your body.'

'O Vaishvanar Agnidev, you are a ghost because of the rain, and your donation cannot be stopped by anyone. The fire that parents like earth and sky are not able to inspire soon gets satisfied, purifies, and is revealed as a friend among humans.' 'The fire that lights humans like a woman with ten fingers wakes up in the early morning hours, accepts offerings, shines with excellent light, and has a beautiful appearance. It destroys enemies like a sharp-edged axe.' 'Oh fire! We call those horses of yours before us. Foam comes out of their mouths. They are red in complexion, walk on a straight path, have a beautiful gait, a glowing body, full of youth, strong, and worth seeing. Your rays are capable of subduing enemies, mobile, glowing, and worthy of worship, making various sounds like the shining Maruts. Like a horse, she is fully capable of taking people to their destination.'

'O resplendent fire god! We have composed this great hymn for you. It is for your sake that learned men utter noble words. The host performs your yajna. Therefore, please grant us wealth. Scholars like Ritwik and others are sitting here to worship the human fire with the desire for wealth like animals.'

Sukta 7, attributed to attributed to Rishi Vāmadeva invokes the deity Agni through the chants Triṣṭup, Jagti, and Anustup. This fire, Agni, is the best, present at the beginning of all, the giver of all happiness, and worthy of being worshiped in all yagyas. These qualities were illuminated by Bhrigu in ancient times. Agni is the best among the yagyas, brilliant, and the destroyer of sins. Scholars who perform sacrifices to Agni revere these gods. Agni is worthy of being worshiped by humans and is extremely radiant, with a light that is favorable. This fire god is full of diverse knowledge, free from illusion, and like the sky full of stars, he makes all the yagyas successful. The visible fire is established in every yagya place by Ritvik and other intelligent people. The fire god gives his bright light for the happiness of the people, is fast-moving like the messenger of the host, and is full of the light of knowledge. The appearance of Agnidev should be beneficial for every citizen. The hota form of Agni has been established in its proper place by Adhvaryu and others, full of dazzling and purifying light. He is very charitable and a friend to everyone. May those seven bright fires be favorable and reside in the yagya place. Human beings have worshiped Agni, the mother earth, present in the waters and in the trees, situated in a cavity unserved by many creatures due to the fear of being burnt, amazingly intelligent, and accepting of sacrificial offerings everywhere. May the gods, after renouncing their sleep, please the fire in the sacrificial fire with praises in the morning, and the great Agnidev of truth, who has accepted the oblation offered with namaskar, should know about the yajna performed by the host. Agni is knowledgeable and performs heroic deeds in the yagya, understanding the space between these people and the sky and the earth. Agnidev is ancient and increases the yajna even more, being very intelligent, the best, and the messenger of the gods. He reaches the highest place in heaven to deliver prayers for the gods. Agni is full of light, with a walking path that is black. His radiance is supreme among all luminous objects. For his attainment, the wood due to his birth is eclipsed, and he is born and becomes the messenger of the host. Ritvigya Aavi sees the brightness of the fire that arises after churning Arani. When the air flows on the target of the flames in the form of branches, the fire spreads its sharp flame in the group of trees and consumes the wood with its speed. Agni Dev burns Atradi wood very quickly with his fast rays. Agni Mahan becomes a fast-moving messenger, burning wood together like a horse rider strengthens and inspires his horse.

Sukta 8, attributed to attributed to Rishi Vāmadeva invokes the deity Agni with the chant Gayatri. "O fire! You are the master of all wealth, the one who offers sacrifices to the gods, imperishable, performing great sacrifices and heroic deeds for the gods. We praise you, Agnidev, with simple praises." Agni is described as great, a light of fire who fulfills the wishes of the hosts and knows the sequence of salutations to Indradi deities. He is invited to the yagya. Bright with fire, Agni knows the order of saluting the Indradi gods and gives the desired wealth to the host desirous of performing the yagya. As a connoisseur of Dautyakram, Agnidev in his Hotaarupa form knows the place worthy of ascension to heaven and moves between the sky and the earth. The host who lights Agni with wood and pleases him by increasing the offerings invites others to offer fire by performing the same actions. The host worships and takes care of Agni, becoming rich and enjoying various luxuries, filled with eternal happiness. Ritvik and others wish for wealth to come every day so they may gain various knowledge, science, and power. Agni, a scholar, destroys the sufferings of human beings by attacking with force like fast-moving arrows.

Sukta 9, attributed to Rishi Vāmadeva invokes the deity Agni with the chant Gayatri. "O fire, give us happiness. You are the desire of the gods and great. You come to the host with the desire to sit on the nearby Kush." Agni is indestructible, unable to be violated even by demons, and able to roam freely in the mortal world as the god of fire and the messenger of all the gods. Agnideva is worthy of praise, brought to the sacrificial house of priests or coming to the sacrificial place after being praised. He is represented as the Agnideva Adhvaryu, the god-wife form, Jupiter in the sacrificial house, or seated in the form of Brahma in the sacrifice. Agni desires the offerings of men who wish to sacrifice, embodying the form of Brahma and knowing the works of the priests and others, becoming a preacher of sacrificial deeds. Agni also desires to perform heroic deeds in the sacrifice of the host, consuming the offerings to carry them. O glorious one, consume our yagya, accept our oblation, and have the grace to listen to our invocation hymn. The chariot on which Agni rides, protecting the host of sacrifices while traveling in all directions, can never be violent. May that chariot spread all around us and protect us.

Sukta 10, attributed to Rishi Vāmadeva invokes the deity Agni with the chants Padpankti, Mahapad Pankti, and Ushnik. "O fire! We priests enhance you with praise, just as a horseman enhances his steed. You carry the offerings, and those who perform Yagya find you favorable, worthy of performing Yagya, extremely lovable, and pleasant." Agni is worthy of sacrifice, achieving desired results, foundational and great in truth, and leading like a charioteer. He is full of light, as bright as the sun, and has the best heart, coming before us with a good mind. Today, Agni is praised through speech and provided oblations. The sun is like his purifying flame or his roar like a cloud. Agni's most beloved light adorns things like ornaments day and night. He is full of food, his form as free from sin as pure ghee, and his pure radiance as bright as a jewel. Even though Agni is continuous, he is created by hosts and is capable of removing the sins of the hosts. He is luminous, and our feelings of brotherhood and friendship towards him should be beneficial. May this spirit of friendship and brotherhood be our auspicious form in the entire Yagya.

Sukta 11, attributed to Rishi Vāmadeva invokes the deity Agni with the chant Triṣṭup. "O fire! You are full of strength, and your sacrifice is worthy of the bright sun, swift and glorious, visible even in the night. You are very beautiful, and through your inspiration, food containing ghee and other offerings is produced." Agni, the Lord with many births, opens the doors of the sacred world for the stota Yajman worshiped by those performing Yagya. He is full of beautiful radiance and provides wealth to the host along with the gods, and we seek that desired wealth as well.

Agni carries offerings and facilitates the arrival of the gods. The speech in the form of praise originates from him, and he alone is worthy of worship. For those performing righteous deeds and sacrifices, the increasing wealth and food are generated by Agni. The powerful bearer of the oblation, the devotee of sacrifices, the great son endowed with the power of truth, all emerge from Agni. The auspicious opulence inspired by the gods, and the horse with special speed and power, are born from him.

Agni is indestructible, and those who wish to fulfill the desires of the gods serve him through praises. He is the original god among the gods, radiant, and his tongue strengthens the gods. Agni removes sins and seeks to destroy demons. O mighty Agnidev, you remain alert for our welfare, being auspicious and luminous at night. You strengthen the hosts, remove distractions, sins, and evil wisdom from us.

Sukta 12, attributed to Rishi Vāmadeva invokes the deity Agni with the chant Triṣṭup. "O fire! The host who enlightens you by stabilizing happiness and provides you with food in the form of offerings in all three seasons every day, gains knowledge of your glory through actions that satisfy you and thus wins over his enemies." Agni blesses those who bring him the Dhashasadhaak wood and worship his glory day and night, bestowing upon them a host of children and animals, the destruction of their enemies, and the acquisition of wealth.

Agni, the lord of great power and wealth in the form of excellent food and animals, enriches the very young and inexperienced hosts of fire service with handsome wealth. O eternally young Agnidev, save us from the crimes and sins we commit against you out of ignorance. You are found everywhere; remove our sins. As our friend, may we never face obstacles due to the crimes or sins committed against Indradi gods or all human beings. You provide happiness to our children by protecting them from troubles in the form of sin. Agni, worthy of worship and abode, just as you saved the cow tied to the ropes, save us from sin. Our age has been increased by you, O fire, and may you increase it even more.

Sukta 13, attributed to Rishi Vāmadeva invokes the deity Agni with the chant Triṣṭup. "O fire god with great mind, you become enlightened before the light of dawn that destroys darkness. Hey Ashwinikumars, you enter the host's house. The Sun rises with its glory in the morning to inspire Ritvik and others." Suryadev develops rays, and when these rays rise in the sky, Varuna, Mitra, and Agni follow their Kamas just as the strong bull follows the cows, throwing up dust in desire.

The Sun, which the Creator Gods created to destroy the darkness without abandoning the work of the world, is the one who knows all living beings. O luminous Sun, you increase the rays for the sake of the food that sustains the world, driving away the black night and traveling with horses that can carry even the heaviest burden. The moving rays of the Sun should dispel the darkness present in space. No one can bind the directly received Sun, and no one can do violence to the Sun living below. By what force do they move higher? The Sun, rising like a pillar in the sky, provides shelter to itself. Who sees this?

Sukta 14, attributed to Rishi Vāmadeva invokes the deity Agni with the chants Triṣṭup and Pankti. "Just as the bright sun illuminates the dawn, Agni, the lord of wealth, illuminates his rays emanating from great wealth. O Adhidvaya, you are mobile. Both of you should come and perform this Yagya by riding on the chariot." The luminous Sun illuminates all the worlds and moves on the shelter of its rays, completing the sky, earth, and space with his light. The bearer of wealth, the mighty Jyotibhaya, and the Usha of Arun complexion appear bright through Rashmiya, animating every living being and moving in a decorated chariot for welfare.

Hey Ashwinikumars, when the dawn rises, may the moving horses with great carrying capacity take you to the Jhar Yagya. Both of you are wish-granters. This Soma is presented for you; hence, drink Soma in this Yagya and attain confirmation. No one is able to save the directly available Savitadev. Even if they remain down, it is not possible to do violence to them. By what force do they move higher? He is like a pillar of heaven, sheltering heaven. Who sees this? That is, no one knows this element.

Sukta 15, attributed to Rishi Vāmadeva invokes the deities Agni, Somak, and Ashwano with the chant Gayatri. "Among the gods who perform sacrifices, worthy of sacrifice and bright, the fast-moving horses that bring Agnidev to our Yagya move like a moving chariot three times a day." The brilliant Agnidev, who protects the Aas, bestows beautiful wealth on the host offering and spreads Haviran from all sides. The fire god, capable of destroying enemies by becoming more luminous in contact with air, is worthy of being attained by scholars and is at the forefront of the task of conquering the enemy.

Your stota should be one of brilliance, capable of overpowering enemies and having authority over the moving fire. Let the host of fire serve Agnidev repeatedly, who is like a horse, as bright as the sun, and like the son of the sky. King Somak, son of Sahdev, expressed the idea of giving these two ashes to us, and we went to him and brought both of them. From King Somak, son of Sahadeva, who was worthy of introduction, we took the beautiful horses the same day. Hey Ashwinikumars, you both are bright and shining. King Somak, son of Sahadev, satisfied both of you, attaining the age of a hundred years. Hey Ashwinikumars, you grant long life to King Somak, son of Sahadev.

Sukta 16, attributed to Rishi Vāmadeva invokes the deities Agni, Somak, and Ashwano with the chant Triṣṭup. "May Indra, lord of the moon, endowed with truth, come to us. May their horses come closer. We will offer Soma, the essence of food, for the sake of Lord Indra, so that he may fulfill our wishes by being worshiped by us." Indra, who scares the enemies, is invoked to free us just as the blind are freed after reaching their designated place. Indra, the destroyer of enemies and giver of all, is praised by the host with beautiful hymns, much like Ana. Poets who edit mysterious years compare Indra, who showers wishes, to the works they edit. When confirmation is achieved by drinking Soma suitable for consumption, the seven rays from the sky become enlightening for humans.

When the sky is visible through the rays, gods reside in that heaven, shining with brilliance. Savitadev, the leader of all, appears and destroys the grave darkness for humans to see. On Monday, Indra becomes extremely glorious, enriching both the sky and the earth with his glory, and pervading all the worlds. Indra, knowing all the works beneficial for humans, causes water and rain, showering water on the desert people full of good wishes. The deserters who split mountains with just their voices wish for Indra and open the herd full of cows. Indra's thunderbolt protects the worlds, sets in motion the cloud covering the waters, and fills the living earth, being extremely brave and aggressive.

Indra is called by the multitude, and when he stole the mesh after seeing the net, 'Sarma' revealed the cow stolen by the Panis for him. Praised by the Angiras, Indra gives joy and welfare to our children. Indra, respected by people, went before the 'Kuls' to give them money, saved them from enemy attacks, and provided shelter. With his advice, he destroyed the deceitful Rityaks out of desire for the wealth of the 'Kuls'. Indra decided to kill the enemies and reached the house of 'Kutsa', who was eager for his friendship, and both settled at their place. His wife Shachi, seeing the truth, became suspicious after seeing their similar appearance.

When the wise man and two horses move fast like perfume, Indra attaches trouble to his chariot and travels together to protect on his path. Indra, the master of the achchas who move like the wind and destroy enemies, killed Shushana and the demon Kuyava, breaking the cycle of the Sun. Indra also killed the demons Pipru and Pravrik, created 'Rijishva' the son of Vaidathi, and killed fifty thousand black demons. Indra destroyed enemy cities like old age destroys beauty.

Indra, indestructible and radiant, appears near the sun, outshining it. In battles, Indra protects those seeking his shelter and desiring wealth, praised through hymns. Indra becomes their protector, full of opulence like beautiful wealth. Indra has done many famous works for the welfare of humans, blessed with wealth and desire. Indra brings food quickly for seekers like us, and devotees make beautiful invocations for him. Indra protects the yagya performed by Vamdev, cannot be tortured, behaves kindly in battles, and has a beautiful mind. Indra comes near and is always praised by praisers. Indra, rich and glorious, is wished well in battles, and we continue to praise him joyfully, shining with wealth and surrounded by sons, grandchildren, and relatives. We compose beautiful hymns for young Indra, who showers wishes, ensuring our friendship with him remains unbroken. Indra, worshiped by ancient Rishis and saluted by us, increases food and wealth for those who praise him, filling a river with water. New hymns are created for Indra, worshiping him with words of praise laced with chariots.

Sukta 17, attributed to Rishi Vāmadeva invokes the mighty Indra, extolling his unparalleled strength and valor. The earth and sky themselves attest to Indra's power, which vanquished the formidable Vritrasura, liberating the rivers previously subdued. Indra's mere presence instills fear, causing the heavens and earth to tremble. His power binds the clouds, ensuring rain for the parched lands. Indra, wielding his thunderbolt with radiant might, cleaves mountains and annihilates enemies, restoring the flow of water. Prajapati, in his brilliance, regarded Indra as a magnificent creation. Indra, revered by many, dispels the fears brought by adversaries and is celebrated by all with hymns. As the embodiment of opulence and radiance, Indra's influence extends to the celestial bodies and the Soma, symbolizing his omnipotence. From birth, he shielded his people from Vritra's menace, ensuring the world's regions thrived. Indra, the indefatigable warrior, is praised for his wealth-bestowing thunderbolts and his role as the sustainer of lush forests. His friendships are unbreakable, and his wrath is feared by all, causing the entire world to tremble. Indra's victories over demons and enemies are legendary, marking him as the supreme protector and distributor of wealth. His divine lineage and immense strength, bestowed by his father Prajapati, are celebrated. Indra, the benefactor of wealth and remover of sins, inspires awe and reverence. His blessings extend even to the darkest nights, bringing prosperity and protection. Attributed to Rishi prays for Indra's continued guardianship, friendship, and provision of sustenance. In their praises, they seek Indra's attention, wealth, and protection, affirming his role as the ultimate guardian and benefactor of humanity. The chant forms Triṣṭup, Ekpada, and Virat, encapsulating the rhythmic and poetic devotion to the glorious Indra.

Sukta 18, attributed to Rishi Vāmadeva extols the deity Indraditi through the chant of Triṣṭup. This ancient path has birthed countless individuals—men, women, and the wise—who embrace love and enlightenment. This path has also seen the rise of the powerful and the distinguished. Vāmadeva cautions against dishonoring one's mother, emphasizing that straying from this ancestral route, resulting in a life of suffering akin to that of animals or birds born through deviated paths. Aditi, the divine mother, held Indra for months and years, nurturing him to accomplish extraordinary feats. No one past or future can match his greatness. Indra, empowered by Aditi, brought light and perfection to both the heavens and the earth.

The rivers, flowing with water and unspoken reverence, celebrate Indra's might, breaking the clouds that once hindered their praises. Indra's act of slaying Vritra is sanctified by the Vedas, where the waters absolve his sin by absorbing it as foam. Indra's birth was marked by immediate challenges, as the demon Krishwa sought to devour him, yet the waters brought him joy and strength to overcome his foes. His valor is further highlighted when he crushes the demon Vyans with his thunderbolt, despite being struck.

Aditi, like a nurturing cow birthing a strong calf, brings forth the omnipotent Indra, who is the inspirer and benefactor of all, fulfilling desires and granting the fruits of deeds. Aditi's wish for her son's victory is profound, and Indra, in turn, seeks to vanquish Vritra with the aid of Vishnu. Indra's unparalleled prowess is such that no enemy can subdue him, nor can any god surpass his divine status. In times of poverty and disgrace, it is Indra who offers protection and sweet sustenance, underscoring his role as the ultimate guardian and provider. Thus concludes the fifth chapter, celebrating the invincible and benevolent Indra.

Sukta 19, Rishi Vāmadeva praises the mighty Indra through the chant of Triṣṭup. Indra, adorned with the Vajra and revered by all gods and the heavens, is worshipped for his protective prowess and destructive power against evil. The gods, like an old father inspiring his son, urge Indra to defeat demons, recognizing him as the embodiment of truth and the master of all universes. Indra, with precise aim, killed the dormant Vritra, unleashing rivers to quench all beings.

Indra vanquished the ignorant and weak Vritra, breaking clouds and mountains to scatter water and fill the sky with radiance. The Maruts, like mothers to their sons, rallied to Indra, aiding him in defeating Vritra and filling the rivers with life-giving water. Indra provided fertile land, abundant food, and quenched the thirst of travelers, restoring the cows seized by demons.

By defeating Vritra, Indra liberated the dawns and rains, releasing the rivers to flow freely. He rescued 'Ayuputra' from a termite's hole, restoring his sight and reuniting his separated limbs. Indra's wisdom and knowledge of all deeds are praised by Vāmadeva, who recounts Indra's rituals for rain that bring prosperity. Indra, worshipped by ancient Rishis and praised by the present, increases the sustenance of his devotees, filling rivers and ensuring abundance. The new hymns sung in Indra's honor continue to exalt his divine actions and guardianship.

Sukta 20, attributed to Rishi Vāmadeva extols the deity Indra through the chant of Triṣṭup. "Hey Indra! You are the giver of wishes and full of radiance. Whether you are far or near, come and protect us. In the battlefield, you wield the thunderbolt and stand alongside humans, blessed with the radiant Marudgana. May Indra, who comes before us, bring his horses to provide shelter and wealth. As the wielder of the thunderbolt and the bearer of great wealth, may he assist us in times of war. Indra, keep this Yagya, performed with friendship, and complete it. We praise you, Vajrin. Just as a hunter hunts deer, let us be victorious in battle and obtain wealth with your strength."

Indra, the master of grains, is called to drink the intoxicating Soma Rasa made with devotion, enjoying it in the middle of the day along with bright hymns in the Stavana Savan. For the brave Indra, worshiped by new Rishis and compared to a fruitful tree and a skilled conqueror, hymns full of praise are recited. He is as massive as a mountain, dazzling with fire, born to subdue enemies, and wields a great thunderbolt. Since his appearance, no one has been able to stop him or waste the wealth given for good deeds. Indra, the mighty and wish-granting deity, oversees wealth and homes, protects cow herds from demons, leads educational activities, and commands in war, being a productive doer.

Indra's intelligence, power, and actions are unparalleled, allowing him to perform many tasks repeatedly, destroy sins, and grant wealth to his devotees. He is implored not to destroy his followers but to provide opulence to those dedicated to him. Indra is praised by both ancient Rishis and the current generation, likened to the fulfilling waters of a river that nourish praises. New hymns are created to continually praise and take care of him, joining paths with the horseman Indra.

Sukta 21, attributed to Rishi Vāmadeva extols the deity Indra through the chant of Triṣṭup. "Indra, the lord of heroes, come to protect us with praises. Be pleased with the hospitality we offer and follow us with your strength, skill, and brightness as radiant as the Sun. O humans, praise the Marudgan in this sacrificial place for the power and opulence of the renowned Indra, who performs auspicious deeds like a king in a yagya, capable of defeating enemy armies and protecting us."

Indra, come to provide us shelter from heaven, earth, space, the solar system, or any distant place, along with the Marudgan. We gather at this sacrificial place to praise Indra, the destroyer of enemies, owner of stable and great opulences, who defeats enemy armies with life force, and who bestows rich wealth on his devotees. Indra, who creates a thunderous sound that stuns the world and gives rain through offerings, is called to the yagya with the best hymns.When residing in the house of one who wishes to praise Indra, the stotas present their praises to him. Indra, the sustainer of the world and shower of desires, protects and nourishes the hosts, appearing in their deeds for prosperity and desired attainment. Indra, who opened the door of the cloud and perfected the speed of water, grants wealth to the uninitiated when good deeds are offered to him.

Indra, your hands are capable of great deeds. What is the status of your high position, and why are you not ready to provide us with wealth? When this praise is given to Indra, the destroyer of Vritra and the lord of truth-rich wealth, he bestows it on the host. Indra, worshipped by many, grants wealth upon hearing our praise, allowing us to enjoy divine wealth.Indra, praised by ancient Rishis and now by us, increases the food of those who praise him, like filling a river with water. O horseman Indra, we compose a new hymn for you, continually praising and taking care of you equipped with the best chariot.

Sukta 22, attributed to Rishi Vāmadeva and Gautama extol the mighty deity Indra through the chant of Triṣṭup. They describe Indra as a powerful god who devours sacrificial offerings and adorns himself with the Vajra, the thunderbolt. Indra, the granter of wishes, wields thunderbolts in both hands, showering them upon his enemies. He has blessed the Parushni river, enabling the performance of sacred mantras. Indra, from his birth, was filled with immense power and food, causing the sky and earth to tremble with his presence.

At Indra's appearance, the mountains, seas, sky, and earth quaked in fear. The mighty Adityas hold the sky and earth, inspired by Indra. Vayu, inspired by Indra, speaks like a human. Indra's great deeds and bright intelligence are praised, as he forcefully destroyed Ahi with his thunderbolt, upholding all worlds. Indra's actions are filled with fear; cows protect their milk, and rivers flow because of him. When he released the rivers stopped by Vritra, they praised Indra for his protection. Soma, a source of pleasure, reached Indra, inspiring praises. Indra is asked to grant great strength to always defeat enemies, subdue opponents, and destroy their weapons.

Attributed to Rishi s implore Indra to listen to their praises and provide various types of food and cows. They acknowledge that Indra was worshiped by ancient Rishis and now by them. Indra increases the food of his devotees, filling rivers with water. They compose new hymns for Indra, continually praising him and introducing him as charioteers.

Sukta 23, attributed to Rishi Vāmadeva extols Indra, the deity, through the chant of Triṣṭup. The hymn begins with a question: how will their praises reach Indra, and why does Indra, the great one, come to the Yagya with love? Indra, who enjoys Soma and desires Haviratra, holds bright wealth for his devotees. They ask who will drink Soma with Indra and receive his favor, and when his astonishing wealth will be distributed. They wonder whom Indra will protect to amplify their hymn.

"Hey Indra," they ask, "how do you listen to the Hota when filled with great opulence? How do you understand the protection of the praiser just by listening to hymns? What are your ancient gifts that fulfill the wishes of the devotees?" Attributed to Rishi s question how those who praise Indra in distress and attain enlightenment through Yagya can achieve Indra's wealth. When the luminous Indra, after defeating an elephant, prostrates himself before them, he understands their praise deeply.They ponder when and how Indra forms bonds with humans at dawn and when he will express himself towards those who enhance his glorious deeds. Indra's friendship, which defeats enemies, is sought, and they wish to promote his brotherhood. Indra's actions, beneficial for his praisers, make him as visible and desired as the Sun. He sharpens weapons in advance to defeat demonic forces, nurturing the dawns like a debtor eliminating debt.

Ritdev, filled with water, removes sins through his praise. His knowledge-giving praises reach even the deaf. Ritdev's many forms are invoked by devotees for food, and cows are given as Dakshina in Yagya. Those who praise Ritdev perform Yajna to honor him, their strength yearning for water, and the earth provides milk for Ritdev. Indra, praised by ancestors and Rishis, increases the food of devotees like a river fills with water. The hymn concludes with attributed to Rishi s composing new hymns for Indra, the horseman, becoming charioteers to continually praise and discuss him.

Sukta 24, attributed to Rishi Vāmadeva extols the deity Indra through the chants of Triṣṭup and Anustup. "What shall we do to bestow wealth upon Indra, the son of Bala, through our beautiful praise?" they ponder. They call upon the brave Indra, who cares for animals, to grant them the wealth of their enemies and express their reverence through praise.

Indra is invoked in battle against Vritra, being worthy of the highest praise. When praised excellently, he manifests to bestow wealth upon his devotees, desiring Soma and receiving offerings from the hosts. In times of war, humans call upon Indra, and both the host and the stota approach him for the benefit of their children.

Indra, strong and powerful, is worshipped by people from all four directions who come together for puja. When warriors gather on the battlefield, some brave warriors worship the powerful Indra while others bring offerings to him. Those who perform Soma rituals for Indra during Yagyas become wealthy, whereas those who do not are rendered destitute. Indra, who resides in the heavenly world, grants wealth to those who desire the moon and perform rituals single-mindedly for him. Indra fulfills the wishes of those who bring offerings, sing hymns, and perform somersaults in his honor. Recognizing his devotees in battle, he showers them with blessings. Even in fierce battles, the Ritvik invokes Indra by drinking Soma, seeking his vision and benevolence.

The hymn reflects on those who earn money through good deeds but lose it due to poor transactions, emphasizing that Indra cannot be bought with mere wealth. Indra bestows his favor and wealth upon those who genuinely praise him. The hymn concludes by invoking Indra, worshipped by ancient Rishis, to increase the food of those who praise him like a river full of water. Attributed to Rishi s compose new hymns to Indra, their horseman, to continue praising and serving him as charioteers.

Sukta 25, attributed to Rishi Vāmadeva extols Indra through the chant of Triṣṭup. The hymn begins with a question: which benefactor, desiring the gods, seeks friendship with Indra today? Who worships Soma and praises Indra when the fire is lit, seeking his shelter? Indra is praised for his protection, and those who bow down in his honor, take the cows given to him, and seek his help, are celebrated.The hymn continues to ask which host requests the gods, like Indra, for protection and praises deities such as Aditya, Aditi, and Udaka. Ashwini Kumar, Indra, and Agni drink the filtered Somras as per the wishes of the hosts who recite their hymns. Those who resolve to perform Soma for Indra, the friend of humans and the best leader, are blessed by Agni, who makes them see the ever-rising sun.

Aditi ensures that Indra loves the hosts who perform beautiful Yagyas and auspicious events. Those who wish to praise Indra should be filled with affection and devotion. The hymn emphasizes that Indra rejects the sins of those who approach him with Soma offerings, and those who fail to praise him face his wrath. Indra does not favor the rich and greedy who do not perform the sacred rituals; instead, he destroys their useless wealth. He establishes a great kinship with the host of Somabhishvakarta and the cook of Haviratra.The hymn concludes by acknowledging that people of all types—high, low, and medium—invoke Indra. All living beings, whether moving, living in houses, going to the battlefield, or desiring fire, call upon Indra for his protection and blessings.

Sukta 26, Attributed to Rishi Vāmadeva extols the deity Indra through the chant of Triṣṭup. begins by identifying themselves as the Creator, an inspirer, and a scholar of 'Daurabatma.' They are the son of attributed to Rishi 'Kaxivan,' the poet 'Ushna,' and the son of 'Arjuna.' Celebrated like 'Kuts,' they are revolutionaries and beloved by all. Rishi recounts how they inspired the waters with their words and guided all the gods according to their wishes. By invoking Soma, they destroyed the defenseless cities of 'Shambar.' When protecting the king during a yagya, they provided a hundred cities for his residence.

The hymn calls upon the Maruts, who attain prominence among the eagle birds and are swifter than others. The gods brought Soma, performed as offerings, from the celestial world in a wheelless chariot and bestowed it upon humans. When Shyen brought Soma from the sky out of fear, he flew with the speed of the mind, traversing the vast expanse of space swiftly with the identical honey, spreading his fame. Shyen, with the illustrious gods, retrieved Soma from a distance and brought the praised and joyous Soma from the high sky to the earth with firmness. Performing thousands of sacrifices, Shyen found and returned Soma. Upon Soma's arrival, the multi-talented and intelligent Indra harnessed the power generated from Soma to vanquish the ignorant enemies. Thus, through the words of Vāmadeva, celebrates Indra's strength, the achievements of the divine beings, and the significance of Soma in their victories.

Sukta 27, attributed to Rishi Vāmadeva extols Indra through the chants of Triṣṭup and Shakvari. The hymn begins by recounting attributed to Rishi 's profound understanding of all the gods, including Indra, even while still in the womb. They describe their upbringing in iron-fortified towns and their knowledge that freed them from bodily bonds, allowing their soul to soar like an eagle.

Vāmadeva continues, recounting how, even in the womb, they were free from attachment, overcoming the sorrows of pregnancy with the power of knowledge. The Lord, who inspires all, destroyed the enemy germs in the womb, grew, and extinguished the troubling air. Attributed to Rishi then tells of bringing Soma, when the eagle turned towards the sky and shouted. Protectors of Soma tried to snatch it from Shyena, and Shushudana, the protector of Soma, fired an arrow at Shyena. Despite this, Shyena brought Soma safely. Attributed to Rishi likens this to how the Ashwinikumars kidnapped King Bhujyu from Indra's domain, and Rijugami brought Soma from the great sky, protected by Indra, even as one of its wings was pierced by an arrow during a battle with Krishna.

Finally, the hymn calls for the mighty Indra to drink the sacred, sweet-smelling, poetic-mixed, satisfying, and joyful juice of the seven forms of Soma given by the Adhvaryus, celebrating Indra's strength and the divine protection over Soma.Thus, through the words of Vāmadeva, venerates Indra's might, the divine wisdom imparted from the womb, and the significance of Soma in their celestial endeavors.

Sukta 28, Rishi Vāmadeva extols the deity Indra through the chant of Triṣṭup. The hymn begins by addressing the moon, celebrating Indra's alliance with Soma. With Soma's help, Indra shed water for humanity and killed Vritra, introducing water by opening the doors blocked by Vritra.

"Hey Soma," attributed to Rishi continues, "with your assistance, Indra scattered the single wheel of the two-wheeled chariot fixed on Surya's chariot. In competition, Indra took away all the moving wheels of the Sun." This highlights Indra's power and agility, aided by Soma.

Indra, with Soma's support, defeated enemies in battle even before noon, while Agni also destroyed many foes. Indra's prowess is compared to a thief killing a rich man on an unsafe path, emphasizing his relentless victory over innumerable enemy armies.

"Hey Indra," the hymn praises, "you strip all the wicked of their virtues, making them worthy of condemnation. O Indra and Soma, both of you become a hindrance to enemy attacks, killing them and accepting praises for your victories." The hymn acknowledges their might and their role as protectors. Indra and Soma are also praised for their generosity, having donated vast herds of horses and cows. Both deities are wealthy and capable of killing enemies, with all their deeds being true and righteous. Thus, through the words of Vāmadeva, venerates Indra's alliance with Soma, their combined might, and their benevolence and truth in protecting humanity and defeating enemies.

Sukta 29, Rishi Vāmadeva extols the deity Indra through the chant of Triṣṭup. The hymn calls upon Indra, urging him to come to their colorful yagyas for protection, even bringing the blind. Indra, known for his strong mind, is worshipped by hymns and revered as the true form and master of the universe.

Indra, the benefactor of humans and knower of all knowledge, attends the Yagya when called by those accomplished in Saum. He is fearless, praised, and brings confirmation with the blossoming desert, embodying beauty and strength. The hymn implores humans to make Indra listen to the stotra with both ears, seeking his favor for hair growth and overall strength. The mighty Indra, empowered by Soma juice, is asked to free the best places for their wealth from fear.

Indra, who holds the thunderbolt in his arms, unites his numerous horses to move in the night, providing protection. The wise Indra responds to the pleading hosts with pleasantries and eulogies, ensuring the scholars are preserved. Radiant, blessed, and worthy of praise, Indra is honored through yajnas, performed at the time of giving wealth.

In Sukta 30, attributed to Rishi Vāmadeva extols the deity Indra through the chants of Gayatri and Anustup. The hymn begins by praising Indra as the destroyer of Vritra, proclaiming that there is no one greater or more famous than him in the world. Indra is revered for his brilliance and renowned qualities among the gods. Indra's omnipresence is likened to a wheel following a cart, with people following him faithfully. The gods, desiring victory, received strength from Indra, who protected them by firing a disc at the Sun and aiding the warring 'Kula' and his assistants. In battle, Indra single-handedly fought against violent demons and vanquished them all. Indra is celebrated for his protective prowess, having defended attributed to Rishi Etash in battle by attacking even the Sun. He is described as the remover of darkness and the punisher of the wicked, destroying demons who threaten the people. Indra's manly deeds are compared to the Sun destroying the dawn, as he crushes enemy armies desiring victory. Indra's might is further illustrated by his destruction of Usha's chariot, causing her to flee in fear. He manifested the Tishtamana river and various nets on earth, rained upon the land, destroyed the cities of 'Shushan,' and looted their wealth. Indra defeated the demon Shambar by throwing him from a mountain and killed countless enemies surrounding the Dasyu named 'Garchi.' Indra is praised for saving sons and daughters from suffering, making them famous, and rescuing kings 'Yadu' and 'Turvash' from a curse. He swiftly killed the kings Arna and Chitrarath across the Saryu, and showed mercy to a blind and lame man abandoned by his brothers. Indra provided many cities to the host 'Divodas' who performed sacrifices, and through his illusion, he subdued a massive bandit army. The hymn concludes by hailing Indra as the violator of Vritra, the distractor of enemy forces in battle, and the protector of cows. Indra's glory and majesty remain unchallenged, and he is implored to bestow beautiful wealth upon his devotees, with the blessings of Dantwinin Pusha and Bhag. Thus, Sukta 30, through the words of Vāmadeva, venerates Indra's unparalleled strength, protection, and generosity, celebrating his heroic deeds and divine supremacy.

Sukta 31, attributed to Rishi Vāmadeva extols Indra through the Gayatri chant. The hymn opens with an inquiry: by what worship will the ever-growing, worshipable, and friendly Indra come before us? Which wise man's best deeds will impress Indra enough to make him appear before us? "O Indra! Among the true forms and the Soma juices, which Soma juice will empower you to destroy the wealth of our enemies? You protect the friendly form of the praisers and come before us with various means of protection. Pleased with our praises, come before us like a circular wheel. Indra, come here knowing your place in the sacrifice. With the sun, we perform your sacrifice."

Indra, the protector of the less fortunate, is wealthy and fulfills the wishes of devotees and ascetics. He immediately grants abundant rewards to those who prove and praise Soma. Even the demons cannot stop his hundreds of opulences, and various adversaries cannot hinder him. "Indra, may your hundreds of defense instruments and thousands of means of protection guard us. May all your inspirations aid in our protection." In this Yagya, Indra is asked to make the hosts entitled to imperishable and radiant wealth. He is called upon to protect us daily with his great wealth. Like a brave man, Indra should strengthen the abode of the cows with new means of defense. Indra, the destroyer of enemies, is bright and moves everywhere in a chariot with imperishable cows, protecting us along the way. The hymn also acknowledges the sun's role, inspiring everyone and making the sky capable of fulfilling desires, and prays for the Yagya to increase among the gods.

Sukta 32, attributed to Rishi Vāmadeva extols the deity Indrashvo through the chant of Gayatri. The hymn begins with a call to Indrashvo, the destroyer of enemies, urging him to come near with great protection. Indrashvo is praised as worthy of worship and a traveler who provides desired results and wealth for nourishment. Indrashvo's friendly hosts help him destroy unruly enemies with great might.

The hymn expresses gratitude for Indrashvo's blessings, acknowledging his undefeated nature and his rich protections. The praisers, useful to men with cows like Indrashvo, seek his help to acquire abundant eternal wealth, including cows and horses. Indrashvo, who is worthy of praise, has the power to give wealth to his devotees without hindrance.The descendants of Gautama praise Indrashvo through hymns for food, urging him to destroy the cities of 'Kshepak' demons. The praisers chant the powers manifested by Indrashvo, seeking his favor for food containing sons and daughters. Indrashvo, the famous god of hosts, is called to perfect residences and come before the hosts, receiving confirmation from Soma-form Atra.

The praisers ask Indrashvo to listen to their words and accept their offerings, desiring thousands of fast-moving horses and Soma Kalashas. They seek hundreds or thousands of cows and abundant wealth from Indrashvo, urging him to be a great giver and not provide small amounts. Indrashvo, known for his generosity among the hosts, is asked to make the praisers masters of wealth. The hymn concludes by praising Indrashvo's two red horses and his role as a donor of cows. The praisers request that these horses grace their path, aiding them whether traveling by chariot or on foot. The hymn, thus, venerates Indrashvo's strength, generosity, and protection, celebrating his divine powers and the blessings he bestows upon his devotees.

Sukta 33 of the Fourth Anuvaka, attributed to Rishi Vāmadeva extols the deity Ribhava through the chant of Triṣṭup. The hymn begins with the praisers, likened to messengers, inspiring speech in the form of praise and praying for a milch cow to present Soma near the hosts. The Ribhugana, moving like the wind, performs activities benefiting the world, reaching space in a moment with their swift horses.

The Ribhugana, known for their benevolence, gave youth to their mother and became renowned for their work, such as making chamas, forming friendships with gods like Indra. They are described as kind-hearted, patient, and strong, dedicated to their hosts. These gods, shining like the sun and rejuvenating fallen parents, are invoked to protect the Yagya, singing Soma along with Vibhu and Ribhu Indra. Ribhugana served a dead Dhenu (cow) for a year, endowing her body with vital organs and protecting her, eventually attaining divinity through their works. Elder Ribhu expressed the desire to divide one Chamas into two, Boch's Ribhu made three, and younger Ribhu made it sharp. Their mortal soul accepted these tasks, demonstrating their divine capabilities.

The Ribhus, in human form, fulfilled their statements and became entitled to Swadha in the third Sawan. Seeing the four chamas as bright as the sun, Tvashta desired them. Residing as guests in the world of the sun, the Ribhugana caused twelve rain-bringing constellations to make crops flourish, rivers flow, and medicines to grow in arid places. Those who created the chariot with beautiful wheels and gave birth to the world-inspiring cow are invoked to manage wealth with their good deeds and accomplished service. The deities, including Indra, accepted the Ribhugana's work of constructing horses and chariots, acknowledging their blessed deeds. The Ribhus, praised for strengthening the two horses, are asked to provide wealth, water, cows, and all happiness like a benevolent friend.

Sukta 34, Rishi Vāmadeva extols the deity Ribhava through the chant of Triṣṭup. The hymn opens by inviting Ribhu, Vibhu Baaj, and Indra to the Yagya for wealth, expressing love through praise to achieve Soma. The joy emanating from Soma is asked to remain consistent with the deities. The Ribhus, once human and now gods, are adorned with perfume, and the hymn seeks confirmation from the gods for their joyful Soma and stotra. The Ribhus are requested to provide wealth for their descendants.

The hymn continues, highlighting that this Yagya is performed for the radiant Ribhugana, with the servant Soma present near them. The Ribhus are the main goal of the Yagya. The sacrificial host desires a gem worthy of donation by the Ribhus' grace in the third season, offering nourishing Soma for the gods to drink. The deities are urged to come near, praised for their great opulence, with Soma returning to them like newborn cows at the end of the day.

The Ribhus, friends of Indra and wise due to their connection, are invited to the Yagya by the stotra, to drink the sweet Soma with Indra and bestow precious wealth. Indra is also called to drink Soma with Varuna, Marudgan, and other gods, praised for his radiance. The Ribhus are asked to find happiness by meeting the Adityas, worshipable gods, and Savitadev, becoming strong with the gods who are immovable like mountains and give gems.

The hymn acknowledges the Ribhus' deeds, such as making the Ashwinikumars affectionate, giving youth to old parents, creating the cow and horse, making armor for the gods, separating the sky and earth, and creating sound. The Ribhus are seen as providers of cow, food, children, and residence, guardians of wealth, and praisers of wealth. They are asked to prepare to give wealth after drinking Soma.

The hymn concludes by urging the Ribhus not to leave, promising not to let them remain hungry, and seeking joy in the Yagya along with Indra for handsome wealth. The Ribhus are asked to become strong with Marudgana and other brilliant gods, celebrating their divine abilities and benevolent actions.

Sukta 35, attributed to Rishi Vāmadeva extols the deity Ribhava through the chant of Triṣṭup. The hymn begins by calling upon the young sons of Sudhanva to come to the third Savan and stay, not to go elsewhere. The Ribhus are invited to partake in the Ishtikaraka Soma after Indra, who has donated gems. They are praised for their craftsmanship, having made four chamas from one and drinking the renowned Soma. The hymn recounts an instance where Ribhuran, while licking a spoon, asked Agni to be pleased, to which Agni responded, acknowledging their skill and path to immortality. The Ribhus are asked to prove Soma for happiness and drink the sweet Soma. The hymn celebrates the Ribhus for giving youth to their parents through their artistry and revealing horses made from a single chamas. They are recognized as masters of Atra, best wish-givers, and wealth providers for hosts who sift Soma for their enjoyment. Indra is also called to drink the well-known Soma in the third Sawan with the gem-donating Ribhus. The Ribhus are acknowledged for attaining divinity and immortality through noble deeds and are requested to grant wealth. They are celebrated for their excellent craftsmanship, making the Soma-yukt Tosare Sawan successful, and are invited to drink Soma with a joyful heart.

Sukta 36, attributed to Rishi Vāmadeva extols the deity Ribhava through the chants of Triṣṭup and Jagti. The hymn begins by praising the Ribhus for their commendable deeds, such as creating a three-wheeled chariot for the Ashvinikumars that moves through space without a horse, maintaining the sky and earth. This act is a testament to their divinity. The Ribhus are celebrated for their craftsmanship, having created a chariot with beautiful wheels through inner meditation. Devotees invite them for Soma consumption. The Ribhus gave youth to their aged parents, making them able to walk again, a deed renowned among the gods. They also divided one chamas into four parts and covered a cow with leather, earning them an imperishable status among the gods. All their deeds are worthy of praise. The wealth revealed by the Ribhus, especially the main wealth of Annayukta, came to them. The chariot built by the worshipers at the Yagya place is praised. The person protected by the Ribhus becomes mighty, skillful, and wealthy, excelling in battle and acquiring progeny and strength. The hymn is composed beautifully for the brilliant, knowledgeable, and poetic Ribhus, praying to them through psalms. The Ribhus are asked to accept all beneficial food items and provide the bright food and wealth that generates strength and nourishes the devotees. The Lord of Lords is urged to love the fame of the devotees, granting them fame, wealth, servants, and the power to conquer others.

In Sukta 37, attributed to Rishi Vāmadeva extols the deity Ribhava through the chants of Triṣṭup and Anusthup. The hymn invites Ribhugana to follow the Yagya of human beings to make the days auspicious and come to their Yagya through the divine path. It prays for all Yagyas to bring affection to their hearts and for Soma mixed with ghee to inspire love and good deeds in them. The Ribhus, praised for benefiting the gods through Soma offerings in all three seasons, are called upon to accept the Soma offered to them with great pleasure. The hymn describes the Ribhus' strong horses, resplendent chariots, and iron-like chins, recognizing them as the masters of the present and the best givers. The Ribhus are invoked to increase wealth, act as powerful protectors in times of war, and always be charitable in good deeds. Those protected by Ribhus and Indra are considered the best, earning wealth and blessings through their work and Yagya. The hymn calls for Ribhus to guide them on the path of Yagya, granting success in all directions. The devotees are inspired by the Lords, Indra, and Ashwinikumari to donate wealth and horses.

Sukta 38, attributed to Rishi Vāmadeva extols the deities Dhara Prithvio and Dadikra through the chant of Triṣṭup. The hymn opens by acknowledging the generous king Trasadasyu, who received immense wealth from the sky and earth and distributed it generously. He was bestowed with a horse, a son, and a sharp weapon to defeat demons and opponents. The deities Dhara Prithvio and Dadikra are praised for their protective power, special light, and might, likened to a swift-moving, enemy-destroying horse that benefits humanity. The hymn describes all humans as joyful warriors who traverse directions with speed, crossing terrains like the wind. Dadikra, who stops gathered enemies in battle and moves swiftly, ensures the enemies of the host do not succeed.

Enemies scream in fear upon seeing Dadikra, just as people would upon seeing a thief. Dadikra, graceful and horse-like, chews the bridle and licks the dust from its feet, embodying strength and agility. This horse, tireless and war-capable, runs swiftly through enemy lines, blowing dust from its feet. Those who desire war fear Dadikra's power, as deadly as a thunderbolt, becoming unstoppable in battle. Dadikra, full of speed and fulfilling human wishes, is praised for ensuring victory. The deity increases crops with water, akin to the Sun enhancing water with its brightness. The hymn concludes by asking Dadikra to bless the praisers with desired results, celebrating the deity's generosity and protective might.

Sukta 39, attributed to Rishi Vāmadeva extols the deity Dadikra through the chants of Triṣṭup and Anusthup. The hymn begins with humans expressing their intent to worship the swift-moving Dadikradeva by spreading grass in front of him, invoking the protection of dawn that dispels darkness and safeguards them from troubles. As performers of the Yagya, they praise Dadikradeva, chosen by many and a fulfiller of wishes. Varun, a friend to humanity, wears Dadikra for the benefit of mankind, saving them from sorrows like a bright fire. Those who praise Dadikra in horse form at dawn, when the fire is lit, are protected by Mitra, Varun, Aditi, and Dadikra. The hymn calls upon those who wield power and bless their praisers to chant the name of the great Dadikradeva, seeking happiness through their friend Varun and thunderbolt-wielding Indra in the fire. Both warriors preparing for battle and those performing Yagya invoke Dadikradeva like Indra. Varun, the friend, adopts Dadikradeva in horse form to inspire humans. Dadikra, full of victory, comprehensive and swift, is praised to please the senses and increase lifespan. Thus, Sukta 39 venerates Dadikra's divine protection, swiftness, and the prosperity he brings, celebrating his essential role in ensuring victory and well-being for humanity.

Sukta 40, Rishi Vāmadeva extols the deities Dadikra and Surya through the chants of Jagti and Triṣṭup. The hymn begins with a commitment to worship Dadikradeva repeatedly, invoking all the dawns to engage them in their works. The hymn supports Vishnu, the descendant of water, fire, Surya, Jupiter, and Angira. It calls upon Dadikra, who lives with attendants and inspires clever, moving cows, to wish for Atra during the auspicious Usha-vela. These Dadhikras should be swift, manifesting strength and divine qualities. Just as all birds follow their traditional paths, all moving creatures follow the swift and desirable path of Dadhikra. These swift-moving, protective beings like Shyen gather around Dadikra and move for the sake of food. Depicted as a horse, this deity, tied at the throat and mouth, moves quickly on foot, valiantly crossing crooked roads with their faces toward the Yagya. Dadikra resides in the sky, air space, and at the Yagya altar, as worshipable as Aditi, occupying preferred places among humans and in Yagyas. This deity is born in water, light, truth, and mountains. Thus, Sukta 40 venerates Dadikra's divine strength, swiftness, and protective qualities, celebrating their essential role in guiding and supporting the rituals and daily activities of humanity.

Sukta 41, attributed to**Rishi Vamadeva and dedicated to the deities Indra and Varuna in the Trishup chhanda,** the hymn extols their virtues and beseeches their blessings. Hey Indra, Hey Varun, O one who would attain immortality, which hymn with the power of fire can attain the blessings of both of you? May that stotra, filled with the offerings made by us, enter into the hearts of both of you. Indra and Varuna, known for their fame, bestow the power to destroy sins, kill enemies in war, and gain renown with immense defense equipment. They are the providers of beautiful wealth to their devotees and the givers of immense love like a father to his son. They are beseeched to attack enemies with swift force, protect devotees, and ensure the fulfillment of wishes through their praises. As protectors with innovative means of defense, they are called upon to provide horses, chariots, and wealth, ensuring victory in battles and prosperity for their devotees.

Sukta 42, attributed to Rishi Asadasyu, Paurukutsya, and dedicated to the deity-soul, Indra, and Varuna in the Trishup chhanda, the hymn highlights the supremacy and divine protection granted by the deities. We are Kshatriyas, the masters of all humans, our nation divided yet united under divine protection. Just as all gods are ours, so are all people. We are beautiful in appearance and as famous as Varuna, with the gods safeguarding our yagya. As Varun Tejaswi Raja, it is for our sake that the gods assume the might to kill demons, embodying the essence of Varuna. Indra and Varuna inspire and sustain every living being, holding the sky and earth, and irrigating waters in the form of rain. The sons of Aditi have performed the Yagya for water, transforming the vast sky into three worlds. Leading the battle, horse-riding warriors follow us, calling us in determined war, performing Yagya in the form of glorious Indra, filled with strength to defeat the enemy. Our divine power, unstoppable, completes all tasks. Strengthened by Somras and Stotras, the vast sky and earth become movable. Varuna's deeds are known by all, praised by all living beings. Indra, renowned for vanquishing enemies and making rivers flow, has blessed us. Under the grace of Indravarun, Purukutsa's yagya for his wife birthed Trasadasyu, the enemy destroyer, attaining semi-divinity like Indra. Inspired by Rishi Indravarun, Trasadasyu, the demigod destroyer, received hymns and praises. Satisfied with wealth, the gods with Haviratra, and cows with Trinadi, we praise both Indra and Varuna, the creators and destroyers of the world, seeking a stable cube.

In Sukta 43, attributed to attributed to Rishi s Purumila and Hajmilahi of the Sauhotras, and dedicated to the Aśvinī-kumāras in the Triṣṭup chhanda, the hymn seeks the blessings and presence of the divine twins. Which of the gods of the sacrifice will hear this praise? Which gods will accept this stotra worthy of worship? To which deity among the gods should we sing our loving, bright, beautiful praises of Haviratra, who deserves this? The Ashwini Kumars are the ones who bring happiness and are most present in our Yagya, with their swift, beautiful chariot respected by Surya. They are called to show their might, come from the sky route, and display their divine qualities. The hymn asks which praise suits them best and seeks their protection from enemies. Their chariot, moving swiftly around the sky and sea, signifies their power to create sweet water and destroy foes. The horses, anointed by the cloud, move like birds, highlighting the chariot that saved Surya. The Ashwini Kumars are invited to the Yagya together, praised for their beauty and generosity, and implored to protect and fulfill the wishes of the devotees.

Sukta 44, attributed to attributed to Rishi Purumilahajamilaho Sohotro and dedicated to the Ashvinau deities in the Trishup chhanda, the hymn venerates the Ashwinikumars and their divine attributes. O two horses! We call upon your cowboy and famous fast chariot that has given shelter to Surya. The seating area in it is made of wood, a carrier of praises, and full of food and wealth. The Ashwinikumars, adorned by their good deeds, embody Soma's vigor, with their chariot pulled by excellent horses. Which host of soma-suppliers praises you for drinking soma and seeking protection? The Ashwinikumars, known for their numerous deeds, are called to the Yagya with their golden chariot to drink the sweetest Somras and provide a beautiful cube to seekers. They descend from the sky in their golden chariot, ensuring other hosts do not hinder their arrival. The Ritvijas of 'Purmeen' and 'Ajmihn' have combined their stotras to call upon the Ashwinikumars, asking for wealth and many children. The hymn unites the Ashwinikumars in the Yagya, praising their excellent food and seeking their protection, fulfilling the devotees' wishes upon their arrival.

Sukta 45, attributed to Rishi Vamadeva and dedicated to the Ashvin deities in the Jagati and Trishup chhanda, the hymn praises the Ashwinikumars and their celestial chariot. As the bright sun rises, the best chariot of the Ashwinikumars travels everywhere, adorned with stunning decorations and stones. Various Atras and Chamas are filled with Soma, illuminating the universe at dawn with light as bright as the sun, erasing darkness. The Ashwinikumars, practitioners of drinking Soma, are called to bring their chariot to the host's house, complete their journey quickly, and bless the Soma-filled vessel. Their beautiful horses, swift and golden, inspire the waters and bring sweetness. When the virtuous Adhvaryus crush the sweet Soma, they sing praises of the Ashwinikumars, who illuminate like the sun and complete their path with somersaults. The priests praise the ever-new chariot of the Ashwinikumars, inviting them to the Haviratra Yagya with their beautiful horses and celestial chariot.

In Sukta 46, attributed to Rishi Vamadeva and dedicated to the deities Indra and Vayu in the Gayatri chhanda, the hymn invites the gods to partake in the sacred ritual. Hey Vayu, come and drink this anointed Somras in the Yagya that will elevate you to heaven, for you are the first to drink Somras. Hey Vayu, Hey Indra, may both of you find satisfaction in drinking Soma and Paan. Vayu, appointed to work for the welfare of the people and creator of Indra, come here to fulfill our strong desires. May thousands of horses quickly bring both of you here for Sompan. Indra and Vayu, with a chariot made of bright gold wood and great power from the sky, come near the host offering the sacrifice. Both of you are for the sacrifice, come to this great Yagya. O Indra, O Vayu, this is well-known Soma. Both of you, having equal love, come to the sacrificial place of the host and drink Somras. In this Yagya, horses should be untied to give you the drink. Both of you come to this sacrificial place.

In Sukta 47, attributed to Rishi Vamadeva and dedicated to the deities Indra and Vayu in the Anushtup chhanda, the hymn venerates the deities and invites them to partake in the sacred Soma ritual. Hey Vayu, purified by the best rituals, we, wishing to attain the divine world, first bring Somras for you. You are worthy of desire. Come from that place along with your vehicle to drink Soma. Hey Vayu, you and Indra are eligible to drink that Soma. Just as water goes towards a pit, similarly all types of Soma flow towards you. Both of you are masters of power, extremely brave, and equipped with horses. United, you sit on the chariot, drink Soma, and come here to give us shelter. Hey Indra and Vayu, both of you are the ones who perform Yagya and are the leaders among all the gods. We are the hosts who provide you Havinantra. Whatever wish you have, please provide it to us.

Sukta 48, attributed to Rishi Vamadeva and dedicated to the deity Vayu in the Anushtup chhanda, the hymn extols the power and majesty of Vayu. O wind, you are like a king who makes his enemies tremble. Drink the Somras, which has not been drunk by others in advance, and bring blessings to those who praise you. Come here to drink Soma in your auspicious chariot. Hey Vayo, along with Indra, you take the form of a charioteer, riding a golden chariot with strong, mild-natured horses, free from evil. You come to drink the joyous Soma. The black-complexioned, world-like form of Vasus, the sky, and the earth follow your footsteps. Ninety-nine horses, as swift as the mind, bring you here. You come on a beautiful chariot full of Soma to drink Soma. Hey Vayo, you attach hundreds of horses to the chariot and come here with them.

Sukta 49, composed by Rishi Vamadeva and dedicated to the deities Indra and Brihaspati in the Gayatri chhanda, the hymn seeks the blessings and presence of the deities. O Indra and Jupiter, we put the most beloved Somroop Haviranna in your mouths and offer joyful Somras to both of you. For the sake of your pleasure and for you to drink, we pour that delicious Soma juice into your mouths. Both of you, come to our sacrificial fire to drink Soma. O Indra and Jupiter, grant us wealth consisting of hundreds of cows and thousands of horses. We invite you to drink Somras. While residing in the house of the host who is offering Havi, both of you should drink Soma and become strong.

Sukta 50, composed by attributed to Rishi Vamadeva and dedicated to the deities Brihaspati and Indra in the Trishup chhanda, the hymn venerates the powerful and wise Brihaspati, protector of the Vedas, who controls the ten directions of the earth and pervades all three worlds through his words. The ancient Rishis installed Brihaspati, who possesses a special tongue that brings happiness, as the priest. O brilliant Lord Jupiter, your enemies tremble due to your movements. You are fruitful, ennobling, non-violent, and support those who praise you and perform great yagyas. From the distant heavenly worlds, your horses come to this yagya, spreading sweet nectar like water boiling around a well. When Brihaspati first appeared in the solar system, his brightness destroyed darkness. Along with the praising Angiras, he destroyed the demon 'Bal' with fierce words and brought out cows giving excellent milk from the cave. We will worship Brihaspati, the maintainer and fulfiller of desires, in the yagya praised by Haviranna to gain children and opulence. The king who protects and praises Brihaspati, offering the first oblation, defeats his enemies and prospers. His subjects always bow to him, and the earth bears fruit in every season. The king who helps a poor scholar conquers his enemies' wealth, with gods as his protectors. O Jupiter and Indra, be pleased in the yajna, granting wealth and children. May your kindness inspire and protect us, and may you attain consciousness through our praise.

Sukta 51, attributed to Rishi Vamadeva and dedicated to the deity Usha in the Trishup chhanda, the hymn praises the luminous and all-knowing dawn. The glory that is praised by us is all-known, extremely luminous, and appears in the east direction, piercing the bright darkness. The daughter of the Sun, Usha, full of light, is fully capable of helping the hosts in their movement. Just as the Yupanshas carved in Yagya are stable, the beautiful dawn spreads in the east, dispelling obscuring darkness and giving pure, bright light. The light that dispels darkness and is full of opulence inspires the host offering food for the sake of Somadi food. Similarly, prosperous housewives reveal their virtues and warn their husbands when the intense darkness ends. O luminous dawn! May your ancient chariot, which made Navagva eternally young and Dagva Angiras brilliant, come to this place of our yagya. You move around the houses in a moment on your moving horse, inspiring the sleeping four-legged animals with your movements. Where are those ancient dawns for which Ribhugan created Chamas etc.? When the bright new beautiful dawns shine, they remain uniform, indistinguishable from old or new. The dawns worshiped by the Yajna performing host, bringing wealth and welfare, appear for the sake of Yagya, giving true results. Uniform rays descend from space in the east and go everywhere, full of light, worshiped like rays aiming at the place of sacrifice. The dawns, uniform in beautiful color, bright and radiant, luminous with their bodies, roam everywhere hiding the darkness. O daughter of the luminous sun, fill us with children and wealth. We request our happiness, so we can become masters of opulence with children. O daughters of the bright sun, we pray that we become famous and prosperous among all humans, may the sky and the earth be full of light and provide happiness for us.

In Sukta 52, attributed to Rishi Vamdeva and dedicated to the deity Usha in the Gayatri chhanda, the hymn glorifies the radiant dawn. You stretch out the sky with your rays, illuminating the heavens. Usha, shocked by Venus, appears as the daughter of Surya, leading praiseworthy creatures and producing beautiful fruits. Like her sister, she destroys the darkness at the end of the night. Usha, who looks beautiful like a horse, is luminous, the mother of rays, and performs the Yagya, being related to the Ashvinikumars. Hey Ushe, you are the presiding deity of opulence, driving away enemies and granting knowledge. We greet you with praises. The dawn of great brightness, like a stream of rain, has filled the world with rays worthy of praise. Hey Ushe, your beautiful light destroys darkness with brilliance and makes the world prosperous. You follow this Haviranna, spreading your luminous glory through the rays in the sky and vast space.

Sukta 53, attributed to Rishi Vamdeva and dedicated to the deity Savita in the Jagti chhanda, the hymn extols the strength and intelligence of Savitadev, praying for wealth and prosperity. Savitadev, strong and intelligent, is prayed to for wealth worthy of choice and worship, to be given to the offering host as per their wish. The brilliant Savitadev, who sustains the sky and all worlds, nurtures living beings through light and rain, wearing golden armor, fills the world with brilliance and manifests happiness worthy of praise. Savitadev fills the sky and earth with brilliance, attracting praise through excellent deeds, inspiring the world towards work, and extending arms for the construction work of the universe. Savitadev enlightens the world with non-violence, follows resolutions, protects creatures in all worlds, observes fasts, and is the master of the vast world. Pervading all three universes with glory, Savitadev is prevalent in society, pervading fire, air, Aditya, and the three heavens and earths, kindly protecting through fasts. Savitadev, who determines actions, possesses great opulence, is known by everyone, controls all living beings, destroys sins, and grants equal happiness in all three worlds. The luminous Savitadev maintains the world through seasons, increases opulence, grants wealth with children, and shows affection day and night, bestowing prosperity with sons and grandchildren.

Sukta 54, attributed to Rishi Vamdeva and dedicated to the deity Savita in the Jagato and Trishup chhanda, the hymn praises the sun and seeks its blessings in the Yagya. The sun has appeared, and we will greet it soon in the third hour. It should be praised by everyone present in the savana. The sun, provider of wealth like gems and jewels, is the best provider of wealth for us in this Yagya. You should first reveal the best part of Soma, the best means of immortality, in the Yagya. Hey Savitadev, you fill the sacrificial host with light and grant long life to humans in the order of father, son, and grandson. If, due to ignorance, greed for money, or arrogance of power and family, we have committed any crime against you or other gods and learned people, please free us from that sin in this Yagya. Savitadev, the sustainer of the world, performs non-violent actions that cannot be destroyed by anyone. Hey Savitadev, the great and opulent Indra is worshiped by us. You elevate us higher than a mountain, give all these hosts a residence with houses, and regularize all travel times scheduled by you. With your blessings, the living hosts perform the beautiful Soma for you in all the three sathans. May those hosts be blessed with immense happiness along with the sky, the earth, the great and solemn Sindhu Gods, and the Adityas, and make us happy as well.

Sukta 55, attributed to Rishi Vamadeva and dedicated to the Vishvedevas in the Trishup and Gayatri chhanda, the hymn calls upon the deities for protection and prosperity. Hey Vasu, who among you can save from suffering? Who will protect? Sky and earth, you too are indivisible, protect us. Hey friend Varun, be our protector. Which god among you will provide wealth in Yagya? The gods who grant ancient status to their praisers, remove sorrows, and dispel the host's darkness, fulfill human desires with truth and beauty. We praise Mother Aditi for happiness and well-being, so the sky and earth protect us, and day, night, and dawn fulfill our wishes. Arthama and Varun show the right path, and Lord Agnidev guides beneficial yagya. Indra and Vishnu, adorned and worshipped, bestow happiness, children, strength, and wealth. We seek protection from Indra's friends, deserts, mountains, and Bhagdevata. May Lord Varuna protect us from sin, and friendly gods safeguard us. O goddesses in the form of sky and earth, we praise you for our desired work like a man praising the ocean for a sea voyage. May Goddess Aditi and other gods protect us, and Indra, who frees from sorrows, be our protector. We cannot stop the Atra of Mitra, Varun, and Soma, but we can increase them through Yagya rituals. Agnidev, lord of wealth and fortune, bless us with wealth and good fortune. O Satyavani Usha Devi, mistress of wealth and food, grant us beautiful wealth. Indra, along with Savitadev, Bhagdevata, Varun, and friends, go to the Yagya place and donate their wealth to us.

Sukta 56, attributed to Rishi Vamadeva and dedicated to the deities Heaven and Earth in the Trishtup and Gayatri chhanda, the hymn extols the celestial and terrestrial realms. May the best, most important Heaven and Earth be filled with light with this beautiful stotra and somersault. For this purpose, the Parjanyas, capable of irrigation work, establish the vast and important sky and earth, conveying special words to the desert people. Worthy of Yajna, bearers of desires, free from violence, void of treachery, full of truth, supreme doers of the gods, and editors of Yagya, both the gods in the form of sky and earth are filled with Haviratras compatible with other gods. The one who created this sky-earth, running it beautifully, is worthy of glory among all worlds. O sky and earth, you wish to provide us with food, are compatible with each other, omnipresent, and worthy of Yagya, granting us homes with housewives and protection. May we attain chariot-equipped servants by our best deeds. O sky and earth, you are radiant. We receive this great hymn for your sake. You both are holy, and we come to praise you. May you both purify and beautify each other with your brilliance and strength, always carrying the Yagya. O sky and earth, you become helpful to those who praise you as friends, seated with various types of wealth and circling the Yagya place.

Sukta 57, attributed to Rishi Vamadeva and dedicated to the deity Kshetrapati and others in the Gayatri and Trishup chhanda, the hymn seeks blessings for prosperity and agricultural success. With a field lord like a brother, we, the priests, will conquer the field. May Kshetrapati strengthen our cows and horses, and bless us with the wealth we deserve. Hey Kshetrapate, just as a cow gives milk, grant us sweet, pure water as tasty as ghee. O Lord of the waters, make us happy in every way. May the medicines be of sweet quality, the earth be full of grains, and rivers have fresh water. May the space shower sweet water and the ruler be blessed with sweet food. We commit no violence and remain friendly to all. May the plowmen and all involved in plowing be happy, and may the animals and equipment work harmoniously. O Annapati and Mistress, hear our praises. May Indra irrigate the earth with the water created in the sky. Hey Sita, you are lucky and capable of bestowing beautiful fruits as you go under the earth. We praise your Guru for your fortune-bringing powers. Lord Indra should accept Sita, and Pusha should hold it well, ensuring prosperity. May the plow blade dig the land joyfully, farmers drive their bulls happily, and clouds shower sweet water, filling the earth. O lords of food and fields, make us happy.

Sukta 58, attributed to Rishi Vamadeva and dedicated to the gods of fire, needle, steam, and cows or ghee praise in the Trishup and Jagti chhanda, the hymn exalts the nourishing and purifying qualities of ghee and fire. Honey rays have emerged from the sea, granting immortality to human beings. The widespread form of ghee, embodying nectar, serves as a divine shelter. We praise Yanaman Ghrit and accept it in this Yagya with salutations. Brahya, listen to this invocation. The one knowledgeable in the four Vedas, like a deer with four hundred calves, preaches the Vedic science. The physical fire, with its four wings, three feet as a house, two heads as Brahmodana and Prakmya, and seven hands as verses, fulfills all desires. This mantra, recited in three ways by Kalpa and Brahmin, exists among mortals as a divine presence. Birds preserved milk, curd, and ghee among cows, which gods discovered and cherished. Indra created milk, Surya another substance, and the gods obtained the essence through food. Water descends from space with immense speed, unseen by enemies but visible to us, revealing fire. Like affectionate rivers, nectarous words flow from purified minds, swift as deer fleeing hunters. The Ghrit stream flows rapidly like river water, crossing boundaries and fighting waves like the self-respecting Asdha. Just as a devoted woman loves her husband, the ghee stream moves lovingly towards fire, illuminating equally. Brilliant fires always desire these ghee streams. Just as a girl seeks her husband, revealing her beauty, the ghee stream flows to radiant Dhrit-Bharaye Agni at Soma-Yaga. Hey Ritvijo, approach the cows and praise them, filling our Yagya with opulence for the gods. Let water flow melodiously. O fire, the entire world relies on you. Your great strength manifests in the ocean, heart, life, and purification processes. We seek to attain that sweet essence.

The fourth Mandala of Rig-Veda concludes with this Sukta, emphasizing the unity of divine power and the importance of praise and worship in seeking divine blessings and protection.

SEVEN
RISHI BHARDWAJA (MANDALA 6)

Bharadvaja (Sanskrit: भरद्वाज, IAST: Bharadvāja), also spelled Bharadwaja, was one of the esteemed Vedic sages (maharishi) of ancient India, celebrated for his profound contributions to Vedic literature and his enduring influence on various fields of knowledge. As one of the Saptarishis, the seven great sages in Hindu tradition, Bharadvaja's legacy is intricately woven into the fabric of ancient Indian culture and religion.

He is credited with authoring the sixth book (mandala) of the Rigveda, one of the oldest and most revered texts in Indian literature. His hymns reflect a deep understanding of the social, spiritual, and philosophical contexts of his time, offering invaluable insights into the Vedic civilization.

Bharadvaja was not only a scholar and sage but also an accomplished grammarian, economist, and physician. His name appears in various significant texts, including the Mahabharata, where he is recognized as the father of the illustrious teacher Droṇācārya, the guru of the Pandava and Kaurava princes. Moreover, the ancient medical treatise, Charaka Samhita, mentions Bharadvaja as a pioneer in the field of medicine, attributing his knowledge to the teachings of Indra, who responded to Bharadvaja's plea to alleviate human suffering caused by poor health.

The etymology of his name, "Bharadvaja," which combines the Sanskrit words "bhara(d)" (nourishment) and "vaja(m)" (bringing about), symbolizes his role in nurturing knowledge and wisdom. Bharadvaja's influence extends beyond religious texts; he is also revered in later Puranic legends and even in Buddhist Pali canonical texts, where he is acknowledged as one of the ancient rishis whose wisdom transcended religious boundaries.

As the progenitor of the Bharadvāja gotra, Bharadvaja holds a significant place in the genealogical traditions of Brahmins and Kshatriyas, further solidifying his importance in the socio-religious history of India. His teachings and contributions continue to be honored, making him a pivotal figure in the spiritual and intellectual heritage of Hinduism.

(First Anuvaka)

Sukta 1, Rishi Bharadwaja, son of Brihaspati, offers a hymn dedicated to Agni, the deity of fire, using the Trishup chanda. Bharadwaja recitation begins with an invocation to Agni, "Oh fire! You are the best among the gods. The mind of the gods is fixed on you. You are worthy of being seen. You are the one who invites the gods in this Yagya. Oh Lord of Fire who showers wishes; give us strength to defeat all the powerful enemies." The Sukta continues to extol Agni's virtues, highlighting his role as the divine performer of sacrificial rituals, the bright and luminous one who enlightens the paths of those seeking wealth and prosperity. Bharadwaja emphasizes the significance of Agni in sacrificial ceremonies, his ability to bestow strength and protection, and his eternal presence that fulfills the desires of worshippers, ensuring their prosperity and happiness. The hymn concludes with a prayer for Agni's blessings, seeking wealth, protection, and success in all endeavors.

Sukta 2, Rishi Bharadwaja, son of Brihaspati, offers a hymn dedicated to Agni, the deity, through the Anuṣṭup and Shakvari chanda. Bharadwaja hymn extols Agni's virtues, beginning with, "O fire, you are the master of splendor and a friend to us. You are the sacrificial fire, sustaining us with perfumes and nutritious substances. Worshippers invoke you with air and hymns as part of their sacrificial offerings." The Rishi continues, highlighting Agni's role in inspiring non-violence and supporting trade among living beings, "O Atvik, with energy like fire, you are renowned. You are the sound of Yagya, invited by the hosts of Manu's descendants who desire happiness. You are generous-minded, praised in rituals for your brilliance and wealth-giving power." Bharadwaja emphasizes the blessings Agni bestows, ensuring the hosts are blessed with children and reside in beautiful homes, "O fire, the host who strengthens you with mantra-based offerings is blessed throughout the year." The hymn also underscores Agni's purifying and all-encompassing nature, spreading brightness like Aditya in the morning and being revered as a guest who performs public welfare, "O fire, you are worthy of praise, shelter, and reverence, your existence proven through Arani Manthan." Bharadwaja concludes with a prayer for prosperity and protection, "O fire, enter the house of those wishing to perform a Yagya, wear our offerings, and bless us with a beautiful residence, free from enemies and troubles, securing us from sins and ensuring our safety with your protective strength."

Sukta 3, attributed to Rishi Bharadwaja Brihaspati and dedicated to the deity Agni with the Trishup chanda, the hymn extols the virtues and protective powers of Agni. The Rishi invokes Agni, the divine host of Yajna, to grant long life and salvation from sins to those who perform rituals with devotion. Agni's brilliance, comparable to the love of Varuna and Mitra, ensures great protection and prosperity to the devotees, shielding them from false pride and sin. The hymn vividly describes Agni's terrifying and all-encompassing flame, likening its movement to a cow's mooing and its ferocity to that of a goldsmith melting gold or an archer's sharp arrow. Agni's light is praised for its ability to inspire work and spread light, akin to the sun's radiance. The hymn celebrates Agni's power to defeat enemies and bestow celestial and earthly opulence, highlighting the flame's brightness and speed, which increases the strength of Agni Marudgan.

Sukta 4, attributed to Rishi Bharadwaja Brihaspati, dedicated to the deity Agni, and written in the Trishup chanda, the hymn invokes Agni as the divine son of Bala who summons the gods to partake in the Yagya. The Rishi beseeches Agni to treat the Indrani gods with favor and perform the Yagya for them, just as he has done in past sacrifices. Agni is praised for his brilliance, comparable to the sun, and his role as the illuminator and protector. The hymn extols Agni's power to bestow praiseworthy wealth and his ability to purify and reveal all objects with his brightness. Agni is depicted as the destroyer of enemies, the dispeller of darkness, and the swift-moving force that governs the world like the wind. The Rishi prays for Agni's favor to conquer adversaries, bring supreme opulence, and grant long life and happiness to the devotees. The hymn concludes with a plea for beautiful children and a prosperous life, emphasizing Agni's divine qualities and the joy he brings to those who worship him.

Sukta 5, Rishi Bharadwaja and dedicated to the deity Agni with the Trishup chanda, the hymn venerates Agni, the son of strength and the eternal, intelligent, and treachery-free Yusha. The Rishi calls upon Agni through the hymn, praising his qualities that are extolled by great Rishi s. Agni is invoked as the summoned of gods, free from many flames, who assists the hosts day and night. The hymn describes Agni's role in quenching desires and bestowing opulence upon worshippers, as well as his power to destroy both visible and hidden enemies with his brilliance. Agni's brightness is linked to causing rain and warding off adversaries. The hymn further celebrates Agni's ability to grant the best wealth to those who serve him with hymns, sacrifices, and human activities, ensuring that they become adorned with prosperity. The Rishi prays for Agni's protection and prosperity, seeking beautiful children, ample food, and immortal fame through Agni's luminous brilliance, thus becoming renowned and ageless.

Sukta 6, attributed to Rishi Bharadwaja Brihaspati and dedicated to the deity Agni with the Trishup chanda, the hymn celebrates the divine power and brilliance of Agni. The priests, filled with wishes and sacrificial rituals, approach Agni with vessels of praise, recognizing his divine form and bright wishes. Agni, the great purifier, spreads his ageless vocabulary through the bright rainy space and moves through the desert, consuming countless woods. The hymn vividly describes Agni's flames, which, combined with air, spread everywhere, burning forests to ashes with their radiant movement. Agni's flames, likened to abandoned horses, reside dynamically in the earth and arise repeatedly with the rain, just as Indra's thunderbolt does in battle. Agni's monstrous form destroys forests, spreading opulence across the earth, eliminating troubles, subduing enemies, and providing great prosperity. The Rishi praises Agni's strange yet famous appearance and prays for blessings of sons and grandchildren, seeking Agni's favor for immense prosperity.

Sukta 7, attributed to Rishi Bharadwaja, son of Brihaspati, and dedicated to the deity Vaishvanara Agni with the Trishup and Jagatai

chanda, the hymn venerates Vaishvanara Agni, who moves upon the earth like the head of the sky, born from Yagyadi for the benefit of the people. Agni is described as knowledgeable, well-decorated, and akin to a guest for Vajmanau, equipped with means of protection and acting as the face of the gods. The worshipers manifest Agni with reverence, recognizing him as the deity who evaporates the Yagya's liquids and symbolizes the Yagya's flag. The host endowed with Haviranna attains knowledge from Agni, and brave men subdue their enemies by his grace. Agni, with the quality of immortality, appears like a son from two forests and is praised by all gods. When Vaishvanara Agni ignites between the sky and the earth, the host attains an imperishable status through sacrificial actions. Agni's deeds are unhindered, and he establishes the sun that shows the days. His brilliance creates the higher places of the divine world, causes water to flow from clouds, and generates seven rivers. Lord Vaishvanara, the protector of the waters of fire and creator of shining stars and four directions, remains unconquered by anyone.

Sukta 8, attributed to Rishi Bharadwaja Brihaspati and dedicated to the deity Vaishvanara Agni with the Jagati and Trishtup chanda, the hymn exalts Vaishvanara Agni, the radiant light and brilliant fire present everywhere, praised in the Yagya. Agni is depicted as sacred, inspiring beautiful hymns, and as a protector of true beings, performing both Vedic and worldly activities in the superior sky. Vaishvanara Agni, beneficial like a friend, stabilizes the earth, covers the sky, hides darkness with his brilliance, and stretches the sky and earth like animal skins. Marudgan established Agni in space, and humans worship him as their master, with Matrishva bringing this divine fire from the solar system to earth. Agni is worthy of Yagya, grants successful children and beautiful wealth to devotees reciting hymns for her. Immortal and honored, Agni destroys enemies like a thunderbolt striking a tree. Agni bestows supreme power, wealth, and drives away enemies, enabling devotees to conquer hundreds and thousands with his protection. The hymn concludes with a prayer for Agni's indestructible protection and praise for his role in safeguarding sacrifices and relieving sorrows.

Sukta 9, attributed to Rishi Bharadwaja Brihaspati and dedicated to the deity Vaishvanara with the Rishtrapa chanda, the hymn celebrates the divine power of Vaishvanara Agni, who destroys darkness with his brilliant light, like the king of fire. The hymn reflects on the changing cycles of night and day, painting the world with colors. Vaishvanara Agni, knowledgeable about the warp and weft, preaches wisdom and shines as Aditya, protecting the waters and illuminating the earth. The hymn extols Agni as the eternal light among humans, guiding them with his steady flame, more powerful than the mind. All gods approach Vaishvanara with reverence, recognizing his supreme role. The Rishi expresses the desire to perceive Agni's qualities through the senses, meditating on his distant light, and seeking his protection. Vaishvanara Agni, revered by all gods, is depicted as a lamp in darkness, providing defense and refuge with his immortal qualities, ensuring the well-being of his devotees.

Sukta 10, attributed to Rishi Bharadwaja, son of Brihaspati, and dedicated to the god Agni with the Trishtup and Dvipad Virat chanda, the hymn praises Agni, free from all defects and the knower of all created things, who performs beneficial tasks in the Yagya. Agni, with his nectar-like flames, is capable of summoning the gods and listens to the hymns of those praising him. The host who offers oblations and beautiful hymns to Agni becomes prosperous, receiving cows, wonderful flames, and means of protection. Agni's birth filled the sky and earth with glory, removing darkness with his light. The hymn seeks Agni's blessings for wonderful wealth, a brave and wealthy son, and prosperity for those performing Yagyas. Agni is implored to drive away enemies, increase wealth, and grant a hundred virtuous years with beautiful children.

Sukta 11, attributed to Rishi Bharadwaja Brihaspati and dedicated to the deity Agni with the Trishtup chanda, the hymn celebrates Agni as the great force in Yagyas, guiding Maruts and humans away from the wrong path towards good deeds. Agni is depicted as friendly to both gods and earth, engaged in the Yagya, and always charitable towards the devotees. As the bearer of offerings, Agni purifies and manifests through flames representing the faces of gods. The hymn acknowledges the significance of Agni in ensuring the success of Yagyas for the Indradi gods, praised by Rishi s like Angira and Bharadwaja. Agni is described as brilliant, graceful, and a caretaker of the vast sky and earth, adorned with beautiful hair. The ritual of consecrating kush and offering pure ghee signifies the preparation of the Yagya altar, with Agni central to its success, akin to the sun's glory. The hymn concludes with a prayer to Agni, the stunning lord with innumerable flames, to increase his glory, bestow wealth, and free the devotees from the bondage of sins.

Sukta 12, attributed to Rishi Bharadwaja, son of Brihaspati, and dedicated to the deity Agni with the Trishtup chanda, the hymn venerates

Agnidev, the master of Yagya and invoker of gods, who is established in the host's house to complete the connection between the sky and earth. Agni, the son of force, illuminates the entire world like the sun with his radiant light. The hymn praises Agni's brilliance, comparing his radiance to the sun, spreading across the three worlds and delivering offerings from humans to the gods. The omnipresent flames of Agni ignited in Mars, spread through the space path and illuminate the world. The knowledgeable worship Agni is at fire sacrifices, recognizing him as the father of calves and a quick worker like a bull. When Agni consumes forests and spreads over the land, people praise his flames. The hymn concludes with a prayer to Agni, the destroyer of enemies, to protect and save from condemnation, bestow prosperity, destroy sorrow-causing enemies, and grant a life filled with happiness and the best warriors.

Sukta 13, attributed to Rishi Bharadwaja Brihaspati and dedicated to the deity Agni with the Trishtup chanda, the hymn extols Agni, the Lord of Fire with beautiful opulence. Agni is recognized as the source of various opulence's and the power that conquers enemies in the world of creation. As the originator of rain, Agni is worshipped by all. The hymn requests Agni to bestow beautiful wealth and to let his glory be visible. Agni, pervasive like the wind, is praised for giving abundant knowledge and opulence's worthy of enjoyment. Agni, appearing for the Yagya filled with excellent knowledge, inspires wealth and empowers the protector of good people to destroy enemies. The hymn further celebrates Agni, son of strength, whose bright light through worship and yajna-karma brings prosperity and benefits. The Rishi prays for Agni to provide beautiful perfumes, the best sons, and abundant food, seeking Agni's advice and blessings for a long, prosperous life with happiness and beautiful children.

Sukta 14, attributed to Rishi Bharadwaja, son of Brihaspati, and dedicated to the deity Agni with the Anushtup and Shakvari chanda, the hymn praises the brilliance and prominence of the devotee who serves Agni with hymns while performing Yagya rituals. This devotee receives ample food from enemies to support his family. Agni, the most knowledgeable and unique, performs Yajna-karma and is all-seeing, invoked by the sons of the hosts during Yagya. Agni protects his worshipers, taking wealth from their enemies and aiding in their conquest over non-worshippers. He grants a son of good deeds, who conquers enemies and protects noble deeds, instilling fear in adversaries. Agni, with his brilliant knowledge, subdues critics and protects men, his strength evident in wartime. The hymn concludes with a plea to Agni, the radiant fire of the earth and sky, to convey praises to the gods, provide happiness and pleasures to devotees, and free them from enemies, sins, and sufferings, ensuring they overcome all defenses.

Sukta 15, attributed to Rishi Bharadwaja Baṛhaspati & Vitahavya Angirasas, and dedicated to the deity Agni with various chandas including Trishtup, Shakvari, Jagati, Atishakvari, Brihati, and Anushtup, the hymn venerates Agni as the divine fire that serves both gods and humans. Agni is praised for his role in the Yagya, illuminating the world like the sun, and being the protector and purifier. The hymn highlights Agni's ability to bestow wealth, opulence, and protection upon those who serve him with hymns and offerings. Agni, who is ever-present and omnipotent, is described as the bearer of praises, capable of invoking the gods, and performing Yagya rituals. The hymn also emphasizes Agni's role in driving away enemies and ensuring prosperity for his devotees. Agni is invoked to provide beautiful wealth, protect the yajamana, and ensure that offerings reach the gods. The Rishi prays for Agni's blessings to overcome sins, achieve happiness, and live a prosperous life with beautiful children, honoring Agni's eternal significance and his role in the cosmic order.

Second Anuvaka

Sukta 16, attributed to Rishi Bharadwaja and dedicated to the deity Agni with the chants Gayatri, Trishtup Vardhamana, and Anushtup, the hymn profoundly praises Agni, the divine fire, for his essential role in the cosmos and Yagya rituals. Agni, revered as the summoned of gods and master of Yagya, is depicted as a beacon of purity, illuminating the universe with his radiant flames and connecting the realms of earth and heaven.

The hymn begins by addressing Agni as the home-maker, established by the gods in the Yagya performed by the descendants of Manu. Agni is invoked to praise the gods in the Yagya with his blissful flames, summoning the Indradi gods to partake in the havir (sacrificial offerings). Agni, described as blessed with charitable qualities and profound knowledge, is acknowledged for his ability to understand both the detailed and small methods of Yagya, guiding those who have strayed back to the righteous path. The hymn then reflects on historical instances where Agni played a pivotal role in bestowing wealth and prosperity. The Rishi recounts how Agni granted many types of wealth to Divodasa, who performed the Soma Yagya, and prays for similar blessings upon the sacrificers. Agni's immortality and divine qualities are celebrated, with a request for him to bring the gods, inspired by the praises of learned Rishi s like Bharadwaja, to the Yagya. The hymn emphasizes that through Agni, desires are fulfilled, evils are pacified, and prosperity is achieved.

Agni's brilliance and omnipresence are extolled, as he is described as pervading the universe, bearer of praises, and filled with flames rising upward. The Rishi s of the Bhrigu dynasty are noted for keeping Agni like a friend in their homes, praising him daily with the best hymns. Agni, the protector of the worlds and the one who consumes havir, is invoked to provide a house full of opulence to the sacrificers, protect the Yagya, and offer blessings. The hymn also delves into Agni's role as a divine messenger and the protector of the Yagya, appointed by Manu and praised by the learned. Agni is acknowledged for his ability to consume offerings and deliver them to the gods, sitting on the sacred kush and receiving praises. His luminous presence is said to bring vast, praiseworthy opulence, and his enlightenment by Rishi s like Atharva and Dadhyang is recounted, showcasing his role in destroying enemies and bestowing wealth.

In addressing Agni, the hymn requests protection from sins and enemies, asking for the strength to overcome adversaries and live a life filled with happiness and prosperity. The Rishi prays for Agni's radiant blessings to bring great benefits to the hosts, wishing for longevity, beautiful children, and success in all endeavors. Agni's role in expanding the space with his brilliance, protecting the Yagya, and ensuring the success of the hosts is highlighted, emphasizing his importance in the cosmic order. The hymn concludes with a profound invocation to Agni, praising his luminous qualities and asking for his continued protection and blessings. The Rishi seeks Agni's favor to ensure that all sacrifices are successful, enemies are defeated, and the hosts are blessed with opulence and happiness. The eternal significance of Agni in the Yagya and his vital role in maintaining harmony and prosperity in the world is underscored, making this Sukta a profound tribute to the divine fire and his essential place in Vedic rituals and the cosmos.

Sukta 17 , Rishi Bharadwaja Brihaspati, extols the mighty deity Indra in the Triṣṭup meter, also referred to as the two-stepped Triṣṭup. Indra, praised by Angiras, is lauded for searching for the cows stolen by the Panas and drinking Soma. He is celebrated for his bravery in defeating enemies and fulfilling the wishes of those who praise him. Indra is recognized as the one who breaks mountains and reveals wonderful wealth. The hymn calls on Indra to drink Soma as he did in the past, grow strong, manifest the sun, and destroy enemies. Indra is eternal and bright, and the Somras makes him happy and powerful. By drinking Soma, Indra removed darkness, appointed the Sun and the Dawn, and healed the unmoving mountain where the stolen cows were hidden. He made the cow's milk-loving, removed stones to allow their pasrishi , and filled the vast earth with his deeds. Indra, the leader in the battle against Vritrasura, helped the Maruts in the war and killed Vritra with his thunderbolt created by Tvashta. Marudgana praises Indra, and with the help of Soma, he is able to destroy Vritra. Indra released the waters stopped by Vritra, making rivers flow and mixing their waters in the ocean. Indra is the doer of all great works, giver of immortal strength, and wielder of the thunderbolt. The hymn calls for Indra to provide affirmation, strength, food, wealth, and protection, ensuring happiness and prosperity for the devotees for a hundred years.

Sukta 18 , attributed to Rishi Bharadwaja Bārhaspati, the deity Indra is praised in the Triṣṭup meter. Indra, brilliant and a destroyer of enemies, is called upon to satisfy and increase his power through these hymns, as he fulfills the wishes of mankind. Indra, the warrior, is strong, benevolent, and a protector of humans. He controls and blesses those who perform famous deeds with sons and servants, showcasing his strength repeatedly. Mighty Indra, who has appeared in many yajnas, destroys enemies with vigor and invincibility. His long-standing friendship with the praising Angiras and his prowess in opening city gates and killing demons like Bal are highlighted. Indra empowers singers, grants sons, and is worshipped on the battlefield as the thunderbolt-bearer. Known for defeating enemies, he is a source of wealth and power. Indra, the destroyer of demons, mounts his chariot of strength, holding the thunderbolt, and removes the illusions of the wicked. He fiercely burns demons and removes all troubles in battle. Indra, called by many, is impervious to evil and endowed with wealth, greater than the sky and earth, and has no rival. He protects 'Kulla' and 'Ayu', provides wealth to storms from Shambar, and kills Shambar with his thunderbolt. Praised for protecting Divodas, Indra is celebrated as the best among scholars, pleasing those who praise him. After performing Pakshaadi Karma, he reveals new hymns, continuing to be a source of praise and protection.

Sukta 19 , attributed to Rishi Bharadvani Baispatya, the deity Indra is praised in the Triṣṭup meter. Indra, who fulfills the wishes of his devotees and spreads his might across both worlds, remains unconquered by his enemies and prosperous. He is celebrated for his praiseworthy deeds and knowledge. The hymns invoke Indra's abundant generosity, likening his provision to a shepherd caring for his flock. Indra, mighty and youthful, brings his hands full of abundance to provide food and peace of mind. Just as rivers flow into the sea, the devotion of his followers flows towards Indra, who is the lord of wealth and strength. Indra is asked to grant the best strength, quickness to defeat enemies, brilliance, and wealth for humans to enjoy. He is called upon for military power, protection, and victory in battle. Indra's wish-fulfilling forces are desired from all directions, bringing wealth and fame. Indra, the owner of divine and earthly wealth, is invoked for protection, prosperity, and dominance in war. The hymns request Indra's help to kill enemies, gain immense wealth, and bring happiness under his shelter, ensuring strength and success through his mighty presence.

Sukta 20 , attributed to Rishi Bharadvaja Brihaspati Bārhaspatya, the deity Indra is praised in the Virat meter. Indra, like the sun filling the earth with light, grants sons and prosperity to his devotees, bestowing immense wealth, fertile lands, and the power to overshadow enemies. Indra's power is likened to the sun, and through hymns, he is presented with strength. Along with Vishnu, he vanquishes Vritra, who restrained the waters. Indra, possessing the thunderbolt that destroys all Panas, becomes the recipient of sweet Soma juice. His violence and valor provide food to those who commit violence, and his energy and brightness increase. Fearing Indra's helper Kutsa, the Panas flee, and Indra shatters Shushna's illusion, seizing all her food. Shushna's strength is destroyed by Indra's thunderbolt, and Indra commands his charioteer Kutsa to worship the Sun. Indra protects the people by crushing Namuch's head and enriches the Rishi Nidrit with animals and wealth. Indra breaks the strong forts of the illusive Pipn, grants wealth to Rijishwa, and controls many demons. Indra, never defeated by his enemies, rides his chariot and horses to destroy Vritradi with his deadly weapon. Worshippers invoke Indra to gain new wealth, praising him in yagyas. Indra pulverizes Shardasura's seven puris and kills the demon Navavastva, presenting his god-son to Samadhyamvan Ushna. Indra makes his enemies tremble, unblocks flowing waters, and aids the crossing of oceans. Indra, the mighty one, is offered the ultimate sacrifice, the source of all sacrifices, by his devotees.

Sukta 21 , attributed to Rishi Bharadwaja Bārhaspatya, the deity Indra is extolled in the Trishtupa meter. O mighty Indra, the beautiful praises of the much-desired Bharadwaja call upon you. You, with your immortal and innovative form, are a charioteer followed by Haviran. We praise Indra, who grows through the sacrifice of the all-knowing man and is attained by praises. This extremely brilliant Indra surpasses the glory of the sky and the earth. Indra destroyed the darkness spread by Vritra with the glory of the Sun. Mighty Indra, you are indestructible, and people always desire your place, remaining non-violent. Where is Indra, who has performed famous deeds like killing the Vritra demons, found today? In which country and among which worshippers? What kind of sacrifice pleases you, Indra? What mantra is suitable for invoking you, and who is capable of worshipping you? Indra, you are the guardian of those who praise you, quickly listening to their prayers. Present-day praisers seek to honor you with new hymns. O Indra, you were a friend of the ancient Angiras, and now hear our praises too. O Bharadwaja, praise Varuna, Mitra, Indra, Marut, Poosha, Vishnu, Agni, Savita, the gods of plants, and mountains for the fulfillment and protection of our desires. Mighty Indra, these psalmists praise you with hymns worthy of worship. Indestructible Indra, hear my praise, for there is no other god like you. Omniscient Indra, come before my praiseworthy hymn, accompanied by all the gods. Those gods who are the tongue of fire, consuming the offerings in the sacrifice, and who empowered the Rajarshi mind to destroy enemies, come here with them. Indra, you are intelligent and path-finding. Be our leader on the paths to be traveled joyfully and in difficult times, bringing us food with your great and tireless horses.

Sukta 22 , Rishi Bharadwaja Brihaspati extols the virtues of the deity Indra, utilizing the Trishup chanda. The hymn begins by lauding Indra as the destroyer of desires, mighty, learned, truthful, and a tormentor of enemies. Our ancient ancestors, such as Angira and the seven Rishi s who performed the nine-month yagya, praised Indra, making him mighty and prosperous. Indra is celebrated as the destroyer of enemies, mobile, and sovereign over all. The hymn beseeches Indra for pleasant wealth, offspring, relatives, servants, and animals, invoking his opulence for happiness. The worshippers seek the same joy that the ancient stotas attained, acknowledging Indra's might and his ability to vanquish evil demons. Yama, the lord of death, worships Indra, who wields the thunderbolt and provides shelter, multitasking capabilities, and strength to his devotees, ensuring their happiness and bravery. Indra, known for killing the Vritra and destroying Asuri's temples, is praised for his ancient might and protective nature. He fills the sky, earth, and space with fiery glory, burning the wicked and spreading his opulence. Indra is revered for dispelling the illusions of demons and granting great, non-violent happiness, making enemies conquerable. The hymn concludes by calling upon Indra to appear soon with his unparalleled horses, revered by gods and demons alike.

Sukta 23 , attributed to the Rishi Bharadwaja, the son of Bārhaspati, the deity Indra is venerated through the Triṣṭup chanda. The hymn begins with an invocation to Indra, calling upon him to yoke his horses to his chariot when the Soma ritual is performed and the great stotra is recited correctly. Indra, the opulent one, arrives with his thunderbolt in hand, riding a chariot drawn by two horses. He becomes the companion of the praised host, protecting them in battle and vanquishing demons that hinder the virtuous. Indra, who drinks Soma, clears the path for those who praise him, grants beautiful abodes to those who perform Soma Abhishek, and bestows wealth upon the stota. He traverses three forests with his horses, bearing the Vajra, drinks Susiddha Soma, and grants sons to those who donate cows. Devotees chant the desired stotras and offer gifts to strengthen Indra, who performs protective functions. Indra is called upon to drink Soma mixed with curd, sit on the host's throne, and enhance the host's place. The hymn concludes by praising Indra, the lord of the havirannayukta host, who guides praisers on the best path and is the giver of desirable wealth.

Sukta 24 (Third Anuvaka) , attributed to the Rishi Bharadwaja, the son of Bārhaspati, the deity Indra is praised through the Triṣṭup chanda. The hymn begins by highlighting how Indra's Soma-born joy in the Somayag fulfills the wishes of the host. Indra, worshipped through the praises of Indra Stota, is the Lord of heaven who protects. The wise and mighty Indra, destroyer of enemies and protector of devotees, grants homes and food and is praiseworthy. His glory stabilizes the sky and the earth, with protection as abundant as tree branches. Indra's brilliance and strength are vast, likened to the wide path of cows and the binding of berries. Indra continues to perform wonderful deeds, ensuring tasks are seen equally by deities like Mitra, Varuna, Pusha, and Savita. Indra's protection is sought in the forest, and his praises ensure devotees receive their desires like water from mountains. Indra, who remains ever youthful and strong, moves forward with the strength of hymns. His influence protects devotees from the wicked, and even great mountains and abysses are insignificant before him. Generous-hearted Indra is asked to provide food, strength, and protection day and night. The hymn concludes with a plea for Indra to protect the Stota on the battlefield, near or far, ensuring a long, happy life with beautiful sons for the devotees.

Sukta 25 , attributed to the Rishi Bharadwaja, the son of Bārhaspati, the deity Indra is extolled through the Triṣṭup chanda. The hymn opens with a plea to Indra for protection against all sizes of monsters on the battlefield and for sustenance with consumable food. Indra is invoked to safeguard the forces from enemy attacks and to thwart those who obstruct sacrificial works. He is called upon to destroy enemies, near or far, with his might, and to empower his devotees to defeat brave foes. The hymn praises Indra's unparalleled strength and victory over adversaries, asserting that none can rival him. It emphasizes that wealth comes to those whose yajna is dedicated to Indra and that he protects his devotees in times of anger and sorrow. Indra is acknowledged as the great power, endowed by the gods to subdue violent demonic forces and to grant his devotees, including Bharadwaja, homes filled with food.

Sukta 26, attributed to the Rishi Bharadwaja, the son of Bārhaspati, the deity Indra is glorified through the Triṣṭup chanda. The hymn begins with an invocation to Indra, calling upon him with Soma-rasa for the gain of food and protection during battles. Indra is praised by Bharadwaja for securing great food and for being the protector of the good and the destroyer of the wicked. Indra's might is recounted in his defeat of Shushnasur for Kutsa and the beheading of Shambrasura to bring happiness to his guest. Indra created weapons for King Vrishabha, protected him in a ten-day battle, and enriched King Tuji. The hymn continues to praise Indra's destruction of enemies, his remarkable deeds, and his protection of Divodas. Indra's valor in killing Chumuri for King Dabhiti and granting a girl named Raji to Pithinus is highlighted, as well as his defeat of eight thousand warriors at once. The hymn concludes with a prayer for Indra's supreme happiness and strength, expressing a wish for prosperity for 'Kshatrashree', son of 'Pratardan', through Indra's favor and wealth acquisition.

Sukta 27, attributed to the Rishi Bharadwaja, the son of Bārhaspati, the deity Indra is venerated through the Triṣṭup chanda. The hymn begins by questioning what Indra accomplished after being strengthened by drinking Soma. Indra, empowered by Soma, performed beautiful and auspicious deeds, befriending Soma and excelling in his actions. He is praised as the greatest doer of both ancient and new hymns. Indra's unparalleled glory and wealth are acknowledged, with no other deity matching his power. His bravery in killing the demon Varshik's sons with his thunderbolt is celebrated. Indra granted desired wealth to Abhyavati, the character of King Chhayman, and killed the sons of Vrichivan, a descendant of Varshik. Indra is summoned by many, and in a notable battle, he destroyed one hundred and twenty sons of Varshik who attacked him. Indra, whose horses move between the sky and earth, subdued the sons of Varashikha near Devavahak

Vanshirana Abhiyavati and provided King Turvash with wealth. The hymn concludes with praise for Abhiyavat, the son of Chayaman, who performed the Rajasuya Yagya and provided generous offerings, including a chariot, cows, and female slaves, ensuring the indestructibility of his Dakshina.

Sukta 28 , attributed to the Rishi Bharadwaja Brihaspati, the deities Gava and Indra are revered through the chandas Trishup, Jagati, and Anuṣṭup. The hymn begins with a prayer for cows to come to their homes and bless them, becoming a source of prosperity by giving milk to Indra at dawn. Indra is praised for granting wealth to sacrificers and stotas, always increasing their wealth and providing them with protection. The hymn expresses a wish for the cows to remain unharmed, free from thieves and enemy attacks, ensuring the owner's happiness. It emphasizes the importance of cows as a form of wealth and prays for their well-being, nourishment, and freedom. Indra is asked to provide cow's milk and food in the form of Soma, with cows being cherished and revered. The cows are invoked to strengthen the people, beautify their bodies, bring auspiciousness to homes, and thrive in the Yagya Mandap. The hymn concludes with a plea for the cows to enjoy beautiful grass, clean water, and protection from thieves and violence, while seeking Indra's blessing for their prosperity and strength.

Sukta 29 , attributed to the Rishi Bharadvaja Brihaspati, the son of Barhaspatiya, the deity Indra is praised through the Trishup chanda. The hymn begins with an exhortation to men, highlighting how their priests serve Indra in friendship, reciting the best hymns that are beautiful and generous. Indra, who holds a rod in his hand, grants great wealth and protection. He is praised for collecting wealth for the benefit of humans, riding a chariot with ropes held firmly and well-watered horses. Lord Bhardwaan offers his services to Indra to attain wealth, praising Indra's might and beautiful, ever-mobile form that shines like the sun. The hymn describes the proper preparation of soma and the offering of cooked purodash, emphasizing the praise of Indra through the hymns of the Ritvijans. Indra's unparalleled strength, which even the sky and earth fear, is likened to a caretaker satisfying cows with water, as yajnas are performed with offerings of praise. Indra, invoked with butter, grants wealth to his devotees and appears to kill many demons and enemies like Vritra, demonstrating his great valor.

Sukta 30 , attributed to the Rishi Bharadwaja, the son of Bārhaspati, the deity Indra is celebrated through the Triṣṭup chanda. The hymn begins by describing Indra's resurgence to carry out the task of vanquishing demons like Vritra. Indra is invoked to bestow wealth upon those who praise him. He is depicted as encroaching upon the sky and the earth, with half of the entire sky and earth being equal to him. The hymn praises Indra's power, which is capable of burning demons, and highlights that no one can impede his actions. Indra makes it possible to see the sun through the clouds each day and has expanded the worlds with his great deeds. Indra's work of keeping rivers flowing continues as before; he has created paths for rivers and commanded mountains to remain stationary, thereby stabilizing all worlds. The hymn asserts that there is no god or human greater than Indra, who killed Vritra and released the water mass to flow into the sea. Indra is acknowledged as the master of the entire world, illuminating both the sun and dawn simultaneously.

Sukta 31 , attributed to the Rishi Suhotra, the son of Bhāradvāja, the deity Indra is honored through the chandas Trishup and Shakvari. Indra is invoked as the giver of glory and the primary owner of wealth, wielding his power to support the people. The sons and grandsons of enemy plowmen and humans praise Indra in various ways to invoke rain. Indra's might causes waters to fall from the clouds out of fear, and his arrival instills fear in the sky, earth, mountains, trees, and all living creatures. Indra's valor is recounted in his battles, such as fighting Sushna to aid Kutsa, killing Kuyava, and stealing the wheel of Surya's chariot, reducing it to one wheel. Indra destroyed the hundred cities of the demon Shambar, granting wealth to Divodas and Bhardwaj. As the leader of invincible warriors and immense wealth, Indra is called upon to mount his monstrous chariot for fierce battles, bringing his defense equipment and making his devotees renowned among all humans.

Sukta 32 , attributed to the Rishi Suhotra, son of Bharadwaja, the deity Indra is celebrated through the Triṣṭup chanda. The hymn begins with the recitation of articulate, detailed, pleasant, and unique hymns in honor of Indra, the great destroyer of enemies, swift and praiseworthy. Indra, praised by the brilliant Angiras, illuminated heaven and earth with the light of the sun and pulverized the mountain. In response to the pleas of Angiras, Indra freed the cows from bondage and, along with the yagya-performing Angiras, defeated enemies and destroyed demon cities. Indra, who fulfills the desires and wishes of worshipers through praise, is invoked to come before his worshipers with the Badhwa cow, a symbol of great aura, strength, and many calves. Indra, the subduer of evil, releases water as the sun sets to the south, allowing it to fall into the pure ocean from which it never returns, signifying the continuous flow of blessings and fulfillment.

Sukta 33 , attributed to the Rishi Shunahotri, son of Bharadwaja, the deity Indra is praised through the Trishup chanda. The hymn begins by calling upon Indra, who fulfills desires, to bestow a son upon the sacrificer and to ride the best horse, defeating enemies in battle with beautiful horses. Indra is invoked by those seeking protection in war, recalling his deeds of killing sinners with Angiras and providing refuge to his worshipers. Indra, the brave warrior, punishes both Dasyu and Aryan enemies, wielding his weapons like an axe in the battlefield. He is everywhere, a friend who enhances wealth with his excellent means of protection. Warriors and their men call upon Indra for the attainment of wealth. Indra is acknowledged as their protector, providing happiness according to their needs and granting bright butter to those wishing for cows. Indra's greatness and benevolence are extolled, highlighting his pivotal role in ensuring prosperity and safety.

Sukta 34 , attributed to the Rishi Shunahotra, son of Bharadwaja, the deity Indra is extolled through the Trishup chanda. The hymn highlights Indra's reception of countless hymns and the ample praise from those who worship him. In ancient times and even now, there is mutual competition among the Rishi s in the worship of Indra through stotras and mantras. The devotees consistently worship Indra, calling upon him through many means. Indra is celebrated as great, unique, and well-worshipped by the hosts. The hymn likens the devotees to charioteers of Lord Indra, always praising him for benefits. Indra, who is free from the binds of karma and praise, receives praises from a hundred thousand praisers. On the day of Yagya, mixed Somras is presented to Indra along with worshipful stotras. Just as a person moving through the desert cares for water creatures, the hymns and offerings increase Indra's power. Indra, who moves everywhere, is invoked as the protector and provider of prosperity in fierce battles, with the hymns of praisers recited for his sake.

Sukta 35 , attributed to the Rishi Nara Bharadwaja, the deity Indra is celebrated through the Trishup chanda. The hymn begins with a plea to Indra, the charioteer, asking when he will bestow the glory of a thousand men upon the praiser and reward the stota with wealth. Indra is invoked to beautify the yajnas with food and to unite the praiser's men and sons with those of the enemies, granting victory in battle and securing milk, curd, and butter from the foes. The hymn asks when Indra will provide various types of food to the praiser, include the stotra in his yajna, and make the praisers worthy of providing cows. Indra, known for providing cows and food through horses, is requested to strengthen the calves and easily milkable cows, showing kindness to those with a beautiful glow. The hymn concludes by praising Indra as the giver of the best things, noting that the stotras do not hold back in reciting his hymn, and asking Indra to please Angiras with food.

Sukta 36 , attributed to the Rishi Nara Bhāradvāja, the deity Indra is honored through the Triṣṭup chanda. The hymn begins by acknowledging the joy Indra brings through Soma drinking, which is beneficial to all. Indra's wealth, present in all worlds, is seen as a source of universal prosperity. Indra, more powerful than other gods, is recognized as the true provider of food. For fertility's benefit, the host worships Indra's power, wearing it on their forehead, and relies on Indra to kill Vritra and other enemies. The Marudgans serve Indra harmoniously, with their strength and chariot horses, and praises filled with worship and strength meet Indra like rivers entering the sea. Indra, after receiving praise, is expected to distribute food that provides sustenance and homes to many. As the chief master of all living beings and the god of all created beings, Indra is praised for listening to hymns and empowering the army to conquer enemies' wealth. Indra, continually praised and illuminated with food, is asked to remain with the devotees always.

Sukta 37 , attributed to the Rishi Bharadvaja Brihaspati Barhaspatiya, the deity Indra is venerated through the Trishup chanda. The hymn begins with a call to Indra, asking for his chariot-mounted weapons to appear before the devotees. Bharadwaj invokes Indra to grant strength and wisdom. The Somrasa flows in the yajna, filling the pot, and Indra, the lord of joyful Soma, is asked to worship this Soma. The powerful Indra is brought forth by the chariot, and the devotees pray that the wind does not destroy the Somroop Havi before Indra can drink it. Indra, the Vajin, is invoked to destroy sin and bestow wealth and sons upon the devotees. The hymn seeks Indra's bestowal of perfume and strength, strengthened by the praises of the devotees. Indra, the destroyer of enemies, is called upon to kill enemies and grant all wealth to the devotees.

Sukta 38 , attributed to the Rishi Bharadwaja, the son of Barhaspati, the deity Indra is extolled through the Trishup chanda. The hymn begins by inviting the wonderful Indra to drink Soma and hear the call of the devotees. During the yajna, the host praises Indra and offers oblations, with Indra's ears reaching from afar to listen to the stotra. The stota praises Indra loudly, wishing for their praises to bring Indra before them. Indra is described as ancient and intact, worthy of continual praise. The stotra and havya are dedicated to Indra, whose power increases through yajna, Somrasa, praise, worship, and the pasRishi of day and night, month, and year. The hymn concludes with a plea for Indra's strength, wealth, fame, favor, and prowess in enemy-killing deeds, asking for his service today and always.

Sukta 39, attributed to the Rishi Bharadwaja, the son of Bārhaspati, the deity Indra is revered through the Trishup chanda. The hymn begins with an invocation to Indra to partake in their Soma, described as the divine giver of happiness. Indra is asked to bestow the best perfumes and is praised for his heroic deeds, such as taking the Augras and defeating the Panas to rescue the cows hidden in the mountain. Indra's consumption of Soma is said to give strength to night, day, and year, establishing Soma as the illuminator of dawn. Indra, the solar deity, dispels darkness and brightens the dawn with his light, fulfilling human desires. The hymn concludes by requesting Indra to provide infinite resources, including water, herbs, horses, cows, and human beings, ensuring prosperity for all.

Sukta 40, attributed to the Rishi Bharadwaja, the son of Bārhaspati, the deity Indra is extolled through the Triṣṭup chanda. The hymn invites Indra to drink the Soma prepared for his pleasure, to harness his horses to the chariot, and to sit among the worshipers at the Yagya. Indra is asked to become a companion of the praises and to provide food to the devotees. Indra is reminded of how he drank Soma immediately after birth and is encouraged to do the same now, with cows, Ritvijas, Abhisavan, Prastar, and other elements gathered for him. The fire is lit, and the blessing of Soma has taken place, with the devotees appealing wholeheartedly for Indra to come and enrich them. Indra, who has come many times for Soma-rasa, is called upon to attend the Yagya, listen to the praises, and confirm the Soma offered by the host. The hymn concludes with a plea for Indra to come from wherever he is, along with the Marudgan, and perform the Yagya for the devotees.

Sukta 41, attributed to the Rishi Bharadwaja, the son of Bārhaspati, the deity Indra is praised through the Triṣṭup chanda. The hymn begins by inviting Indra to the yajna, where the Abhisut Soma is kept for him. Indra, known as Vajrin, is called to approach the Soma in the Kalash just as a cow enters the cowshed, being the chief among sacrificial gods. Indra is urged to drink the Soma with the same tongue he always uses, with the Ritvij of Soma present before him. The hymn prays for Indra's thunderbolt to slay enemies. The auspicious rain is blessed for Indra, and he is asked to drink the Soma he rules over, considered as Annarupa Abhishut. The refined Soma, superior to the unrefined, is said to bring happiness to Indra. Indra is called to this Soma like a yajna to enhance all his organs. The hymn concludes with a plea for Indra to find the Soma sufficient for his body, enjoy it, and protect all the devotees.

Sukta 42, attributed to the Rishi Bharadwaja, the son of Bārhaspati, the deity Indra is honored through the Bṛhatī and Anuṣṭup chandas. The hymn calls upon the priests to offer Somaras to Indra, the master of sacrifice and omniscient deity who knows everyone and is always active. The Ritvijas are urged to present themselves before Indra, the Sompayee, with vessels full of Nishyantra Somras. They are encouraged to serve Indra with brilliant and accomplished Somaras, to kill the enemy and complete their service. The consecrated Somras should be offered to Indra, and the hymn concludes with a plea for Indra to save them from the wrath of all wicked enemies.

Sukta 43, attributed to the Rishi Bharadwaja, the son of Bārhaspati, the deity Indra is praised through the Uṣṇik chanda. The hymn addresses Indra, reminding him of the same Soma that inspired him to defeat Shambara for Divodas. Indra is urged to defeat his enemies again with this disillusioned Soma. When Soma is anointed in all the dreams of Yagya, Indra is invited to accept and drink this sacred Soma. The hymn recalls how Indra freed the cows hidden in the mountain after consuming Soma and encourages him to drink the Soma that brings him extraordinary power and joy. This tortured Soma is offered to Indra for his consumption, reinforcing his strength and vitality.

Sukta 44, attributed to the Rishi Shanyu Brihaspati, the deity Indra is extolled through the chandas Anuṣṭupa, Viratta, and Triṣṭup. The hymn begins by praising Indra, the wealthy and moon-keeper, who provides immense joy and opulence. Indra, the protector of strong cows and the glorifier of poets, brings great joy to his devotees. Indra is called upon to drink the Soma that grants strength and joy, used to defeat enemies alongside the Marudgan. The hymn lauds Indra as the master of strength, the world conqueror, and the ultimate giver and protector, who destroys enemy wealth through praises. Indra is recognized for his exceptional awareness of yajna rituals and for granting wealth to his devotees. The Soma, drunk in the yajna, attracts Indra, who then turns towards the devotees, providing them speed, strength, abundant food, and protection.

The hymn beseeches Indra to be a friend, protector, and the destroyer of Vṛtrāsura with his thunderbolt. Indra, the bearer of wishes, is asked to destroy enemies and obstacles created by those who do not perform Soma rituals. The hymn celebrates Indra as the creator of clouds and praises, urging him to remain kind to devotees. Indra, happy with Soma, kills enemies and provides homes. The hymn concludes with a plea for Indra to drink Soma, bring happiness, drive away sins, and grant unlimited wealth, victory, and prosperity to his worshipers. Indra, the fulfiller of wishes, is praised for filling rivers and meeting the needs of living beings, and for making the Sun bright, illuminating the solar system, and securing nectar from the heavens.

Sukta 45 , attributed to the Rishi Shanyur Varhaspatya, the deities Indra, Vryu, and Taksha are revered through the chandas Gayatri, Atinivrt, Padanivrt, and Anuṣṭup. The hymn begins by invoking Indra, who brought Turvash and Yadu from distant lands, to be a friend and protector. Even those who do not praise Indra receive his blessings, winning the property of their enemies. Indra's various praises ensure his unwavering protection. Friends are urged to worship Indra, who bestows the best wealth. Indra, the destroyer of Vritra, is asked to protect the worshipers and enrich them by removing obstacles. Indra's hands hold divine and earthly wealth, and he destroys enemy cities and their illusions. Indra is invoked for food and prosperity, as he was in ancient times, to conquer enemy wealth. The hymn praises Indra's speed, his enemy-conquering chariot, and his role as the master of humans and protector of all. Indra, the giver of happiness and a protective friend, is called upon to defeat rivals and fulfill desires with controlled horses and wealth. The hymn concludes with a call to praise Indra, the conqueror of enemies, who, upon hearing the praises, grants food and cows, reveals hidden cows, and repeatedly receives the praises like cows returning to their calves. Indra is asked to satisfy himself with Soma, protect worshipers, and grant strength to destroy enemies, establishing himself like the high banks of the Ganga and bestowing great boons to the devotees.

Sukta 46, attributed to the Rishi Shanyu Varhaspati, the deity Indra is praised through the Pragatha verse. The hymn calls upon Indra for food and protection of the Rishi's wealth, seeking his favor to grant abundant wealth to those who conquer enemies. Indra is invoked as the destroyer of enemies, asked to bring prosperity in the battlefield and act like a bull attacking foes in fierce battles, ensuring the protection of the worshipers and their children. Indra, the nourisher of heaven and earth, is requested to bestow the best wealth that increases strength. The hymn emphasizes Indra's role as the strongest protector and conqueror of enemies, driving away demons and aiding in victory. Indra is asked to grant strength, wealth, and food, ensuring victory over enemies and providing a safe house for the sacrificial hosts, free from the harsh elements and enemy weapons. Indra, the protector from those who steal cows, is invoked to shield the worshipers and warriors in the battlefield, helping them repel enemy attacks and protect their native places and children. Indra is also asked to guide the warriors to victory in great wars and to ensure they can retrieve cows from the battlefield, despite their fears.

Sukta 47, attributed to the Rishi Gagarga Bharadwaja, the deities Soma, Indra, the chariot, Danastuti, and Dundubhi are honored through the chandas Triṣṭup, Anuṣṭup, Bṛhatī, Gayatri, and Jagatī. The hymn begins by highlighting Soma's sweetness, which Indra drinks, ensuring no one survives in the battlefield before him. Soma provides strength to destroy Vritra and the ninety-nine cities of Shambar. It energizes the speaker's words, bestows desired wisdom, and creates the elements of the world. Soma expands the earth, strengthens the heavens, and holds the cosmos together, illuminating the sun and the celestial realms. Indra is called upon to drink the Soma, defeat enemies, and provide wealth. He is the guide and protector, bringing wealth and strength to the devotees. Indra's chariot, associated with overcoming obstacles and achieving victory, is praised. The hymn emphasizes Indra's role in protection, wealth bestowal, and fulfilling desires, invoking his presence in battles and seeking his guidance. Indra is celebrated for his numerous forms, his ability to harness divine forces, and his role in ensuring victory and prosperity for his worshipers. The chariot and Dundubhi (drum) are also praised for their role in battle, providing protection, and driving away enemies, with a plea for Indra to ensure victory and recover all lost cows, signifying abundance and prosperity.

Sukta 48 , attributed to the Rishi Shanyu, the son of Brahaspati, the deities praised are Agni, the Maruts, and Pūṣā Prishnianvabhoomi, with the Chanda being Brihti, Trishup, and Anustrabadini. The hymn extols Agni, the omniscient and indestructible friend, offering oblations and seeking protection and prosperity. The hymn highlights Agni's brilliance in dispelling darkness and bestowing wealth, while invoking his aid in sacrifices. The Maruts and Pūṣā are also invoked for their wealth-giving powers and protection. The hymn calls for the well-being of sons and grandchildren, the removal of anger and disease, and the flourishing of vegetation and wealth. The verses encapsulate the essence of Vedic rituals and the integral role of Agni in connecting the earthly realm with the divine.

Sukta 49, attributed to the Rishi s Ṛjiśvā and Bhāradvāja, the demigods praised are the Viśvedevas, with the chants being Triṣṭup and Śakvarī. This hymn begins with praise for Mitravarun, seeking their attention in the yagya. Agni, the egoless lord of heaven and earth, is invoked as the central figure in every yagya, symbolizing the connection between the divine and the terrestrial. The hymn celebrates Surya's daughters, Sen and Ratri, highlighting their luminous roles. The wind god, Marut, is called upon to enhance praise through wealth, while Ashvins are invoked for protection and fulfillment of wishes. Saraswati, the strange-moving goddess, is asked to oversee the sacrificial rituals and grant welfare to the hymn-singer. The hymn also seeks the presence of rain and wind to inspire water, and praises Maruts for prosperity. It concludes with a call to Vishnu, who measured the worlds, Ahirbudhna mountain, and Savita to provide sustenance, and to Vishvedevs for chariots, attendants, sons, and food, ensuring victory over enemies and shelter for worshipers.

Sukta 50, from the Fifth Anuvaka, attributed to the Rishi s Ṛjiśvā Bhāradvāja, the demigods praised are the Viśvedevas, with the chants being Triṣṭup. This hymn calls upon Aditi, Varuna, Mitra, Agni, Arthama, Savita, Bhaga, and other gods to bless the worshipers. The Sun is invoked to make the radiant gods favorable, and the heavenly and earthly deities are asked for strength, wealth, and the removal of sin. The hymn beseeches the son of Rudra and the desert for aid in times of trouble, acknowledging their connection to the sky and earth. Indra is praised for providing food, while Hiranyapani and Savita are requested to bestow wealth. Agni is asked to bring the gods to the yagya, ensuring protection and blessings. The Ashvins are called upon to relieve sorrow, and the demigods are requested to grant wealth and happiness. The hymn concludes with a plea for protection and prosperity from Rudra, Saraswati, Vishnu, Vayu, Ribhuksha, and other deities, invoking the charitable fire, Tvashta, and the Visvedevas to safeguard the performers of sacrificial rituals. The hymn celebrates the invincible gods and their wives, seeking their continued blessings and favor.

Sukta 51, attributed to the Rishi Ṛjiśvā Bharadwaja, the deities praised are the Viśvedevas, with the chants being Trishup, Ushnika, and Anuṣṭup. This hymn celebrates the Sun, radiant and beloved by Mitravarun, as an ornament of space, the knower and wise deity of the three worlds. It praises Aditi, Mitra, Varuna, Arthama, and Bhaga for their purifying works and protective roles. The hymn calls upon the sons of Aditi as guardians and givers of wealth, seeking their refuge. The Vasugana are invoked for blessings alongside heaven, earth, and fire, while Vishvedevas are asked to destroy the enemy's body and safeguard the worshippers from sin. The hymn emphasizes the power of salutations, which hold sway over heaven and earth and even the gods, and offers respect to the ancestors for atonement. Indra, Prithvi, Pusha, Bhaga, Aditi, and Panchajana are beseeched to enhance the home and provide protection and happiness. Fire is invoked to drive away evil, while Soma is asked to defeat adversaries. The hymn concludes with a plea to Indra and the gods for guidance on a path that leads to victory over enemies and financial prosperity.

Sukta 52, attributed to the Rishi Ṛjiśvā Bharadwaja, the deities praised are the Viśvedevas, with the chants being Trishup, Jagati, and Gayatri. The hymn begins by invoking Vasupati, the god of the Vasus, and calls for the great mountains to humble those who belittle the sacrifices. It seeks protection from harm for those who criticize the stotras and asks for the divine weapon of Soma against the haters of Brahmins. The dawn, rivers, mountains, gods, and ancestors are invoked for protection, while Agni is asked to carry oblations to the gods. The Saraswati River is called upon for medicinal pleasures and protection, while Vishvedeva is requested to listen and bless the sacrifices. Indra with Marut, Mitra with Tvashta, and Arthama are praised for accepting offerings, and Agni is asked to perform the yagya for the chief gods. The hymn calls upon the gods from all realms to sit on the Kushas, drink Soma, and be prostrated, asking Agni, the grandson of heaven, earth, and water, to listen to their praise. It concludes with a plea for the gods to provide good fortune, food, and children, and for the fire and Parjanya to protect the sacrifices and be satisfied with the oblations and salutations.

Sukta 53, attributed to the Rishi Bharadwaja Bārhaspatya, the deity praised is Pūṣā, with the chants being Gāyatrī and Anuṣṭup. The hymn begins with an invocation to Pūṣā, expressing a commitment to serve him for both work and sustenance. Pūṣā is hailed as a benefactor of mankind, a charitable householder, and a protector. The hymn beseeches Pūṣā to soften hearts hardened by greed and to simplify the acquisition of food and profit while eliminating thieves and completing yagyas. Further, it calls upon Pūṣā to subdue the hearts of adversaries, awaken harmony, and reduce the hardness of bandits and misers, urging them to be benevolent. The worshipers pray for Pūṣā to provide cows, horses, servants, and food for their yagya rituals, ensuring their welfare and prosperity.

Sukta 54, attributed to the Rishi Bharadwaja, the son of Bārhaspati, the deity praised is Pūṣā, with the chant being Gayatri. The hymn implores Pūṣā to guide them to a man who can recover their stolen wealth and reunite them with lost animals. It acknowledges the ceaseless and unfaltering path of the sun. The priest who offers Havi to Pūṣā is blessed with wealth and protection. The hymn requests Pūṣā to safeguard their cows, horses, and provide sustenance, ensuring that their cattle and wealth remain unharmed and do not fall into danger. It expresses the hope that Pūṣā will listen to their praises and remove their poverty, helping them remain safe and prosperous during the Yagya. The hymn concludes by asking Pūṣā to protect their cows and wealth from evil and return any kidnapped cattle, thus ensuring their continued prosperity.

Sukta 55, attributed to the Rishi Bharadwaja Bārhaspatya, the deity praised is Pūṣā, with the chant being Gayatri. The hymn begins by expressing a desire for Pūṣā's hymn to reach the worshipers, making him the leader of the Yagya. They seek wealth from the great Pūṣā, acknowledging him as the embodiment of prosperity and a friend to the praise-singers. Pūṣā is lauded as the lord of dawn and night, the master of Ushapati, Surya, and Indra, and a close ally. The hymn concludes with a request for Pūṣā's chariot, driven by the swift chagas, to arrive and bestow their blessings upon the worshipers.

Sukta 56 , attributed to the Rishi Bharadwaja Bārhaspatya, the deity praised is Pūṣā, with the chants being Gayatri and Anuṣṭup. The hymn begins by stating that those who praise Pūṣā, alongside Atyukt Atra, need not seek favor from other gods. It acknowledges the mighty Indra, who, with Pūṣā's help, plucks berries. Pūṣā is praised for skillfully driving the wheel of Surya's deer-like chariot. The worshipers beseech Pūṣā to bestow wealth upon them, expressing their praise in both present and future rituals. They pray for blessings that are free from sin and close to welfare, ensuring prosperity and well-being.

Sukta 57 , attributed to the Rishi Bharadwaja, the son of Bārhaspati, the deities praised are Indra and Pūṣā, with the chant being Gayatri. The hymn begins by seeking the friendship and blessings of Indra and Pūṣā for financial gain. It highlights Indra's preference for drinking Soma and Pūṣā's affinity for Sattu-infused offerings. The hymn describes Pūṣā's vehicle as a chariot and Indra's as an Ashdha, noting Indra's power to destroy Vritra and cause heavy rains, with Pūṣā's assistance. The worshipers express their reliance on the gracious protection of both deities, akin to living on the branch of a pure tree. They seek to draw Indra and Pūṣā towards themselves for their well-being, just as a bridle guides a horse.

Sukta 58 , attributed to the Rishi Bharadwaja Bārhaspatya, the deity praised is Pūṣā, with the chants being Trishup and Jagati. The hymn begins by acknowledging Pūṣā's bright complexion and his significance in both day and night, highlighting their opposite forms. Pūṣā is compared to the sun, radiant and glorified, as a giver and benefactor. The hymn describes Pūṣā's vehicle as a chariot, his role in caring for animals, and his love for devotees. Pūṣā travels through space, illuminating all beings in the form of the sun, and his boats move in space, acting as messengers and offering prayers. The worshipers offer oblations to Pūṣā, who is revered as the best friend of earth and heaven, the lord of the atras, and is known for his affluence and graceful movement.

Sukta 59 , attributed to the Rishi Bharadwaja Bārhaspatya, the deities praised are Indra and Agni (Indragni), with the chants being Brihti and Anuṣṭup. The hymn begins by extolling Indragni's strength and their defeat of demon enemies. The worshipers acknowledge Indragni's precise and comprehensive actions, united by a common father. Invoking Indragni in their yajna for protection, they liken their movement towards Somabhishava to the blind moving towards grass. The hymn emphasizes that Indragni does not partake in the soma of those who praise maliciously. It marvels at the mystery of Indragni's actions when they ride their chariot together. The legless Usha stimulates life and speech, and the hymn calls for Indragni's protection in the quest for cows. It beseeches Indragni to drive away enemies and grant divine and earthly wealth. The hymn concludes with an invitation to supper, recognizing Indragni as the hearer of praises.

Sukta 60, attributed to the Rishi Bharadwaja Bārhaspatya, the deities praised are Indra and Agni (Indragni), with the chants being Triṣṭup, Bṛhatī, Anuṣṭup, and Gayatri. The hymn extols Indragni as the lords of great wealth and destroyers of enemies, who grant food and victory to their worshipers. It recounts their battles for the sun and dawn, and their association with vital elements like the cow, dawn, sun, and water. The hymn calls upon Indragni to appear with great wealth and to destroy enemies with force. Indragni is invoked to make the worshipers successful in war, protect the righteous, and eliminate troublemakers. The worshipers offer praises and invite Indragni to partake in their soma offerings, ride horses born for oblation, and cover them like fire. The hymn concludes with a plea for strong food, swift horses, cows, wealth, and for Indragni to drink the soma, desiring Havya.

Sukta 61, attributed to the Rishi Bharadwaja, the son of Brihaspati, the deity praised is Saraswati, with the chants being the Vishva, Gayatri, and Trishup. The hymn begins by celebrating Saraswati for granting a son named Divodas to the sacrificer Vardhayashwa and purifying the immortal Pani. Saraswati's donations are said to have expanded, breaking the banks of the Saraswati Mountain with her waves. She is praised for killing the detractors of the gods and the son of Tvashta, giving land to humans, and causing rain. The hymn invokes Annavati Saraswati as the protector and provider of satisfaction, comparing her favorably to Indra for those who go into battle seeking wealth. Saraswati is depicted as a protector in battle, giver of wealth like the sun, and destroyer of enemies, with her chariot moving swiftly and bringing victory. Ancient Rishi s served Saraswati, and she is lauded for filling heaven and earth with her splendor. The hymn concludes by invoking Saraswati for great wealth, protection from becoming action less or victims, and acceptance of brotherhood, ensuring they do not attain the lowest place.

Sukta 62, from the first chapter of the fifth octave, attributed to the Rishi Bharadwaja, the son of Brihaspati, the deities praised are the Ashvins, with the chant being Trishup. The hymn extols the Ashvins as the destroyers of enemies who dispel the darkness of night, strengthening the worshipers' praises. It speaks of the Ashvins‘ horses, which carry their chariot across the desert to the yagya with great might. The Ashvins help devotees reach heaven with their mind-speed horses and put to deep sleep those who commit violence against the sacrificial host. The hymn calls upon the Ashvins to come to the beautiful praises of the Adhidraya Stota and let the ancient, malice-free fire perform their sacrifice. It praises the Ashvins Kumars for bringing happiness and wealth. The hymn recounts how the Ashvins rescued Bhujyu from the sea with their chariot horses, and how they break mountains blocking their path, responding to the calls of those wishing for children. It asks the Ashvins to use the gods' fierce anger to kill demons and protect the hosts who worship them. The Ashvins Kumars are requested to ride their chariot to bestow children, cut off the heads of obstacles, and inaugurate the Sampatra seminar, granting divine wealth and receiving the worshipers‘ praises.

Sukta 63 , attributed to the Rishi Bharadwaja Bārhaspatya, the deity praised is Ashvins, with the chants being Virata, Eka pada, and Trishup.

The hymn begins by sending the fifteenth hymn to the dwelling of the two horses, attracting Ashvins Kumars with praise. The Ashvins Kumars are called upon to protect the worshipers' house from enemies by drinking soma. The hymn acknowledges the preparation of Soma and praises laid out for them, invoking their protection. It highlights the fire that rises due to their sacrifice and the capabilities of the stota who sings their praises. The daughter of Surya is mentioned as having adorned their chariot, making them leaders among the gods' people. The Ashvins Kumars are strong, follow the sun's beauty, and their horses lead them towards food. The hymn seeks wealth, steadfast cows, and protection from demons, recalling how King Shanda provided chariots and brave men to their devotees. It concludes by asking the Ashvins Kumars to adorn the worshiper with auspicious wealth and wisdom.

Sukta 64, attributed to the Rishi Bharadwaja Bārhaspatya, the deity praised is the goddess Usha, with the chant being Trishup. The hymn begins by describing Usha as a bright-colored woman who rises like waves in the morning, making all places easily accessible and bringing wealth and prosperity. Usha is portrayed as auspicious, her radiance becoming and beautiful, spreading light gracefully. Her rays carry heat and drive away enemies. The hymn acknowledges that even mountains and airless regions become easy paths for Usha, as she provides useful wealth. Usha is praised for carrying money on Ashdhi and being worthy of worship, granting wealth to the worshiper. As Usha appears, birds leave their nests, and those who earn money rise, symbolizing that Usha provides wealth to the sacrificer.

Sukta 65 , attriuted to the Rishi Bharadwaja, the son of Brihaspati, the deity praised is Usha, with the chant being Trishup. The hymn begins by celebrating the dawn, Usha, whose bright rays dispel darkness and illuminate all creatures. Usha is depicted as the graceful presiding deity of the great Yagya, moving with her red blinds and banishing the night's darkness. She is praised for providing strength, fame, food, and juice to the sacrificer, bestowing wealth along with sons to the servants. The hymn acknowledges Ushas role in freeing cows and dispelling darkness through praise, as lauded by the people of Satyaphal. It concludes with a plea to Usha to destroy darkness and grant wealth and food to the worshiper, just as she did for Bharadwaja.

Sukta 66, attributed to the Rishi Bharadwaja Bārhaspatya, the deity praised is Maruta, with the chant being Triṣṭup. The hymn begins by invoking the steady and learned Maruts, who appear near the hymn-singer and expand to exploit water in the earth while eroding it in space. Described as bright as fire, adorned with golden ornaments, and manifesting wealth and power, the Marudgan are celebrated. They are the mighty sons of Rudra, with space as their glorious mother holding water for human birth. The Maruts, residing in the hearts of devotees, destroy sins and attract the earth with their glory. They make devotees who recite desert hymns free from anger. The hymn praises their brilliance, unmatched by others, and their might in joining the armies of heaven and earth. Despite being horseless and charioteer-less, they inspire water and provide desired gifts. The Maruts protect those they save in battle, ensuring their victory. The hymn concludes by presenting Haviratra to the Maruts, who despise their enemies' power, with their radiance likened to a dazzling flame of fire. The praises of Rudra's sons, the Maruts, are acknowledged for their strength and might.

Sukta 67, attributed to the Rishi Bharadwaja Brihaspati, the deities praised are Mitra and Varuna, with the chant being Triṣṭup. The hymn begins by praising Mitra and Varuna as the best, acknowledging their power to make people hesitate with their arms. It highlights that their strength increases through these praises and asks them to provide a house that protects from cold. The hymn calls upon Mitravaruna to respond to their call, comparing their protective strength to a person who empowers those in need, and recognizes them as great by birth. It mentions that all gods gain strength by singing their praises, and they are the conquerors of heaven and earth, known for their non-violence. Mitra and Varuna are praised for holding the cosmic region firmly, satisfying clouds, space, and Vishwadev through offerings. They are depicted as wearing Pragya Soma to satisfy their hunger, ensuring rivers are clear when sacred rituals are performed. The hymn requests water from Mitra and Varuna, acknowledging their glory and their role in erasing the sin of the offered. It asks them to destroy those who are devoid of hymns and create obstacles, and emphasizes the importance of their presence when praises are sung and Soma is offered, granting a house and blessings to the worshiper.

Sukta 68, attributed to the Rishi Bharadwaja Bārhaspatya, the deities praised are Indra and Varuna, with the chants being Trishup and Jagati. The hymn begins by acknowledging the rituals performed for the happiness of the host, now being conducted for Indra and Varuna. It praises them as givers of wealth and excellence in Yagya, highlighting Indra's bravery and enemy-slaying prowess, and Varuna's protective strength. The stota is urged to praise them, recognizing Indra as a destroyer of obstacles and Varuna as a strong protector. Their glorification and worship result in blessings and mastery over vast heavens and earth. The hymn describes the sacrificer as charitable, wealthy, protected from enemies, and blessed with a prosperous son. It requests Indra and Varuna to grant wealth that dispels defamation and strengthens against enemies. The hymn admires their strength, seeking divine-protected wealth and the power to overcome adversaries. It concludes by praising Varuna's great deeds, brilliance, and eternal presence on earth, and inviting Indra and Varuna to drink the excellent Soma, making them joyous and content during the Yagya.

Sukta 69, attributed to the Rishi Bharadwaja, the son of Brihaspati, the deities praised are Indra and Vishnu, with the chant being Triṣṭup. The hymn begins by directing the hymn and oblation towards Indra and Vishnu, asking them to perform the Yagya and provide a hassle-free path and wealth. It recognizes Indra and Vishnu as worthy of praise, hymns, and being the cause of such praise. The hymn emphasizes their role as lords of Soma, encouraging them to receive the hymns and quotes during the boon-donation. Indra and Vishnu are urged to let the horses that defeat the violent carry them and to heed the requests made in the praises. The hymn celebrates their expansion of space, their role in making the world famous, and their growth from Soma. It asks for wealth, recognizing them as complete as the pot and the ocean. The hymn concludes by inviting Indra and Vishnu to fill their stomachs with Soma, listening to the praises, and acknowledging their invincibility and success against demons despite challenges.

Sukta 70, attributed to the Rishi Bharadwaja, the son of Brihaspati, the deities praised are the heavens and the earth, with the chant being Jagti. The hymn begins by addressing the beautiful earth, acknowledging its watery nature and its adornment by Varuna. It emphasizes the earth's provision of water to noble men and its role as the lord of Bhuvan, beneficial to human strength. The worshipers praise the heavens and earth for nurturing perfect men who grow like branches. The earth, covered by water, provides shelter and adheres to the law of rain, ensuring happiness for the hosts of yagyas. The hymn calls upon the goddess who grants sacrifice, wealth, fame, perfume, and strength to anoint them with honey. It concludes with a plea to Father Heaven and Mother Earth for food, strength, wealth, and children, recognizing their omniscience and benevolence, and seeking continuous inspiration and provision for the sacrificer.

Sukta 71, attributed to the Rishi Bharadwaja, the son of Bārhaspati, the deity praised is the sun-god Savitadev, with the chants being Jagatī and Triṣṭup. The hymn begins by extolling Savitadev, who protects the world by raising his arms. It expresses a desire for the strength to donate money to Savitadev, acknowledging him as the creator of all animals and humans, and seeking his blessings. The worshipers pray that their enemies, who wish them harm, should not become their rulers. Savitadev, described as peaceful-minded, golden-handed, and worthy of fame, is called upon to awaken at the end of the night and inspire the desired food for the sacrificer. The hymn celebrates Savitadev ascent from the earth to the elevated region of heaven, affirming all great things. It concludes with a plea for continuous wealth from Savitadev, recognizing his infinite wealth and the ability to gain prosperity through praise.

Sukta 72, attributed to the Rishi Bharadwaja, the son of Brihaspati, the deities praised are Indra and Soma, with the chant being Triṣṭup. The hymn begins by acknowledging the glory of Indra and Soma, crediting them with the creation of the main spirits, the sun, and water, and their role in destroying blasphemers and darkness. Indra and Soma are praised for raising the dawn and enhancing the brightness of the sun, supporting the heavens through space, and nurturing mother earth. They are recognized for breaking the barriers blocking water, causing rivers to flow and fill the oceans. The hymn also mentions their role in ensuring cows produce mature milk, benefiting all cows regardless of complexion. Finally, Indra and Soma are invoked to bestow wealth and salvation upon the worshipers, and to enhance the strength of the army against overwhelming enemies.

Sukta 73, attributed to the Rishi Bharadwaja Bārhaspatya, the deity praised is Bṛhaspati, with the chant being Triṣṭup. The hymn begins by acknowledging Baṛhaspati as the first to arise, who broke the mountain, and whose actions in both worlds move like a spear. Bṛhaspati makes terrible noises in heaven and earth, symbolizing his power. The hymn praises Bṛhaspati for giving place to strotras in the Yagya, highlighting his role as the destroyer of trees and conqueror of enemies. Baṛhaspati is celebrated for defeating enemies and destroying the cities of demons. He is recognized for conquering demons and killing the enemies of heaven through mantras.

Sukta 74, attributed to the Rishi Bharadwaja, the son of Brihaspati, the deities praised are Soma and Rudra, with the chant being Triṣṭup. The hymn calls upon Soma and Rudra to grant great strength and ensure that all sacrifices are fulfilled through their presence. Acknowledging them as bearers of seven gems, the hymn seeks their auspiciousness for human and animal happiness. It implores Soma and Rudra to remove diseases from the household, drive away poverty, and bestow food and happiness. The hymn requests their protective medicine for the body, forgiveness of sins, and liberation from Varun Pash. With the best bow and sharp arrows, the worshipers offer beautiful praises to Soma and Rudra, desiring their happiness and protection.

Sukta 75, attributed to the Rishi Bharadwaja, the deities praised are the shield, bow, charioteer, chariot, and other implements of war, with the chants being Triṣṭup, Jagti, Anushtup, and Pankti. The hymn begins by describing the king, who looks like a cloud when he dons iron armor for battle, winning non-violently and being protected by the glorious armor. It expresses confidence in victory through the power of the bow, aiming to destroy the enemy's will and remove adversaries. The bowstring, reaching the ear and beloved for its role in overcoming battle, combines with the arrow to form a powerful weapon. The hymn invokes protection from the Dhanushkotis, likening their protection to a mother's for her son, and praises the quiver as the father of arrows, which secures victory in battle. The skilled charioteer and swiftly moving horses, capable of crushing enemies, are celebrated. The chariot is likened to the sacrificial fire, increasing the king's wealth and providing refuge in times of crisis. The hymn prays for the ancestors' protection and for divine favor from Pusha, ensuring enemies do not become rulers. It praises the arrow for its strength and precision, and the whip for guiding horses into battle. The hymn concludes with prayers for protection and victory, likening the mantra itself to armor, and seeking punishment for any treacherous brothers, ensuring divine favor and happiness in battle.

The Sixth Mandala of Rig-Veda concludes with this Sukta, emphasizing the unity of divine power and the importance of praise and worship in seeking divine blessings and protection.

EIGHT

RISHI VASHISHT (MANDALA 7)

Rishi Vashisht (Sanskrit: वसिष्ठ, IAST: Vasiṣṭha), whose name translates to "most excellent" or "best," is revered as one of the oldest and most esteemed Vedic sages. As one of the Saptarishis, the seven great sages of Hindu tradition, Vashisht's wisdom and spiritual prowess have left an indelible mark on Vedic literature and Hindu philosophy. He is credited as the chief author of Mandala 7 of the Rigveda, a collection of hymns that reflect his profound connection with the divine and his role as a guiding light for the ancient Vedic people.

In Rigvedic hymn 7.33.9, Vashisht is described as a scholar who crossed the Sarasvati River to establish his school, symbolizing his role as a bridge between the sacred knowledge of the Vedas and the earthly realm. As the purohita (chief priest) of King Sudās Paijavana, the leader of the Bharata tribe, Vashisht played a crucial role in securing the blessings of the gods, particularly Indra, for his people. His strategic and poetic invocations are credited with ensuring the Bharatas' victory in the legendary Battle of the Ten Kings, a testament to his spiritual authority and deep understanding of the divine forces.

Vashisht's influence extends beyond the Rigveda. He is traditionally associated with the Yoga Vasishtha, the Vasishtha Samhita, and is mentioned in various Puranic texts, including the Agni Purana and Vishnu Purana. His legendary possession of the divine cow Kamadhenu and her offspring Nandini, who could grant any wish, underscores his connection to the abundance and prosperity that come from spiritual excellence.

Vashisht's life and teachings continue to inspire generations, embodying the highest ideals of wisdom, devotion, and excellence. His hymns in Mandala 7 of the Rigveda stand as a timeless testament to his spiritual insight, offering a window into the Vedic understanding of the cosmos, the divine, and the enduring quest for harmony between humanity and the forces that govern the universe.

This chapter dedicated to Rishi Vashisht's hymns aims to explore the depth of his spiritual legacy, examining how his prayers for water and other natural elements reflect the Vedic people's profound reverence for the natural world. As we delve into the verses attributed to him, we gain a deeper appreciation for his role as a spiritual guide and a protector of the Vedic tradition, whose influence continues to resonate through the ages.

(First Anuvaka)

Sukta 1, attributed to Rishi Vashisht, the deity invoked is Agni, and the chanda used is Virata and Trishup. This hymn is a profound expression of reverence towards Agni, the divine fire, who is essential for the Vedic rituals and the sustenance of life. Vashisht extols Agni's virtues, describing him as the sacred fire that protects homes from fear and darkness when kindled. He highlights Agni's role in bestowing abundant wealth and brightness, illuminating the household and bringing prosperity. Agni is portrayed as the youngest and most radiant of fires, surpassing worldly flames in brilliance and auspiciousness, and being capable of granting progeny and prosperity.

The hymn continues with a prayer to Agni to destroy enemies and obstacles with the same intensity with which he burns demons who utter harsh words. Agni is beseeched to eliminate all troubles and diseases, ensuring the well-being of the devotees. The sacrificial fire, kindled by the hosts and circumambulated during the Yagya, is revered for its ability to invoke divine blessings. Agni is requested to deliver delightful offerings to the gods, as all deities' desire participation in the great sacrifice.

The Rishi also prays for protection from childlessness, poverty, and misfortune, seeking Agni's favor for a prosperous life filled with sons and grandchildren. The hymn underscores the importance of Agni's role in maintaining the sanctity and success of the Yagya, ensuring that the sacrificial offerings reach the gods and that the devotees receive Agni's benevolent protection and blessings. The hymn concludes with a heartfelt plea for Agni's continued support, asking for refined food, auspicious protection, and the well-being of both the singer and the host, ensuring their prosperity and protection throughout their lives.

Sukta 2, attributed to Rishi Vashisht, the deity invoked is Agni and the chanda used is Trishup and Pankti. This hymn is a solemn plea to Agni to accept the sacrifices and be luminous, extending his flames to meet the sun rays. Agni's glory is revealed through the deeds of those who perform yajnas and consume offerings with devotion. The Rishi urges the yajmani to always worship Agni, who serves as a powerful messenger between the sky and the earth. The hymn highlights the importance of offering ghee during havans, emphasizing the devotion of those who seek the favor of the gods through yajnas. Agni is depicted as the divine form providing welfare, akin to the mythical cow Kamadhenu, who grants shelter and prosperity. The hymn requests the arrival of goddesses Bharati, Ila, and Saraswati, symbolizing wisdom, speech, and nourishment, respectively, to bless the yajna. The plants are invoked to perform yajnas, recognizing the divine connection between fire and the gods. Agni is called to arrive with divine radiance, alongside deities like Indra, ensuring the satisfaction of the gods with the offerings. The hymn concludes with a plea for Aditi, the mother of gods, to preside over the yajna, ensuring the fulfillment and protection of the devotees.

Sukta 3, attributed to Rishi Vashisht, the deity invoked is Agni, and the chanda used is Trishup. This hymn praises Agni, the purifier and chief among those who perform yajnas, for his brilliance and his role as a messenger to the gods. Agni is described as consuming grass like a horse and residing in trees as Marut, with his path marked by black smoke. His innovative flames are rich and advanced, spreading smoke to the sky as he reaches the gods. Agni's radiance pervades the earth as he consumes wood, his army of flames revered like the Creator. Worshipers pray to Agni, likening him to a horse that always moves, and his radiant flames fulfill their desires.

The hymn beseeches Agni to bestow auspicious gifts upon the devotees, who in turn offer sacrifices with good conscience. Agni's brilliance is compared to the sun, his appearance becoming beautiful as he shines in the electric room and space. The worshipers seek protection from Agni, praising him with offerings and asking for his infinite glory to safeguard them. Agni is recognized as powerful and charitable, his bright flames and protective words safeguarding the yajna hosts. The hymn acknowledges Agni's role in performing yajnas, describing his emergence from wood and his birth from the mother goddess Arani. The hymn concludes with a plea for Agni to grant the best wealth, blessing the performers of yajnas and ensuring prosperity for singers and poets.

Sukta 4, attributed to Rishi Vashisht, the deity invoked is Agni, and the chanda used is Pankti and Trishup. This hymn is a profound adoration of Agni, the divine fire, and its vital role in the lives of gods and humans. The hymn begins by praising the blessed host who offers pure oblations to Agni, whose illumination spreads among all beings. Agni, emerging from two forests with brilliant and shining hair, consumes wood and spreads across the forests. This fire, established by humans in holy places, possesses a brightness that can even be recognized by enemies.

The hymn describes Agni as knowledgeable, indestructible, and radiant, residing among ignorant humans and urging them to keep their intelligence alert for his sake. Agni's intelligence is so great that he defeated the gods, earning his divine status. Trees and the earth serve Agni, who is also capable of bestowing nectar and superior immortality. The hymn expresses a fervent desire not to be born without a son, not to be ugly, and to continue serving Agni. The devotee prays for abundant wealth, freedom from debt, and not to be an adopted child of another caste. Agni is asked to grant wealth, destroy enemies, and bless with new-born children.

The hymn continues with a plea for protection from violence and sin, asking for sacred offerings to reach Agni and for wealth to come in thousands of ways. Agni is requested to give the best money and a son who performs yajnas. The singers and exponents should receive all the wealth, and Agni's welfare should protect the devotees. The hymn concludes with a heartfelt appeal for Agni's blessings, ensuring prosperity and protection for the yajna performers and their descendants.

Sukta 5, attributed to Rishi Vashisht, the deity invoked is Vaishvanara, and the chanda used is Trishup. This hymn dedicated Vaishvanara, the universal fire that pervades the space and the earth, who is exalted through sacrifices and becomes beautiful. The hymn begins with a call to praise the earthly and divine fire in the Yagya, where the presence of gods enhances the fire. Vaishvanara, the leader of rivers and the rain-maker, is recognized for his role in nature and his power to destroy enemies, as evidenced when he illuminated the city of Puru's enemy, causing the inauspicious to flee in fear.

The hymn continues to praise Agni for enlightening the sky and the earth with his radiance, emphasizing his dominion over men and his reception of sinless speech. Vaishvanara is depicted as a friend of the virtuous, empowered by the Vasugana to protect against demons. Appearing as the sun, Agni is the first to drink soma, generating water and providing hope to those in need. The hymn petitions Agni to bestow food that strengthens wealth and preserves the fame of the sacrificer. Finally, it requests blessings from Agni, along with the Rudragan and Vasugana, to ensure the prosperity and protection of the devotees.

Sukta 6, attributed to Rishi Vashisht, the deity invoked is Vaishvanara, and the chanda used is Triṣṭup. This hymn extols Vaishvanara Agni, the divine fire, celebrated for his destructive power against the Puris and likened to Agni Styuya and Bali Samrut Indra. The Rishi praises Agni's radiant brilliance, his ability to bear mountains, enlighten the world, provide welfare, and rule both sky and earth. Gods find pleasure in this fire, and Vashisht sings of Agni's ancient and noble deeds. Agni is invoked to drive away those averse to the Yagya, bitter-spoken, and foolish, ensuring their downfall.

The hymn further lauds Agni for showing the best path to creatures living in darkness, being the master of fire and wealth, and the destroyer of evil. Agni, who vanquished demonic illusions with his weapons and created Usha (the dawn), is celebrated for his power to restrain people and enforce order, as exemplified by making King Nahusha a tax-payer. People seek Agni's blessings for happiness, offering Havya, while Vaishvanara Agni, appearing in the space between sky and earth, is likened to a nurturing parent. As the sun rises, Vaishvanara Agni dispels all darkness, illuminating the sea, sky, earth, and all places, driving away the gloom.

Sukta 7, attributed to Rishi Vashisht, the deity invoked is Agni, and the chanda used is Trishup. This hymn dedicated Agni for his swift and brilliant nature, likening him to a horse and acknowledging his renown among the gods as Dagdhadum. Agni is called upon to perform heroic deeds in the Yagya, being a friend of the gods and arriving with a resounding presence that burns forests with might. The hymn depicts Agni as young and graceful, bringing satisfaction and manifesting intelligent fire to Agni, the leader of the Yagya and invoker of the sky and earth. Agni, who resides monogamously in human homes, is praised for his role in making the sky and earth gPankti , performing Yagya, and bearing offerings to Brahmanda deities.

The hymn honors those who enhance mantras and ignite fire for Yagyas, noting how they amplify nourishing forces through Anil. Agni, the master of Vasus, is celebrated by the descendants of Vashisht for filling the sacrificial host and the stota with great devotion, and for his continuous protection. The hymn encapsulates the reverence and gratitude felt towards Agni, highlighting his integral role in both divine and human realms.

Sukta 8, attributed to Rishi Vashisht, the deity invoked is Agni, and the chanda used is Trishup. This hymn extols Agni, whose form is offered with ghee and whose praises by scholars increase their numbers. Agni's fires illuminate before dawn, spreading radiance everywhere, with their path marked by darkness and enhanced by medicinal offerings. Agni is addressed as a beautiful donor, whose wealth increases with the offerings received. The hymn recalls Agni spreading light like the sun, praised by the yajna host and shining for the fire gods after defeating Puru. Abundant offerings make Agni stand steadfast, absorbing praises to gPankti stronger.

The diligent and intelligent Vashisht, managing a hundred cows and possessing a thousand, has composed this hymn to worship Agni. Agni, born from air and force, is the lord of the air force. Vashisht is devoted to Agni's praise, seeking quick blessings for the host and the stota along with the sacrifice. The hymn concludes with a plea for Agni to protect with the best protectors, ensuring safety and prosperity.

Sukta 9, attributed to Rishi Vashisht, the deity invoked is Agni, and the chanda used is Trishup. This hymn celebrates Agni, who purifies all living beings, brings joy, and awakens with the consciousness of dawn. Agni is praised as the bearer of growth among gods and humans and the bestower of wealth upon the virtuous. Those who guard Agni's path perform noble deeds, receiving fertile cows as rewards. Agni, with a peaceful mind and special brilliance, awakens at dawn, nourishing medicines as food.

The hymn acknowledges Agni's brilliance in human sacrifices and his enhancement through praises. Agni is implored to act as a messenger to the gods, to avoid harming those who praise him, and to facilitate the Yagya, ensuring offerings reach gods like Adhidraya and Saraswati. The hymn concludes with Vashisht's devotion to Agni, requesting the deity to repel harsh-speaking demons, please the gods with praises, and protect the devotees.

Sukta 10, attributed to the Rishi Vashisht, the deity of the fire, Prthu Pāja, gave lightning and shouted. The Chanda is Trishup. Like the Sun, Agni is very bright, bringing rain and inspiring the bright souls of Havis to gain fame. He awakens the worshipers who wish for fire. In the morning, the fire shines like the sun, spreading the Yagya and receiving the best praises. The fire god bows down to all living beings to solicit wealth. The praises of God and Kamya are directed towards the fire, who is a beautiful viewer of flames, an excellent mover, the husband of humans, and the bearer of sacrificial offerings. Oh fire! Meet Vasugana and call Indra. Meet the Rudras and offer prayers to Rudra. Invoke Aditi in harmony with the Adityas, and be consistent in the Angiras to invoke the chosen Jupiter. Men with desires praise the praiseworthy fire, where in the night of fire, there are processions and messengers offering sacrifices in the Devyaan.

Sukta 11, attributed to Rishi Vashisht, the deity is Agni, and the Chanda is Trishup. Oh fire! You are great, the performer of Yagya who pleases the Gods. You arrive with us in a chariot and become the chief, sitting on Kush. Oh fire! You are ever-moving; those who offer you elephants always make you a messenger. The host on whose wings you sit along with the gods, and on the Kushas where you are seated with them, marks the best day. The Ritviggans offer sacrifices for you in three seasons. You become our messenger in this Yagya, carrying the oblation and protecting us from enemies. Anil, the presiding deity of Maha Yagya, is the lord of sacrifices, and Vasugana praises his deeds. The gods have made this fire the carrier of the oblation. O fire, invokes the gods for the sacrificial fire, make the senses happy with this yajna, and protect us while taking the Yagya Dravya to the sky.

Sukta 12, attributed to the Rishi Vashisht, the deity is Agni, offered obeisances to the Yavistha, who gave the sacrificial fire in his own Durona. The Chanda is Trishup. That Anil, full of glory and rising in his place, situated in the middle of the earth, with a wonderful flame and beautiful call, is approached by us with salutations. Through his glory, this fire destroys all sins and is praised in the Yagya. We, who perform the Yagya, praise him and seek protection from sins. Oh fire! You are also Mitravaruna. Vashisht sang your hymn. May your wealth be easily accessible to us, and may you remain our guardian.

Sukta 13, attributed to Rishi Vashisht, the deity Vaisvanara, the omnipresent fire, is celebrated in the Chanda Triṣṭup. O worshipers, as you perform the sacred Yajnanushvaan for Agni, the destroyer of demons, offer Him your devoted praise. I wholeheartedly extol Anil, who fulfills all desires. Agni, you have completed the sky and earth, illuminating them with your radiant light. By your glory, you liberated the gods from their enemies. Oh fire, born of the sun and omnipresent, you see all living beings and are lauded by them. Always be our protector.

Sukta 14, attributed to Rishi Vashisht, the deity invoked is Jatavedasa, the god of fire, with the Chanda Brihati and Trishup. This hymn introduces Havirvan Yajmana Jataveda Agni, offering sacrifices to the fire while praising the gods. O auspicious flames of Sampatra Agne, we are prepared to serve you by offering Havya Pradan. Agni is invoked to be pleased with samidhas and praise, blessing the worshipers with happiness. The fire god is requested to come to the Yagya along with the gods, with the worshipers acting as his guardians, ensuring that he always follows them.

Sukta 15, attributed to the Rishi Vashisht, the deity invoked is Agni, with the Chanda Gayatri and Ushnika. The hymn addresses the Ritvijas, urging them to place the offering in the mouth of Agni, the closest friend and companion who fulfills desires. The youngest Agni, who follows the Charas, resides in every house, guiding the five Panchajanas. This fire, which grants us mantras, is invoked to protect us from all dangers, safeguard our wealth, and free us from sins. Like Garuda, the hymn composers create innovative verses for the eternal fire, seeking great wealth. The glowing Agni, in front of the sacred thread, is as splendid as the wealth of a host with a flaming son. May the fire, carrying the best offerings, be satisfied with the stotra, desiring our offerings? Invoked by hosts, Agni is a brilliant workman and the Lord of the World. The priests who desire wealth offer rituals to Agni, the praiseworthy flame, the holy purifier, to stop harmful efforts and ensure the best deeds.

Sukta 16, attributed to Rishi Vashisht, the deity invoked is Agni, and the chandas used are Anuṣṭup, Brihati, and Pankti. O host, I invoke for you the newly born, dynamic, angelic fire, the sustainer of all, who quickly moves towards the gods with yoked horses and chariot. This fire, worthy of sacrifices and beautiful deeds, brings wealth to the Rishis descended from Vashisht. The auspicious radiance of Agni is ever-increasing, with smoke reaching the skies, as all humans light the fire. Agni, the successful messenger, worships the gods while carrying Havan and provides consumable wealth. All living beings worship you, Agni; become the master of our Yagya, consume the oblations, and provide gems and wealth to the host. Strengthen everyone in our Yagya. Agni, the rich giver, ensures that those who donate money also offer love to the gods. Protect homes from evil slanderers, grant happiness, and receive continuous praise. Intelligent and air-borne Agni, help us attain wealth through sweet words and engage sacrificial men in action. Protect those who come to sacrifice with the desire of performing Yagya from sin. Agni, who wishes for the stota's happiness, carries our Yagya when the vessel is filled with Soma. Appointed as Hota by the gods, Agni bestows handsome wealth on the host.

Sukta 17, attributed to Rishi Vashisht, dedicated the deity Agni through the dvipada Trishup chanda. The hymns implore Agni to serve as a refuge for those seeking divine favor and to invoke the gods who desire the Yagya. The first verse asks Agni to approach the gods and perform the Yagya with the offerings, making it a cause for their worship. The second verse emphasizes Agni's role in imbuing the immortal gods with the Yagya, offering sacrifices, and propitiating them with praises to bestow wealth and blessings. In the third verse, Agni, referred to as the mighty Anil, is acknowledged as the bearer of the offerings appointed by all the gods. The hymn concludes with a plea for Agni, the stunning and great one, to accept the oblations and provide gems and wealth.

(Second Anuvaka)

Sukta 18 attributed to Rishi Vashisht, dedicated the deity Indra through the Triṣṭup and Pankti chanda. The hymns recount the divine acts of Indra, praising him for bestowing wealth and prosperity upon the ancestors and the worshipers through his mighty deeds. In the first verse, Indra is exalted for enabling the cows to yield milk and providing excellent wealth to the devotees, making him an essential benefactor of those who praise him. The second verse highlights Indra's brilliance and poetic nature, emphasizing his role in granting cows, horses, and beauty to his followers, ensuring they are worthy of wealth.

In the third verse, the hymns bring delightful praises to Indra, wishing for his wealth and happiness through his grace. Indra is metaphorically compared to a cow giving birth to a calf in the form of hymns, showcasing his nurturing role. The fourth verse acknowledges Indra's assistance to King Sudas in crossing the difficult currents of the Parushni River and removing curses that hinder movement, reinforcing his protective nature.

The hymns further narrate how Indra, intoxicated with soma paan, freed the cows and defeated demons hiding them, illustrating his power in safeguarding his devotees' assets. Verses recount Sudas's victories, aided by Indra, against enemies and how he brought prosperity and stability to his kingdom by subduing adversaries and stabilizing the Parushni River's banks. Indra's interventions are praised, showing his ability to empower his followers, like the desert protecting Sudas, ensuring their strength and success.

The hymns also praise Indra's unparalleled deeds, both ancient and new, describing how he vanquished enemies like Devak and Shambar. Verses highlight the loyalty of Rishis like Vashishtha and Parashar, who consistently praised Indra for his protection. The hymn concludes with the depiction of Sudas's chariots and horses, adorned and blessed by Indra, bringing prosperity and protecting the realm. It ends with a plea for Indra's continued support, invoking his strength to protect Sudas and his household, ensuring their enduring prosperity and victory over all adversaries.

Sukta 19, attributed to Rishi Vashisht, dedicated the deity Indra through the Trishup chanda. In this hymn, Indra is depicted as a powerful bull with sharp horns, defeating enemies single-handedly and seizing their limbs. The first verse praises Indra for providing wealth to the host and protecting Kutsa while defeating bandits Shushna and Kuyava. The subsequent verses beseech Indra to protect Ividata Sudas, Payadasyu, and Puru in battle, and recount his victories over various enemies, including Vritras and the bandit Chumuri. Indra's might is further illustrated through his destruction of ninety-nine fortresses of Shambar and the defeat of Vritra and Namuchi. The hymn emphasizes Indra's praiseworthy nature and his role in safeguarding the righteous, ensuring their prosperity and success. The concluding verses ask for Indra's protection in the yagna, his favor towards the devotees, and his continuous role as their eternal protector, granting them wealth, and eternal security.

Chapter Three

Sukta 20, attributed to Rishi Vashisht, dedicated the deity Indra through the Trishup chanda. This hymn extols Indra, born for strength, as an unstoppable force that aids in human endeavors and absolves sins. In the first verse, Indra is praised for providing shelter to the brave and bestowing wealth upon the host, particularly the newly created territory to Sudas. The second verse highlights Indra as a great warrior who single-handedly defeats innumerable enemies and creates obstacles for enemy armies. Indra's power is celebrated in the third verse, depicting how he filled the sky and earth, spread thunderbolts on enemies, and was served by Somras. The fourth verse reveals Kashyap's invocation of Indra for war, acknowledging him as the master of humans, the military leader, and the destroyer of enemies. The hymn concludes with a plea for Indra to provide wealth, protect the devotees, and enable them to wholeheartedly engage in his praise and worship, ensuring their prosperity and safety.

Sukta 21, attributed to Rishi Vashisht, dedicated the deity Indra through the Trishup chanda. This hymn celebrates the brilliance of Soma, which draws Indra's interest. The devotees promise to awaken Indra through Yagya, seeking his attention to their praises. The verses describe the ritual preparations, including the spreading of Kush-Vishtar and the harsh sounds of Somabhishavkaari stones. Indra is praised for inspiring the waters held back by Vritra, causing rivers to flow like chariots and making the world tremble in fear. His disruption of demon activities and the destruction of their strongholds with his thunderbolt are highlighted. The hymn also beseeches Indra to protect the devotees from demons and celibate obstructions during the Yagya. The verses acknowledge Indra's unparalleled actions, his subjugation of all beings, and his victory over Vritra. Ancient gods, recognizing their inferiority to Indra, saw him as a protector and benefactor. The hymn concludes with a plea for Indra's continued protection, strength, and glory, ensuring the devotees' success and safety in all their endeavors.

Sukta 22, attributed to Rishi Vashisht, dedicated the deity Indra through the Virat and Trishup chanda. This hymn begins with an invitation to Indra to drink the joyful Soma, prepared with the Somabhishava stones held in both hands. Indra, known as Haryashwa, is praised for his power in the Yagya, which destroys enemies and brings joy. The verses highlight the numerous sacrifices and wise offerings made to Indra by humans. The hymn requests Indra to recognize and accept Vashisht praises and to be pleased with the service rendered, thereby bestowing superior intellect upon the devotee. Indra, the conqueror of enemies, is acknowledged for his strength and the devotee pledges to always chant his name. Indra is called upon to remain close and not distant, as his presence is integral to the devotees' well-being. The hymn emphasizes that all sounds and praises are directed towards Indra, and his friendship is considered highly beneficial. It concludes with a plea for Indra's grace, highlighting that ancient and new Rishis have always revealed hymns to him, seeking his continued support and presence.

Sukta 23, attributed to Rishi Vashisht, dedicated the deity Indra through the Trishup chanda. The hymns, recited by the Atra-Kamy Stota, are filled with praises for Indra, emphasizing his omnipresence and glory that spans all worlds. The hymn calls for Indra to listen to the devotee's call and be present in the Yagya. Indra's unmatched power and age, surpassing all humans, are highlighted, showing his supreme position among the gods. The verses express a desire for Indra to accept the praises and fill the sky and earth with his glory, while also recognizing his role in destroying enemies. Indra is implored to bring abundance, likened to the wind moving towards its destination, and to bestow the best food and wealth through his actions. The hymn concludes with a plea for Indra to be pleased with the Yagya, to grant a joyful heart and progeny, and to remain kind to humans. Vashisht's worship of Indra through the stotra seeks wealth for the best people and continuous divine favor.

Sukta 24, attributed to Rishi Vashisht, dedicated the deity Indra through the Trishup chanda. The hymn begins with an invitation to Indra to join the sacrifice along with the Maruts and to continue being the protector, granting wealth to the devotees and enjoying their Soma offering. The second verse describes the meticulous preparation of the sweet Soma juice, which calls upon Indra to partake. The hymn beseeches Indra to be drawn by his beloved Haryashwa towards their praises. Indra is implored to defeat the enemies with the help of the Maruts and to bless the worshipers with a desired son. The powerful verses aim to attract Indra's favor, seeking wealth and progeny for the devotees. The concluding verses emphasize the desire for Indra's grace, asking for his continuous presence and blessings, ensuring prosperity and a well-off son for the givers.

Sukta 25, attributed to Rishi Vashisht, dedicated the deity Indra through the Trishup and Pankti chandas. The hymn opens with a plea for Indra's thunderbolt to protect the devotees in times of war. Indra is beseeched to vanquish those who oppose and criticize the worshipers, thereby ending their Yagya and enriching the faithful. The verses express a desire for Sudas to receive hundreds of Indra's protections and donations, while calling for the destruction of violent enemies' weapons, and the bestowal of fame and wealth. The hymn highlights the devotees' dedication to worship, seeking Indra's engagement in their actions and his mercy. Through chanting hymns, the devotees seek divine power and blessings from Indra, wishing for sons and continuous divine favor.

Sukta 26, attributed to Rishi Vashisht, dedicated the deity Indra through the Trishup chanda. The hymn emphasizes that Soma offered without hymns does not satisfy Indra; only the Soma prepared with proper praises pleases him. The devotees proclaim their Ukhta as dedicated solely to Indra. In the second verse, it is noted that just as a father calls his son, the Ritviggans call upon Indra for protection. The deeds of Indra, celebrated in ancient times, are recounted, highlighting his role in cleansing enemies of demons. Indra, endowed with numerous means of protection, bestows wealth and alleviates troubles. The hymn concludes with a plea for Indra's best welfare and the granting of various perfumes by Somabhishavkari Vashisht Indra, ensuring his continual presence and support for the devotees.

Sukta 27, attributed to Rishi Vashisht, dedicated the deity Indra through the Trishup chanda. The hymn begins by invoking Indra's aid when preparations for battle are complete, seeking his favor to bestow wealth and prosperity upon the devotees, thereby enhancing their prestige. Indra is called upon to defeat the enemies with his strength and to reveal hidden wealth through his wisdom. Recognized as the god of all beings and the king of earthly wealth, Indra is asked to be pleased with the praises and to grant abundant wealth to the host. The hymn highlights Indra's role in providing food for protection and the best wealth to his chosen friends. The devotees request Indra to make them rich swiftly, expressing their intention to attract his favor through continuous praise and seeking his constant protection.

Sukta 28, attributed to Rishi Vashisht, dedicated the deity Indra through the Trishup chanda. The hymn begins with an invitation to Indra to come to the devotees' praise, uniting his horses before them, as all humans call upon him individually. Indra is requested to listen to their call. The second verse describes how Indra becomes monstrous in his actions when protecting the hymns. Those who praise Indra repeatedly are honored by him on earth and in heaven, and those who perform Yagya for his sake are granted the power to overcome those who do not. Indra is implored to liberate the devotees by taking away the wealth of the wicked. The hymn concludes with praise for Indra, who provides the desired wealth and protection to the devotees, asking him to continue following and safeguarding them.

Sukta 29, attributed to Rishi Vashisht, dedicated the deity Indra through the Trishup chanda. The hymn begins with an invitation to Indra to come quickly and consume the Soma that has been sacrificed for him, requesting him to fulfill their desire for wealth. Indra is called to arrive swiftly with his horses, armed and ready, as the hymns of praise reach him. The beauty of the praises is highlighted, with the devotees seeking Indra's hospitality and urging him to listen. The hymn recalls how Indra heard the hymns of ancient Rishis who benefited mankind, likening him to a father who ensures their welfare. The devotees repeatedly call upon Indra, praising him for the great wealth he provides and his protection, and beseeching him to always safeguard them.

Sukta 30, attributed to Rishi Vashisht, dedicated the deity Indra through the Trishup chanda. The hymn begins by calling upon Indra to arrive with force and increase the wealth of the devotees, enhancing his strength to destroy their enemies. Indra is invoked as the supreme protector and the best commander, capable of conquering all enemies with his thunderbolt. On auspicious days, Indra is said to take the form of fire, allowing devotees to pray to the gods during the Yagya for the best donations. The hymn emphasizes the devotees' devotion to Indra, requesting him to grant them the best blessings, ensuring they remain disease-free and healthy. The concluding verses praise Indra for providing the desired wealth and protecting the devotees, seeking his continual presence and protection.

Sukta 31, attributed to Rishi Vashisht, dedicated the deity Indra through the Gayatri and Virat chandas. The hymn begins by urging friends to please Indra with praises and the drinking of Soma, highlighting Indra as the bestower of wealth and encouraging everyone to seek refuge in his praise. Indra is acknowledged as the generous giver, with a specific request for cows and gold. The devotees particularly praise Indra, asking for his kindness and protection against slanderous and ignorant individuals. The hymn expresses confidence in defeating enemies through Indra's grace. It extols Indra's power, which causes even heaven and earth to bow before him, describing him as a beautiful sight to behold and noting that all living beings bow to him. The hymn concludes by encouraging humans to perform Somabhishav for financial gain and to praise Indra, ensuring his satisfaction with their offerings. It emphasizes that the wise protect the rituals dedicated to the great Indra, whose praises lead to the downfall of enemies, and encourages all devotees to rally their friends to praise Indra.

Sukta 32, attributed to Rishi Vashisht, dedicated the deity Indra through the Pragatha and Dvi Virat chandas. The hymn begins with a fervent plea to Indra, requesting him not to let other hosts deter him from attending their sacrifice and listening to their stotra, even from a distance. The devotees, having completed the Somabhishava, sit in the Yagya and earnestly pray for wealth. Indra is invoked with the same reverence a son has for his father, highlighting the deep bond between the deity and his worshipers. They prepare Soma mixed with milk, inviting Indra to partake in the offering, and express their unwavering hope for wealth, confident that no one can hinder Indra from bestowing thousands of donations upon them.

The hymn extols Indra's might, describing how his followers, the brave warriors, face no opposition when he supports them. Indra is called upon to remove obstacles for the sacrificers, defeat their enemies, and bestow the enemies' wealth upon the faithful. The devotees urge humans to perform Somabhishava for Vajrahast Indra, purify the Purodash, and engage in Yagyas to gain wealth, as Indra is known to grant every kind of happiness. The hymn emphasizes that a man of good deeds becomes strong and victorious over his enemies, while those who engage in evil deeds remain devoid of divine support.

Indra, the protector, is praised for his ability to grant the desired wealth and to safeguard those who extol him. The hymn recalls that Indra listens to the hymns of ancient Rishis who benefited humanity, reinforcing his role as a benevolent deity. The devotees express their dependence on Indra, seeking his continual protection, prosperity, and favor. Indra is implored to grant wisdom, wealth, and daily protection, ensuring the devotees remain free from disease and harm.

The hymn acknowledges Indra's unparalleled power, stating that even heaven and earth bow before him. His praises are described as beautiful and essential for attracting his favor. The devotees express their desire for Indra's continuous support in all battles, ensuring their enemies are kept at bay and their efforts are successful. Indra is recognized as the master of all earthly, cosmic, and divine wealth, and the devotees seek his grace to attain this wealth. The hymn concludes with a heartfelt appeal for Indra to protect their sons and themselves, to grant wisdom and wealth, and to ensure their daily well-being and success in all endeavors.

Sukta 33, attributed to Rishi Vashisht and the sons of Vashisht, dedicated the deity Indra through the Triṣṭup and Pankti chandas. The hymn opens with a request to the descendants of Vashisht, adorned with a chudamani on the right side of their heads, to remain with the devotees and not go elsewhere. It recounts how the Vashisht Gotri Rishis, rejecting Pashdyumna, brought Indra to drink Soma, and Indra favored these Rishis in return. Vashisht's power is celebrated for aiding Indra in saving Sudas during the battle of Dasharaja. The hymn acknowledges that the praises of these Rishis satisfy the ancestors and bestow strength, as Vashisht obtained strength from Indra through excellent verses. In their plea for rain, Vashisht elevated Indra, who granted the best positions to the Tritsuvanshi kings. The hymn recounts how Vashisht's guidance increased the progeny of the Bharatas (Trisu), who were once outnumbered by enemies. The hymn further extols Vashisht's brightness, wisdom, and the acknowledgment by divine entities like Mitravaruna and Agastya of his spiritual significance. It narrates Vashisht's celestial origins as the son of Mitravaruna and Urvashi, recognized by the Vishvedevs, and his omniscience. The hymn concludes with a call to the Pratrtsuo to worship Vashisht, who is revered as the preacher of all deeds, emphasizing his divine birth and unparalleled wisdom.

Sukta 34, attributed to Rishi Vashisht, dedicated the Visvedeva and the serpent deity Ahirbudhnya through the Dvipada, Virat, and Trishup chandas. The hymn begins with a call for their best praise to reach the gods swiftly, likened to a fast chariot. It acknowledges the omniscient nature of rain-water, which knows the appearance of heaven and earth, and listens to hymns. Water satisfies Indra, who is depicted with a golden hand and thunderbolt, and the praises are urged to prepare for his arrival. The hymn guides humans to walk the best road towards the Yagya and to perform rituals to destroy sins. It highlights the significance of Yagya, comparing its support to that of the earth for living beings. The hymn invokes the gods with full heart and praises the noble deeds for the gods. Varuna, with his many eyes, observes the rivers and is acknowledged as the lord of regions. The gods are called upon to protect, defeat detractors, and free the praisers from sin. Friendship with Agni, the companion of the gods, is encouraged, and the fire within water is praised. The hymn implores the fire not to hand them over to the violent, ensuring the sacrifice's offerings are not in vain. It calls upon the gods to hold food for them and destroy enemies, likening a god-favored king's might to the sun's heat. The hymn seeks the favor of Tvashtadev and other gods, wishing for protection, wealth, and the fulfillment of their desires. Mountains, waters, and goddesses are invoked for safeguarding wealth. The hymn concludes by seeking help from heaven and earth, and protection from Indra, Varuna, and Marudga, expressing a desire to live happily under their shelter, with the constant favor of Mitravarun, Indra, Agni, and nature.

Sukta 35, attributed to Rishi Vashisht, dedicated the demigods Vishvedevs through the Triṣṭup and Pankti chandas. The hymn begins with a plea to Indra and Agni to grant peace and protection, asking Indravarun, Indra, and Soma to be auspicious and bring happiness. It seeks blessings from the divine forces for happiness through truthful words and the favor of Arthma. Dhata, Varun, Prithvi, Sarvatra, and other gods are invoked for happiness. The hymn prays for the volcano to be cool and calls upon Mitravarun, Ashvins, Vayu, and virtuous deeds to bring peace. The divine earth, space, medicines, trees, and world lord Indra are also asked to grant peace. Rudra, along with the Vasus, and Tvashta with the Devnaris are mentioned for their peace-giving roles. The hymn further seeks peace from Soma, Somabhishava stones, yajna, stotra, yup, medicines, and altars. The sun, directions, mountains, rivers, and bright waters are invoked for peace, as are Aditi, Marudgana, Vishnu, Pusha, space, and air. Savita, Usha, Parjanya, and Kshetrapathi are called upon to grant peace. Visvadeva, Saraswati, Yajnanushtana, donations, Prithivi-Aakash, Antariksha, Devata, Ashwagane, cows, and ribhugan are requested for peace and strength. Ancestors, Aja Ekapada, Ahirbudhnyadeva, Samudra, Apatrapat, and Prishni are also mentioned for their peace-giving attributes. The hymn concludes with a request for the gods to listen to their new hymn and calls upon the sacrificial gods, sky, and earth to pay attention, asking Manu Prajapati and other deities to grant sons and protect with welfare.

Chapter IV

Sukta 36, attributed to Rishi Vashisht, dedicated the Vishvedevs through the Pankti and Trishup chandas. The hymn begins by directing the hymns recited in the Yagya towards the Sun, acknowledging the Sun's role in creating rainwater through its rays and the fire that shines over the expansive earth. Varuna is specially praised, with new hymns pronounced in his honor, recognizing his role in revealing places and Mitra's role in putting the stota into action. The hymn celebrates the beautiful movement of air and the growth of the Payaswini cow, while also invoking Indra to come to the Yagya arranged by his devotees. Aryama is praised for nullifying the anger of violent sinners, and Atharvan Yajman seeks friendship with Rudra, who bestows blessings when pleased with praises. The hymn then highlights the Sindhu as the mother of rivers and Saraswati as the seventh river, noting how these streams fulfill desires and nourish the land with their waters. The fast Maruts are invoked to protect the rituals and the child. The god of speech is asked to be kind and increase wealth. The hymn concludes by invoking the vast earth, sacrificial Nusha, Bhaga, and Vayu, calling upon the Maruts to be present, seeking protection and blessings from Vishnu, and requesting that the recitations ensure the wellbeing and protection of the devotees.

Sukta 37, attributed to Rishi Vashisht, dedicated the Vishvedevs through the Trishup and Pankti chandas. The hymn begins by calling upon the stunning Ribhugans, asking them to arrive in their tolerant chariot and fill their stomachs with mixed Soma. The sacrificer are encouraged to wear the gem, become brave, drink Soma, and bestow wealth. Indra is invoked to consume food while generously donating wealth, his actions unstoppable. The hymn beseeches Indra to come to the homes of those who praise him, offering sacrifices and praises in return for wealth and protection. Indra's attention to the praises is sought, highlighting his provision of residence and the arrival of his horses with great wealth. The hymn acknowledges Indra as the god whom the earth exalts, the food-loving Varnas accept as master, and the Stota's invite into their homes. Indra's power over non-eating is celebrated. Savitadev is also invoked for praiseworthy wealth, and the wealth given by the mountains is requested. The hymn concludes with a plea for Indra to accept their service and for the gods to always protect them.

Sukta 38, attributed to Rishi Vashisht, dedicated the deity Sun through the Trishup chanda. The hymn begins by acknowledging the Sun rising with its radiant brightness, worthy of human praise, and as a provider of the best wealth to the devotee. Savita, another name for the Sun, is invoked to rise and bless the leaders by initiating rituals and listening to the praises offered. The hymn requests Savita to enhance their praise and protect the stota in all ways. Savita is praised by gods like Aditi, Varun, Mitra, and Aryama. The charitable host Savita is worshipped, and Ahirbudhnya, along with Vani Devi, is asked to listen to the praises and offer comprehensive protection. The hymn calls for happiness from the gods named Vaaji, the destruction of evil spirits and demons, and the removal of all diseases. The gods are implored to protect the devotees in all battles, to derive happiness from Soma, and to proceed on the Devyan path, signifying a divine journey.

Sukta 39, attributed to Rishi Vashisht, dedicated the demigods Visvedevas through the Triṣṭup chanda. The hymn begins with a plea for the moon to grant the devotees the brilliance of the sun, showering them with continual blessings. It mentions Usha Devi's presence at the sacrifice, where the host, alongside his wife, walks the path of fame and performs the Yagya. The Yajaman completes the ritual with Kush and Havya, calling upon Vayu and Pusha to arrive before dawn for the benefit of all. Vasugan is invoked to travel to Bihar in his chariot, serving even those in the desert. The hymn requests the Vasus and Maruts to heed the messenger's call and turn their path towards the devotees. It calls upon Agni to perform the Yagya for the Vishvedeva and to worship Bhaga, Ashvidvaya, and Indra. Indra, Mitra, Varuna, Arthama, Agni, Aditi, and Vishnu are invited, along with prayers for the blessings of Saraswati and Marudgana. The hymn highlights the offering of sacrifices to the worthy deities and the anticipation of their darshan. It concludes with praise for the sky, earth, Indra, Varuna, and Agni, seeking the best food and constant care from the God of welfare.

Sukta 40, attributed to Rishi Vashisht, dedicated the demigods Visvedevas through the Pankti and Trishup chandas. The hymn begins with a heartfelt plea for the best happiness and satisfaction from the gods, expressing the desire to be content with the wealth inspired by Savitadev. It continues by seeking praiseworthy wealth from Mitravarun, Dyavaprithivi, Indra, Aryama, Vayu, and Bhaga, with Aditi bestowing the desired riches. The hymn highlights the protection of worshipers by deities like Agni and Saraswati, ensuring that their wealth remains intact and undestroyed. The omnipotent Mitra, Varun, and Aryama are praised for supporting Yagya rituals, and Aditi is invoked to free the devotees from sins. The hymn acknowledges that all other gods are part of Vishnu, seeking blessings from Rudra and the presence of Ashvidvaya in their homes full of offerings. Pushan is asked not to hinder the wealth granted by Saraswati and other goddesses, while beneficent gods and the wind are called upon to provide protection and rain. The hymn concludes with praise for Dyava-Prithvi, Varun, Indra, and Agni, requesting acceptable wealth and the continuous favor of the gods.

Sukta 41, attributed to Rishi Vashisht, dedicated the deities Agni, Indra, Bhaga, and Ushasa through the Trishup Jagati and Pankti chandas. The hymn begins with a morning invocation to Indra, Mitra, and Varun, and extends praises to Ashvidvaya, Bhaga, Pusha, Brahmanaspati, Soma, and Rudra. Bhaga, the victorious son of Aditi, is especially invoked in the morning prayers by both the poor and the wealthy, seeking disposable wealth. The hymn requests the divine to bestow true wealth, increase livestock, and bless the devotees with sons. It seeks blessings throughout the day, invoking the gods' grace repeatedly. Ushasa is called upon to come first in the Yagya, to face the devotees like a chariot with fast horses. The hymn concludes with a plea for Ushasa to bring all qualities like the horse, cow, etc., to dispel the darkness of night and to continue blessing the devotees.

Sukta 41, attributed to Rishi Vashisht, dedicated the deities Agni, Indra, Bhaga, and Ushasa through the Trishup Jagati and Pankti chandas. The hymn opens with offerings to the morning fire, morning Indra, morning Varuna, and morning horse, extending the morning sacrifices to Pūṣāṇa, the lord of the Brahmins, and to Soma and Rudra. It acknowledges the fierce Bhaga, who is invoked in the morning, with both the rich and the poor seeking his favor. The hymn beseeches Bhaga, the pioneer and Satyaradha, to grant them intelligence and prosperity. The devotees request divine blessings to be bestowed upon them with cows and horses, wishing to be rejuvenated with men and to receive favor throughout the day. They aspire to be well-pleasing to the gods under the sun's rise, seeking Bhaga's lordship over the gods and their own elevation. The hymn portrays the women bowing to the pure feet of the Lord, and likens their devotion to curd settling down. It concludes with a plea for the horses to carry their chariots as swiftly and gracefully as those of the earth, symbolizing strength and stability in their endeavors.

Sukta 42, attributed to Rishi Vashisht, dedicated the Visvedevas through the Triṣṭup chanda. The hymn begins by invoking the Angiras to pervade everywhere, with a wish for rain to desire their praise, and for rivers to irrigate the streams, emphasizing the importance of the host couple in organizing the Yagya. It calls upon Agni, asking for his eternal path to be smooth and for the chariot with black and red horses to carry the great deity to the sacrificial fire. The hymn, situated in the Yagya Mandap, invokes the gods, emphasizing that the devotees worship them closely, seeking the best sacrifices and glory to attain the land. Agni, seen as a guest in the house of a rich person, is praised for providing acceptable wealth when he is conscious and happy. The hymn urges Agni to enjoy their Yagya, to expand it between Indra and Marudgana, and to sit on sacrificial cushions both at night and in the morning, worshipping Mitravarun. Vashisht praises Agni with the desire for wealth, seeking strength, perfume, and continuous wealth, asking Agni to always follow and protect them.

Sukta 43, attributed to Rishi Vashisht, dedicated the gods and the universal gods through the Trishup chanda. The hymn begins by acknowledging the learned, whose praises have spread everywhere, praising for divine attainment and for the heavens and the earth. It calls upon the priests to arrive like swift horses, with rays and light, united in mind, dwelling in the best places of the sacrifice. Agni is invoked to have his sacrificial flames irrigated by Juhu in a proper manner and to act as the destroyer of enemies. The gods are asked to accept the worship while irrigating the water-draining stream, providing the best wealth to the devotees. The hymn pleads for the gods to arrive with a unified mind, and for Agni to grant continuous wealth and never abandon the devotees, ensuring their perpetual happiness and constant protection.

Sukta 44, attributed to Rishi Vashisht, dedicated the deity Dadhikra and other gods through the Jagati, Trishup, and Pankti chandas. The hymn begins with an invocation to Dadhikra for protection, calling upon the two horses, Usha, Agni, Bhaga, Indra, Vishnu, Poosha, Brahmanaspati, the suns, the sky, the earth, the water, and the sun. At the onset of the sacrifice, Dadhikra is specifically invoked, alongside praises for fire, dawn, the sun, and speech. Varun's horse is also praised, with a plea for all the gods to free the devotees from their sins. The hymn extols Dadhikra, noting his leadership among horses and his knowledge of essential truths. It calls for the gods Usha, Surya, Adityagan, Vasugana, and Angiras to lead the chariot. The hymn emphasizes following Dadhikra in the path of truth, justice, and public welfare, likening him to a light like fire that provides strength and guidance to the devotees.

Sukta 45, attributed to Rishi Vashisht, dedicated the Sun deity through the Trishup chanda. The hymn begins with a prayer for the Sun god, who holds all wealth auspicious for human beings, to rise and inspire living beings to perform actions. It calls upon Savitadev to pervade the limits of space, with a pledge to proclaim his glory. The hymn requests the Sun to incline the devotees towards action and to inspire wealth, asking for him to be of a grand form and provide consumable wealth. It concludes with a plea for the Sun to grant the best food and to follow and protect the devotees.

Sukta 46, attributed to Rishi Vashisht, dedicated the deity Rudra through the Trishup and Jagati chandas. The hymn begins by urging the psalmist to praise Rudra, the bow-bearer, invincible, and all-conquering, asking Rudra to listen to their prayers and protect those who sing his praises. It acknowledges Rudra's experience with both earthly and divine opulence and pleads for him to keep diseases away from the devotees. The hymn beseeches Rudra to prevent the destructive power of space electricity on earth from harming them, emphasizing his vast knowledge of thousands of medicines. It requests Rudra to spare their sons and grandchildren from harm and to refrain from violence against them. The hymn concludes with a plea for Rudra not to let them fall into the trap of his anger, to grant them success, and to always follow and protect them.

Sukta 47, attributed to Rishi Vashisht, dedicated the deity of water through the Trishup and Pankti chandas. The hymn begins by invoking the water god, requesting that the Somras, which is worthy of being consumed by Indra and prepared by the Adhvaryus, also be made available to the devotees. It calls upon Apanapat Dev to enhance the juicy Soma, desiring the same pleasure that Indra and the Vasugana derive from it while praying for the gods. The waters are praised for their role in the temples and their non-obstructive nature in Indra's Yagya rituals. The hymn addresses the rivers, urging them to support sacrifices for Sindhu and others, and acknowledges the Sun for increasing the waters with its rays, creating pathways through Indra's influence. The people of Sindhu are encouraged to wear Dhoot and always follow the devotees, ensuring their continuous support and blessings.

Sukta 48, attributed to Rishi Vashisht, dedicated the deities Ribhava and Visvedeva through the Pankti and Trishup chandas. The hymn begins by inviting the Ribhugan to be pleased by drinking their Soma, with their working horses coming forth to benefit humanity. It acknowledges the prosperity bestowed by these powerful deities, expressing confidence in defeating enemies with their support and seeking their protection. The hymn prays for Indra's grace to be spared from harm by Vritra, emphasizing that Indra and the Ribhugan defeat enemy armies and kill foes on the battlefield. It specifically mentions the trio Ribhutraya, Ribhuksha, and Vaj, along with Indra, as destroyers of enemies. The hymn concludes with a plea for the Lord to be a generous provider, offering protection, food, and overall well-being to the devotees.

Sukta 49, attributed to Rishi Vashisht, dedicated the deity of water through the Trishup chanda. The hymn begins by invoking the waters from which the ocean grew, acknowledging their abundant flow. It calls upon the water gods who come from space and the waters freed by Indra to be protectors. The hymn seeks protection from the waters originating in space, those flowing in rivers, and those extracted from ponds, all moving towards the sea. It emphasizes the protective nature of waters filled with light and juice, whose lords journey to Yamalok. The hymn concludes by seeking protection from the waters in which Varun, Soma, Atra, and Vaishvanar Agni reside, noting the pleasure of the Vishvedeva with these waters.

Sukta 50, attributed to Rishi Vashisht, dedicated the demigods Mitra and Varuna, as well as Agni, the Visvedevas, and the rivers through the Jagti and Atijagti chandas. The hymn begins with a plea to Mitra and Varuna to protect the devotees from deadly poisons, ensuring that even stealthy snakes cannot attack them. It calls upon Agnidev to shield them from the effects of poisons produced in tree glands that cause swelling in joints. The hymn also seeks protection from the Vishwadevs against poisons found in the Shalmali tree and in Gulma Lata gPankti ing near rivers, asking that secretive serpents be unable to harm them. Furthermore, it invokes the beneficent rivers that flow through mountainous, low, and advanced countries, fulfilling people's needs, to cure their diseases and not cause any harm. These rivers are praised for their life-giving properties and are asked to continue their benevolent influence.

Sukta 51, attributed to Rishi Vashisht, dedicated the deity Aditya through the Trishup chanda. The hymn begins with a prayer for the suns' grace to provide a happy home, asking them to be pleased with the devotees' praises and to make the sacrificial host blameless and free from poverty. It invokes Aditya, Aditi, Mitra, Varuna, and Arthama to rejoice and protect the devotees, inviting them to drink the Soma. The hymn praises the twelve suns, the forty-nine Maruts, the thirty-three hundred and thirty-three gods, the three Ribhus, the two Ashvinikumara, Indra, and Agni, asking all these divine beings to follow and favor the devotees continuously.

Sukta 52, attributed to the Rishi Vashisht, is dedicated to the suns as deities, and follows the chanda Trishup. In this hymn, the worshippers express their devotion to the sun, seeking protection and blessings. They implore Varuna, the friend, for wealth through worship and pray to the beautiful earth for strength. The verse highlights the wish for Mitra, Varuna, and Aditya to be kind to their descendants, hoping to avoid the repercussions of others' sins. They request that Vasugana prevent them from actions that lead to their downfall. The final verse seeks the wealth granted by Prajapati and all the gods to Angiras upon Savita's prayer, emphasizing the aspiration for divine favor and prosperity.

Sukta 53, attributed to the Rishi Vashisht, is devoted to the heavens and the earth as the deities and follows the Triṣṭup meter. The hymn begins with a praise for the vast heavens and earth, which have been further glorified by the stota's (praisers) through their devotion. The poet calls upon the heavens and earth, emphasizing their praiseworthy nature, to establish their maternal and paternal power at the forefront of fame. Addressing the heavenly earth, the hymn acknowledges its abundance and generosity, requesting infinite wealth and continual blessings for the devotees.

Sukta 54, attributed to the Rishi Vashisht, is dedicated to Vastoshpati, the deity of the dwelling place, and follows the Trishup meter. The hymn begins with an invocation to Vastoshpati to awaken and grant the devotees wealth free from disease, bringing happiness to their animals and humans. The poet beseeches Vastoshpati to increase their wealth and, through divine friendship, bestow immortality and abundance in cattle, likening the deity's protective nature to that of a father towards his son. The final verse asks for a prosperous and joyful abode, with Vastoshpati continually safeguarding their wealth and remaining a constant guardian.

Sukta 55, attributed to the Rishi Vashisht, invokes the deities Vastoshpati and Indra, and follows the meters Gayatri, Bṛhati, and Anuṣṭup. The hymn begins with a call to Vastoshpati, the destroyer of diseases and well-wisher, to protect the worshippers. It describes how Vastoshpati teeth, when drawn, appear as decorated weapons, bringing a sense of security and peace. Addressing Sarameya, the poet instructs this entity to move away from those who praise Indra and cease being an obstacle. The hymn emphasizes the desire for restful sleep for all, including the house, its owner, relatives, and surrounding people. It invokes the power of the Sahasranshu Sun rising above the ocean to help put everyone to sleep, ensuring a peaceful and undisturbed rest for all, including those on vehicles, beds, and those emitting a floral fragrance.

Sukta 56, from the fourth Anuvaka, is attributed to the Rishi Vashisht and is dedicated to the Maruts, following the Trishup and Virata meters. The hymn begins by describing the Maruts as the sons of Rudra, known for their swift horse-like movement. Their origins are mysterious, known only to themselves, and they are often seen wandering and intermingling like a gleam. Scholars understand their significance, and Prishni holds them in space. Maruts are celebrated as destroyers of enemies and givers of wealth and progeny. They travel to deserts, adorned and vigorous, and the hymn calls upon the desert's stable mind and intelligence. The Maruts, adorned with strength and quick like a stota, are implored to take away old weapons and protect the devotees from cruelty. They are praised for their sacredness and truth, purifying others and adorned with beautiful ornaments. The hymn emphasizes the importance of the Maruts in increasing water, accepting offerings, and granting wealth and progeny. The Maruts are depicted as protectors in battle, ensuring victory and sustenance for the devotees. The hymn concludes with a call for the Maruts to continue showering blessings, protecting from enemies, and supporting the well-being of the descendants and the community.

Sukta 57, attributed to the Rishi Vashisht, is dedicated to the Maruts and follows the Triṣṭup meter. In this hymn, the psalmists extol the Maruts, who shake the heavens and the earth and traverse everywhere, bringing rain from the clouds. The Maruts are eager to fulfill the desires of their devotees. The hymn invites them to sit respectfully on the cushion prepared for the Yagya and partake in the Soma. The Maruts, unmatched in strength, are adorned with ornaments, weapons, and swords, illuminating the sky and earth with their brilliance. The worshippers, being human, seek protection from the Maruts' destructive weapons and hope to avoid their anger even in the face of transgressions. The Maruts' fragrance is welcomed, and they are invited to purify the Yagya place, becoming guardians and enhancers of nourishment. The hymn beseeches the Maruts to accept the offerings and provide water for progeny and wealth for the sacrificer. Finally, the Maruts, pleased with the praises, are asked to grant hundreds of sons to the worshippers and to continue their protective presence.

Sukta 58, attributed to the Rishi Vashisht who worshiped the Gana and praised the abode of the goddess, is dedicated to the Maruts and follows the Trishup meter. The hymn begins with a call to the praisers to worship the desert, emphasizing its brilliance and how it pervades the sky and earth with glory. The Maruts, born from Rudra, are described as impressive and powerful, affecting the entire world with their swift movements. They are acknowledged for providing sustenance to the sacrificers and are implored to prosper through praises and bestow desired wealth. The hymn highlights how the worshiper becomes affluent and capable of subduing enemies by the Maruts' grace. It requests the Maruts to accept the hymn, separate enemies, and continue their protective presence. The verse concludes with a call to remove any offenses through praise, ensuring the Maruts follow and protect the worshipers.

Sukta 59, attributed to the Rishi Vashisht, is dedicated to the deities Maruta and Rudra, and follows the meters Brihati, Pankti, Anuṣṭup, Trishup, and Gayatri. The hymn begins with an appeal to the gods, including Agni, Varuna, Mitra, Arthama, and the Maruts, to free the devotee from fear and guide them on the right path. The gods are invoked to bless the yajna performer, enabling them to vanquish enemies and expand their residence. The Maruts, desired for their protective strength, are invited to the Yagya to drink Soma and provide innovative blessings. The hymn emphasizes the consistency of the Maruts' wealth and their role in serving sacred offerings. The desert people, representing the Maruts, are invited to sit on the cushion prepared for them, to donate wealth, and to drink Soma. The Maruts are called to arrive adorned, to destroy those who threaten the devotee's wealth or bind them with Varuna's noose. The hymn praises the Maruts for their beautiful gifts and their role in increasing glory through yajna. It concludes with a worship to the fragrant and appeasing Trimbak, Rudra, asking for liberation from the noose of death and closeness to immortality.

Sukta 60 from Chapter Five, attributed to the Rishi Vashisht, is dedicated to the sun, Mitra, and Varuna, and follows the Trishup meter. The hymn begins with an invocation to the Sun, whose emergence during rituals frees the worshippers from sin. Aditi is also addressed, highlighting the worshippers' devotion to Mitra and Varuna. The poet asks to be liberated by Arthama and to please the deities through praise. Varuna is acknowledged as observing all actions, as the sun rises and nourishes life, discerning human sins and virtues. The hymn describes the sun's journey, drawn by seven horses, and its role in destroying and renewing life. The sun's ascent into space is facilitated by gods like Mitra, Aryama, and Varuna. Mitra and Varuna, along with Arthama, are seen as destroyers of sin, bringing blessings to the Yagya. They impart knowledge, guide the virtuous, and ensure the stability of the earth and heavens. The hymn concludes with prayers for Varuna to protect against enemies, Aryama to shield from demons, and Mitra and Varuna to grant the best places. The deities are praised for their excellent companionship and their power to defeat adversaries, granting beautiful boons to those who extol them.

Sukta 61, attributed to the Rishi Vashisht, is dedicated to the deities Mitra and Varuna, and follows the Trishup meter. The hymn begins with an invocation to Mitra and Varuna, who are described as possessing the sun as their eye, illuminating and overseeing all beings as they ascend into space. They are recognized for their deep understanding of human worship and praised by the yajnakarta (sacrificial performer) and Vashisht . The hymn acknowledges their role in ensuring the success of virtuous actions. Varuna is hailed as roaming the earth and sky, taking form for medicines and living beings, and protecting those who follow the righteous path. The hymn calls on Rishis to praise the glory of Mitra and Varuna, noting their power to separate the sky and earth. It contrasts the fate of the ayakashi (evil-doer), who should be sonless, with the blessed Yagya performer, who should be prosperous with sons. The hymn stresses the importance of sincere praise, free from ignorance, and concludes with a plea for Mitra and Varuna to be delighted by the new hymns, to guide the worshippers through adversities, and to always follow and protect them.

Sukta 62, attributed to Rishi Vashisht, invokes the deities Sun, Mitra, and Varuna and is composed in the Trishup Chanda. The Sukta extols the brilliance of the Sun, calling for its bright radiance to bless humanity. The hymn acknowledges the Sun as the radiant Creator, the supreme light. It prays for friends, wealth, and prosperity, asking for support and the fulfillment of desires through praise. The worshipers seek protection from Akash Kiyi and Aditi and offer praises to Varuna, pleading not to incur his wrath. Mitra and Varuna are implored to spread their arms, irrigate the lands, and bestow success. The Sukta concludes by seeking blessings from Varuna and Aryama to enrich their descendants and make all paths easy and prosperous, affirming their divine presence and guidance.

Sukta 63, attributed to the senior Rishi and dedicated to the deities Sun, Mitra, and Varuna, in the Trishup chanda, the hymn celebrates the rising sun in the form of Mitravaruna, who dispels darkness. The Sun is a creator and inspirer of humanity, rides on green-colored horses, providing strength to all. At midday, the Sun, listening to praises, remains undiminished in brilliance and grants desired boons. The hymn emphasizes the Sun's role in enabling life and action on earth, as the gods created its path through space. Worshipers pledge to perform Yagya at sunrise, honoring Varuna with salutations. The hymn concludes with a plea for Mitravaruna and Aryama to ensure simplicity in their paths and the well-being of their progeny, always guiding and following them.

Sukta 64, attributed to Rishi Vashisht and dedicated to the deities Mitra and Varuna, in the Trishup chanda, the hymn praises Mitra and Varuna as the lords of earthly and divine waters, whose inspiration brings forth rain through clouds. The hymn calls upon Aryama and Varuna to accept their oblations and protect the Yagya. Mitra and Varuna are recognized as the protectors of Yagya and the lords of rivers, inspiring vision in space. The hymn beseeches Earthma to guide them on the best path and acknowledges the happiness shared with the deities. Varuna is asked to consider those who prepare a mental chariot for him and to satisfy them with the best abode.

The hymn concludes with a request for Mitra and Varuna to partake in their Soma offering, to listen to their praises, and to always follow and support their endeavors.

Sukta 65, attributed to Rishi Vashisht and dedicated to the deities Mitra and Varuna, in the Trishup chanda, the hymn begins with an invocation to Varuna, noting his influence at sunrise and his victories in cosmic battles. The hymn praises the strength of Mitra and Varuna, asking them to enhance the vitality of their devotees. It speaks of their mighty loop, binding those who neglect Yagya and being fearsome to enemies. The worshipers commit to serving these deities, expecting their glory to fill the sky and earth. The hymn likens the safe pasRishi of their vehicles to a boat crossing a net, calling upon Mitra and Varuna to aid and nourish them by filling pastures with water. The hymn concludes with a plea for Mitra and Varuna, along with Vayu, to partake in their Yajna, listen to their praises, and continually support them.

Sukta 66, attributed to Rishi Vashisht and dedicated to the deities Mitra and Varuna, as well as the Sun, in the Gayatri Brihti and Umgik chanda, the hymn praises the recurring appearance and deserving honor of Mitravaruna. These deities are celebrated as protectors of the home and body, strengthening the psalmist's work. The hymn requests the sun deities—Mitra, Bhaga, Arthama, and Savita—to bestow wealth and to destroy sins, protecting their household. Mitra and Varuna are acknowledged as protectors of righteous actions and givers of the best bell. The hymn also calls upon Nishyarun and Ritwigi, praising their brilliance akin to the Sun and their role in spreading fame and granting spaces. The hymn further notes the creation of time, sacrifice, and mantras by these deities, and prays for wealth and welfare from them during sunrise. The hymn envisions the charioteer Surya with his seven horses as a provider for the world's welfare, emphasizing the illuminating solar system and the brilliance of Mitra and Varuna. The deities are asked to accept Soma offerings and to lead in fame and prosperity.

Sukta 67, attributed to Rishi Vashisht and dedicated to the deities Ashwini in the Trishup chanda, the hymn begins with a plea to the Ashvins, expressing devotion and commitment to their chariot, much like a son awakening his father. The hymn welcomes the divine chariot, noting how fire illuminates the darkness and makes all areas visible. It continues with a request for the Ashvins to become their servants through service, praising them for bringing wealth and partaking in the soma offering. The hymn asks the Ashvins to protect their intellect and bodies, even in battle, and to bestow protection and wealth on their devotees. It emphasizes the importance of worship, asking the Ashvins to accept their offerings and increase their prosperity, always listening to their appeals and providing continuous support.

Sukta 68, attributed to the Vashisht and dedicated to the deities Ashwini in the Virat and Kristup chanda, the hymn begins by addressing the Ashvins, asking them to defeat their enemies and listen to their praises, consuming their oblations. The hymn invites the Ashvins to partake in their offerings and to respond to their call, not that of their enemies. It describes the Ashvins mounting the chariot of the Sun and arriving at the Yagya in response to their prayers. The hymn acknowledges the Ashvins' divine acts, such as rejuvenating the old Rishi Chyavan and rescuing Bhujya from the ocean. It recounts their generosity in granting wealth to the debilitated Rishi Vrik and responding to the call of Shayu Rishi, likening their generosity to a river filling fields with water. The hymn concludes with a plea for the Ashvins to bless the devoted worshipers, strengthening their livestock and always supporting them.

Sukta 69, attributed to Rishi Vashisht and dedicated to the deities Ashvins in the Trishup chanda, the hymn invokes the Ashvins to arrive on their horse-drawn golden chariot, which spans the sky and earth and is adorned with watery chakras. This resplendent chariot, bearing grains and being the lord of hosts, reveals all living beings and is accompanied by friends and hymns. The Ashvins are invited to the Dev-Kamya Yagya, traveling everywhere through their chariot. Their chariot, accompanied by horses and food, travels with the sun and covers all places. The daughter of Surya surrounds their chariot, and when they protect the host, glorious food moves towards them. The Ashvins are requested to come in their horse-drawn chariot in the morning for the Yagya's welfare, to partake in the soma offering, and to listen to the worshipers' prayers. The hymn recounts their past deeds, such as freeing a submerged arm with swift horses, and asks them to listen to the hymn, visit their house, bestow wealth and gems, and continually support and enhance the praises of their devotees.

Sukta 70, attributed to Rishi Vashisht and dedicated to the Ashvins, in the Shishtup chanda, the hymn calls upon the Ashvins to come and bring fame to their devotees. The Ashvins are welcomed to their earthly refuge, with any horse they desire made available to them. The hymn praises the Ashvins, recognizing their role in fulfilling religious penance in human

Yagya, bringing thrones and sea-like abundance in rainwater. The Ashvins are likened to horses harnessed to a chariot, essential to the Yagya. The hymn asks the Ashvins to grant the same heavenly place among forms, medicines, and creatures as given by swan. It acknowledges their control over medicine and traps given by Rishis, wishing for medicine and water for the devotees. The Ashvins are honored for bestowing gems and treasures upon former hosts. The hymn recounts their numerous Rishily deeds, inviting them to Gajaman's Yagya and seeking their support. The Ashvins are asked to listen to the hymn, adorned with praise, to achieve success through karma, and to follow and support their devotees always.

Sukta 71, attributed to Rishi Vashisht and dedicated to the deities Ashvins, in the Trishup chanda, the hymn begins with the imagery of night giving way to dawn as the sun rises, invoking the Ashvins to bring their blessings. The Ashvins are called upon for their protection, keeping animals at bay day and night, and bringing the best offerings to the sacrificer. They are asked to remove disease and poverty and to protect their devotees continuously. The hymn describes their chariot, drawn by horses and laden with wealth, arriving with three seats and moving towards the day. The Ashvins are praised for their past deeds, such as rejuvenating the Rishi Chyavan, sending a swift horse to King Pedu in battle, rescuing Atri from darkness, and restoring Jahush to his kingdom. The hymn concludes by offering praise to the Ashvins, asking them to be pleased with the praise, achieved through righteous deeds, and to always follow and support their devotees.

Sukta 72, attributed to Rishi Vashisht and dedicated to the Ashvins, in the Trishup chanda, the hymn calls upon the Ashvins to arrive on a chariot full of cows and wealth, adorned with supreme glory. The hymn acknowledges the Ashvins' equal love and stability, noting their fraternity with the worshipers' ancestors and shared wealth. These praises are meant to awaken the Aswini kumaras, making Usha conscious of all actions. Vashisht praises the Ashvins while serving the sky and the earth. The hymn highlights that devotees will praise the Ashvins when dawn removes darkness, as Savita relies on Tej, and Agni receives good worship. The Ashvins are invited to come from all directions, bringing wealth beneficial to the five Vanas, and to always support and follow their devotees.

Sukta 73, attributed to Rishi Vashisht and dedicated to the Ashvins, in the Trishup chanda, the hymn speaks of dispelling ignorance by praising the gods with desire. The psalmist calls upon the Ashvins, the horsemen, who are beloved by worshipers performing their duties. They are invited to partake in the sweet Soma offered by their devotee. Vashisht invokes the Ashvins with offerings, increasing the hymn of destiny to please them. The Ashvins, strong and powerful, are praised as destroyers of demons and are called to come before the worshipers' sons and daughters. They are invited to accept joyful food and bring welfare, ensuring they do not bring harm. The hymn concludes by calling the Ashvins from any direction, asking them to bring wealth beneficial to the five Vanas and to always follow and support their devotees.

Sukta 74, attributed to Rishi Vashisht and dedicated to the Ashvins, in the Brihati chanda, the hymn begins by addressing the Ashvins, invoked by those desiring heaven and protection. Vashisht calls upon the Ashvins, acknowledging their reach to everyone. The hymn requests the Ashvins to bestow their wealth upon their devotees and to bring their chariot to partake in the Soma with an equal mind. The Ashvins are invited to join the worshipers in the Soma ritual without causing violence. Their arrival on horses to the sacrificial host is anticipated, bringing divine food, stability, fame, and wealth. The hymn concludes by noting that those who come to the Ashvins without taking others' wealth and being protectors among the people will increase in strength and attain the best abode.

Sukta 75, attributed to Rishi Vashisht and dedicated to the deity Ushas, in the Trishup chanda, the hymn praises the dawn that appears in the sky, creating light and manifesting her glory. Ushas destroys the enemy and darkness, revealing the path of action for all beings. The hymn requests Ushas to be mindful of their welfare, granting them good fortune and holding wealth for them. Ushas bestows sons and food upon humans. Her rays reveal the deeds of the gods, filling the space and spreading everywhere. As the daughter of heaven, Ushas approaches the five years, bringing amazing divine wealth and being praised and worshiped by Rishis at dawn. The radiant dawn arrives in a chariot with many forms, bestowing precious wealth on her devotees. Ushas comes with deities worthy of the Ushas Yagya, breaking the darkness and providing light for the cows to graze. The cows wish for the same dawn. Ushas is asked to provide wealth rich in cattle and abundant food, always following and supporting the Yagya without criticism.

Sukta 76, attributed to Rishi Vashisht and dedicated to the deity Usha, in the Trishup chanda, the hymn praises Savita Devta for bringing light and welfare to all, rising for the work of the gods. Ushas, the dawn, illuminates the worlds. The hymn speaks of witnessing the divine path full of great splendor as the brightness of dawn appears in the east, moving from the advanced world. Ushas's glory is seen before sunrise, radiating like a great woman. Angiras, through mantras, manifested Ushas, aligning with the gods. This alignment brought compatibility and shared purpose for the cows, moving with their abode Tej. Rishi Vasistha praises Ushas as the protector of cows and food, revealing the morning and being the first to be praised. Ushas leads the hymns, removes darkness, and is consistently praised by the Vasishthas, always following and supporting them.

Sukta 77, attributed to Rishi Vashisht and dedicated to the deity Ushas, in the Trishup chanda, the hymn praises Ushas for gaining brightness near the Sun and inspiring all living beings. Ushas, akin to the fire god, destroys darkness and creates light, making her worthy of human praise. The graceful dawn, appearing with bright clothes, is celebrated as the mother of days, eyes, and all living beings. Ushas brightens the horse with her radiant rays. She drives away enemies and brings amazing wealth, ensuring a transit land free from fear and inspiring praise. Ushas is asked to increase life with her best rays, and to bestow energy from cows and horses. The Vasisthas praise Ushas for providing the best wealth and continually supporting and following them.

Sukta 78, attributed to Rishi Vashisht and dedicated to the deity Ushas, in the Trishup chanda, the hymn describes the dawn, Ushas, appearing first in the form of Ketur with rays facing upwards and spreading everywhere. Ushas arrives in a resplendent chariot, dispelling all sins and darkness. These dawns, seen in the east, are the cause of the morning, manifesting the Sun, Fire, and Yagya, and dispelling darkness. Ushas, the daughter of heaven, is full of wealth and gives the dawn, riding a chariot full of food and drawn by horses. The hymn concludes by awakening Ushas along with the best men, recognizing her as the one who makes the morning and fills the evening with sweetness, and asking her to always follow and support them.

Sukta 79, attributed to Rishi Vashisht and dedicated to the deity Ushas, in the Trishup chanda, the hymn celebrates Ushas for destroying darkness and benefiting humans by awakening them. Dependent on the Sun, Ushas' bright lights work together to dispel darkness, with rays that spread light similar to the Sun's brightness. Ushas, born of fire and the daughter of heaven, brings wealth and produces food beneficial for all. The hymn requests Ushas to grant the same wealth as given to the ancient stotas, acknowledging her role in revealing the mountain door during the kidnapping of cows. Ushas is called upon to inspire truthful words and wisdom to destroy darkness, continually blessing the devotees. The hymn also mentions her encouragement to please the gods and goddesses, and to speak the truth.

Sukta 80, attributed to Rishi Vashisht and dedicated to the deity Ushas, in the Trishup chanda, the hymn begins by celebrating the Vashisht s, who were the first to awaken the dawn with their praises. Ushas, the dawn, covers the sky and earth with her brilliance, providing light to all living beings. She destroys darkness and comes before the Sun, manifesting Surya, Agni, and Yagya. Blessed with cows and horses, these dawns dispel darkness and thrive due to water exploitation. Ushas is invoked to bless the devotees with prosperity and gPankti th.

Sukta 81, attributed to Rishi Vashisht and dedicated to the deity Ushas, in the Brihati chanda, the hymn praises Ushas, the daughter of the sky, for destroying darkness and granting the power of vision and increased brightness to all. Ushas' rays extend to the sun, illuminating planets, stars, and more. The hymn asks for blessings of food and sunlight. Ushas is invoked to bring desired wealth and precious gems to the devotees. As the glorious destroyer of darkness, Ushas animates the world, giving it vision. The worshipers plead with Ushas to be as dear to her as a son is to his mother. Ushas is requested to bring her renowned wealth, to provide the devotees with imperishable Yajna, food, and household prosperity, and to drive away their enemies.

Sukta 82, attributed to Rishi Vashisht and dedicated to the deities Indra and Varuna, in the Jagati chanda, the hymn calls upon Indra and Varuna to bestow the best house upon the worshiper and to defeat violent enemies in battle. Indra and Varuna are praised for their immense wealth, with Indra being self-respected and Varuna being a king, both made brilliant by the gods. They are invoked for their strength, which opens the doors of water and sends the sun into the sky, filling dry rivers with water after enjoying Soma. The hymn calls out to Indra and Varuna amid enemy armies, recognizing them as owners of divine and earthly wealth. Indra and Varuna, creators of all living beings, are adorned with bright ornaments and serve Varuna. The hymn invokes them for the attainment of wealth, noting their special strength in subduing enemies and violent ones. It assures that obstacles, sins, misdeeds, and sorPankti s do not reach those whose Yagya is attended by Indra and Varuna. The hymn concludes by requesting Indra and Varuna to be ready for protection, to listen to praises, and to bring happiness through their friendship. They are called upon to stay ahead in all wars and are praised by ancient and new hymns for blessings of wealth, home, and children. Indra, Mitra, Varuna, and Aryama are invoked for wealth and home, with a prayer that Aditi's glory should not harm them, and praises are offered to Savita Dev.

Sukta 83, attributed to Rishi Vashisht and dedicated to the deities Indra and Varuna, in the Jagati chanda, the hymn begins by praising Indra and Varuna for their friendship, which enabled the host seeking cows to move eastward, and for their protection of Sudas by defeating Vritra and other enemies. In times of war, the hymn calls upon Indra and Varuna to take their side and grant them the vision of victory. As enemy soldiers approach, their noise reaching the sky, Indra and Varuna are asked to arrive with protective equipment. The hymn recalls how they saved Sudas and listened to the hymns of the Tritsus, leading to a successful priesthood through their presence in battle. Surrounded by enemy weapons and hindered in every way, the worshipers plead for Indra and Varuna, owners of all wealth, to protect them. The hymn recounts how Indra and Varuna protected Sudas from the slave kings with the help of the Tritsu, and how even ten kings averse to Yagya could not conquer Sudas, whose leaders' praise grew stronger. Indra, the destroyer of trees, and Varuna, the maintainer of deeds, are invoked for welfare, wealth, and home, along with Mitra and Aryama, while saluting Savita Devi and praying that Aditi's glory does not harm them.

Sukta 84, attributed to Rishi Vashisht and dedicated to the demigods Indra and Varuna, in the Trishup chanda, the hymn invites Indra and Varuna to the Yagya, with the Juhu moving towards them. The hymn praises the rainwater from heaven provided by Indra and Varuna, which brings happiness to all and binds the birds. The devotees pray for Indra to elevate their status and for Varuna's anger to protect them. They seek blessings for a beautiful home sacrifice, excellence in their praises, and divine wealth, asking to be safeguarded from desires. The hymn requests a house of choice and rich wealth, acknowledging Aditya named Apatya for providing abundant wealth to heroes. The hymn concludes with a prayer that their praises serve Indra and Varuna, that their hymns become teachers for their sons, and that they attain the best treasures, with Indra and Varuna always following and protecting them.

Sukta 85, attributed to Rishi Vashisht and dedicated to the deities Indra and Varuna, in the Trishup chanda, the hymn begins with an offering of

Somras to Indra and Varuna. The hymn likens the refinement of praise to the brightness of dawn, and asks the deities to protect the swan in war and travel. It addresses the rivalry with enemies in battle, requesting Indra and Varuna to destroy even the retreating foes when weapons clash. All the Somras are said to brighten and adorn Indra and Varuna, with Indra killing enemies and Varuna holding the subjects. The hymn speaks to the Bali Adityas, emphasizing the importance of knowing the best deeds and sacrifices, and hopes that the blessed host who calls upon the deities with a desire to satisfy them attains the fruits of their labor, even in times of scarcity. It concludes with a prayer for the hymns to pervade Indra and Varuna, protecting the sons and grandchildren, and blessing them with the best home and Yagya, always following and supporting them.

Sukta 86, attributed to Rishi Vashisht and dedicated to the deity Varuna, in the Trishup chanda, the hymn celebrates Varuna, who was born full of glory and established the vast earth by inspiring the sky and the stars. The hymn expresses a deep yearning to be with Varuna, asking when he will accept the oblation and be seen. It reflects on seeking solutions to sins, with scholars suggesting that Varuna's anger is the cause. The hymn questions Varuna about the crime that has led him to wish harm upon the devotee's friend, seeking guidance to rectify the situation through good deeds and salutations. It pleads for the removal of ancestral betrayals and personal sins, comparing the process to freeing a calf from a rope. The hymn acknowledges that sin can arise from various causes such as anger, confusion, gambling, ignorance, or divine will, and sometimes even elders lead the young astray, or sins manifest in dreams. The worshiper vows to serve Varuna purely, asking for knowledge and inspiration for wealth for the devotee. The hymn concludes with a prayer for profit and welfare, asking Varuna to always follow and support them.

Sukta 87, attributed to Rishi Vashisht and dedicated to the deity Varuna, in the Trishup chanda, the hymn extols Varuna for creating the path for the sun in space and for watering the rivers. Varuna, who wishes to travel quickly, separates night from day. The hymn acknowledges Varuna as the soul of the world, sending air and water everywhere, much like how animals carry food after grazing. It expresses love for the vast earth and praises Varuna's followers who are worthy of witnessing the best forms of heaven and earth. The hymn also highlights the brilliance of the Ritvij and the wisdom imparted by Varuna to capable students. Varuna is described as having three heavens, three types of lands, and six directions, creating the ocean like the sun and being powerful, sorPankti -relieving, and the master of all creations. He is also merciful towards crimes, and the hymn concludes with a plea for Varuna's mercy, expressing hope for freedom from sins and continuous guidance and protection.

Sukta 88, attributed to Rishi Vashisht and dedicated to the deity Varuna, in the Trishup chanda, the hymn begins by acknowledging Varuna as the lord of creatures, worthy of Yagya and the master of Dharma, who brings the Sun before everyone. Rishi Vashisht praises Varuna, who is also honored with the flames of Agni. Varuna, engaged in the work of pleasure, drinks Somras, enhancing Vashisht 's body for the sake of darshan. The hymn recounts a joyful experience shared with Varuna on a boat, sailing smoothly in the sea like a swing. Scholars extend the day and night in Varuna's presence, and through protective deeds, Varuna made Vashisht renowned for his great actions. Reflecting on their ancient friendship, the hymn emphasizes their enduring, violence-free bond. Vashisht seeks entry into Varuna's house with a simple door, recognizing Varuna as the master of tears. As eternal friends and worshippers of Varuna, they plead for freedom from bondage and the enjoyment of Varuna's protection, asking Varuna to always follow and support them.

Sukta 89, attributed to Rishi Vashisht and dedicated to the deity Varuna, in the Gayatri and Jagti chanda, the hymn is a heartfelt plea for Varuna's mercy and happiness. Rishi Vashisht asks Varuna to protect him from misfortune, expressing his fear and trembling like a cloud pushed by the wind. He seeks Varuna's compassion due to his inability to perform rituals because of poverty and incapacity. Vashisht describes his paradoxical thirst even while living in the sea, asking Varuna to provide abundant happiness. The hymn implores Varuna not to use violence against humans or gods for any crimes or mistakes committed out of ignorance, seeking forgiveness and protection from Varuna's wrath.

Sukta 90, attributed to Rishi Vashisht and dedicated to the deities Vayu and Indra-Vayu, in the Trishup chanda, the hymn begins by addressing Veerakarma Vayu, inviting him to bring his horses and drink the sweet-tasting Soma presented by the Adhvaryu priests. Vayu is asked to elevate those who consider him a god and offer him sacrifices, making them prominent among humans and bestowing them with superior wealth. The hymn praises Vayu, manifested by the sky and earth for wealth, and served by horses, acknowledging the sinless dawns that dispel darkness and bring special radiance. It recalls how Angiras found wealth in the form of cows and how ancient waters followed him. Indra and Vayu are honored as gods whose chariot is carried by hosts in their Yagya, served by all food items. The hymn seeks blessings from Indra and Vayu for supporters who provide cows, horses, money, and gold, ensuring their victory. Vashisht, carrying the oblation like a horse, invokes Indra and Vayu with excellent praise, asking them to always follow and support their devotees.

Sukta 91, attributed to Rishi Vashisht and dedicated to the deities Vayu and Indra-Vayu, in the Trishup chanda, the hymn speaks of the singers who prospered by chanting hymns to the wind, offering sacrifices to save those in distress, while the sun and Ushas were stopped together. Indra and Vayu are invoked as protectors, requested to avoid violence and be pleased by the best praises that seek the best wealth. The hymn praises the bright-complexioned men sheltered by Vayu, who perform Yagya with single-minded devotion to gain the best child. Indra and Vayu are asked to sit on the cushions and drink Soma as long as they have strength, vigor, and knowledge. Their praise is filled with desires, urging them to prepare their horses, drink the Soma, and free the devotees from sin. Hundreds of horses serve Indra and Vayu, and the food-seeking Vashisht s, with their horses, invoke the deities with excellent hymns, asking them to always follow and support them.

Sukta 92, attributed to Rishi Vashisht and dedicated to the deities Vayu and Indra-Vayu, in the Trishup chanda, the hymn begins by noting that the Soma, which is the first drink for the deities, is present in the vessel for them. The Adhvaryu, performing the best deeds, has presented this Soma for Indra and Vayu, offering the foremost part in the Yajna. Vayu is invited to come with his horses, reaching the house of the sacrificial host to provide wealth containing the best food. The worshipers who praise Indra and Vayu are seen as destroyers of enemies, and with their help, the devotees aim to defeat their foes. Vayu is requested to arrive at the Yajna with hundreds of thousands of horses and to be pleased by drinking the Soma, always following and supporting the devotees.

Sukta 93, attributed to Rishi Vashisht and dedicated to the deity Indragni, in the Trishup chanda, the hymn begins by calling upon Indragni to listen to the innovative hymn, recognizing them as worthy of being invoked with joy. The hymn emphasizes repeatedly invoking Indragni, who provides food to the desired host. Indragni is praised as sacrificial, the destroyer of enemies, and the lord of abundant wealth and food. The sacrificers who engage in sacrificial fire receive the bow of Indragni and invoke them again and again. The hymn praises Indragni for consumable wealth, noting their role as the destroyer of old men and the best, increasing wealth worthy of charity. Indragni is called upon to destroy enemy forces in the battlefield and to annihilate god-hating non-sacrificers. The hymn invites Indragni to visit the Somabhishav Karma, emphasizing their exclusive protection. Through the samidha, the hymn asks Indra and Mitra for protection and the removal of committed crimes, also invoking Aryama and Aditi for absolution. Finally, the hymn seeks food through the Yajna and requests that Indra, Vishnu, and Marudgan show no mercy to their opponents, asking Indragni to always follow and support them.

Sukta 94, attributed to Rishi Vashisht and dedicated to the deities Indra and Agni, in the Gayatri and Trishup chanda, the hymn begins with the stota giving birth to praise, akin to rain being born from the moon. Indra and Agni are invoked to listen to Ashwan and to complete the ritual. The hymn beseeches Indragni to protect from defeat, condemnation, and inferiority. Seeking protection and praising Indra and Agni, the wise and other stotas in distress also praise Indragni for food. Those desiring food and wealth are urged to invoke Indragni in praise. Indragni is asked to reveal themselves to humans and bring food, ensuring they are not ruled by harsh-speaking men nor tortured by enemies. The hymn requests various types of consumable wealth from Indragni and emphasizes invoking Indragni repeatedly after Somgabhishav rituals. Serving Vritrahanta, the hymn praises Indra and Agni, asking them to break the evil kidnapper like a pitcher with their weapon.

Sukta 95, attributed to Rishi Vashisht and dedicated to the deities Saraswati and Sarasvan, in the Trishup chanda, the hymn begins by describing Saraswati as majestic and powerful, like a city made of iron, bowing with water. Saraswati moves like an enlightening charioteer, her glory flowing with all the rivers. The hymn recalls how Saraswati, the best of rivers, flowing from the mountains to the sea, heard King Nahusha's plea and provided him with ghee-milk. Sarasvan, capable of causing rain, proliferates among sacrificial offerings, benefiting humans by providing strong sons and purifying their bodies. Saraswati, possessing beautiful wealth, is praised, and even revered gods bow before her. She is kind to her worshippers, who offer oblations and praises in hopes of receiving her wealth and labor. Saraswati, the bestower of the best wealth, is celebrated by Vasistha for providing food to the devotees and always following and supporting them.

Sukta 96, attributed to Rishi Vashisht and dedicated to the deities Saraswati and Sarasvan, in the Brihati, Pankti, and Gayatri chanda, the hymn begins by urging Vasistha to praise Saraswati, who has great speed among the rivers, and to worship her exclusively. The hymn acknowledges Saraswati's bright and divine presence, attributing the receipt of divine and earthly food to her grace. Saraswati is invoked to protect and provide wealth to the hosts offering sacrifices. The hymn seeks Saraswati's blessings and wisdom, asking her to accept Vashisht's praise, likened to that of Jamadagni. Desiring a pious wife and son, the worshipers praise the Saraswan gods, seeking blessings of rain and the water base of Lord Saraswan. The hymn concludes with a prayer for gPankti th and food from Saraswati, the deity worthy of everyone's reverence.

Sukta 97, attributed to Rishi Vashisht and dedicated to the deities Indra, Brihaspati, Indra, and Brahmanaspati, in the Trishup chanda, the hymn begins by describing the intelligent worshipers who perform sacrifices and rejoice in the gods, particularly during Somabhishav for Indra in the monsoons. Indra is invoked to come first with his horses. The worshipers seek protection from the gods, asking Jupiter (Brihaspati) to accept their sacrifice and bestow wealth, much like a father from afar. They pray not to be guilty in any way towards the gods. Salutations and oblations are offered to Brahmanaspati, with the hope that only superior stotras serve Indra. The hymn requests Brahmanaspati to sit on their altar, fulfill their wishes for food and water, and help overcome obstacles. Immortal God is invoked to provide food, and Jupiter, worthy of Yagya, is called upon. The hymn asks Brihaspati to bring a brilliant horse like Aditya, acknowledging Jupiter's superior strength and many vehicles decorated with pure instruments that provide abundant food. The mother goddess and Jupiter are asked to increase the earth's glory, with Mitravarun's help, and liquefy the waters for food. Brahmanaspati and Indra are praised for protecting the Yagya, destroying enemy armies, and bestowing earthly and divine wealth upon the devotees, always following and supporting them.

Sukta 98, attributed to Rishi Vashisht and dedicated to the deities Indra and Indra-Brihaspati, in the Trishup chanda, the hymn begins by urging the offerers to present Somahuti for Indra, who always seeks the host blessing Soma. Indra is invoked to drink the Soma, just as he did in ancient times. The hymn recalls how Indra drank Soma at birth, as foretold by Aditi, filling the vast space with his radiance and helping the gods gain wealth through war. Indra is asked to lead the worshipers in battle against arrogant enemies, ensuring victory with the help of Marudgan. The hymn recounts both ancient and new deeds of Indra, who destroyed demonic Maya, emphasizing that Soma is solely for Indra. It acknowledges Indra's dominion over the world seen by the light of the sun, his lordship over all cows, and the consumption of his donations. Finally, Jupiter (Brihaspati) and Indra are praised as lords of divine and earthly wealth, bestowing money upon the stota and always following and supporting the devotees.

Sukta 99, attributed to Rishi Vashisht and dedicated to the deities Vishnu, and Indra-Vishnu, in the Trishup chanda, the hymn begins by acknowledging the incomprehensible glory of Vishnu, known only to him. The hymn recognizes Vishnu's embrace of the vast heaven and his unparalleled glory among all beings. It praises the earth, made prosperous with food and cows by Vishnu's grace, and acknowledges Vishnu's role in holding the sky and earth in various ways. Indra and Vishnu are lauded for creating heaven by manifesting the sun, fire, and dawn, and for destroying the illusion of bandits in battle. The hymn celebrates Indra and Vishnu's victory over Shambar's ninety-nine forts and Varchi's hundred thousand warriors. The praise offered in the battlefield aims to increase the strength of Indra and Vishnu, asking them to enhance the devotees' food supply. Concluding, the hymn requests Vishnu to accept the Yagya offering, to be elevated by the praise, and to always follow and support the devotees.

Sukta 100, attributed to Rishi Vashisht and dedicated to the deity Vishnu, in the Trishup chanda, the hymn begins with a plea to Lord Vishnu, asking for protection from the rain while on a ship, acknowledging Vishnu's transformative presence in the sacrificial fire. The hymn praises Vishnu, asking for his continued blessings and protection. The worshiper, offering oblations and mantras, seeks Vishnu's mercy to attain deserved wealth. The hymn celebrates Vishnu's act of placing his feet on the earth three times, creating vast space and showcasing his brilliance. It expresses the desire to chant Vishnu's famous names and praises him, asking Vishnu not to hide his form. The hymn concludes with Vashisht offering oblations to Vishnu, asking for their praise to enrich the deity and for Vishnu to always follow and support them.

Sukta 101, attributed to Rishi Vashisht by the young Agnaya, and dedicated to the deity Parjanya, in the Trishup chanda, the hymn begins by invoking the sacred phrases, Yajurveda, and Samaveda, which exploit water and contain the omkara at the forefront. It describes the electric forms cohabiting and producing a sound like a rain bull, generating fire.

The hymn prays for rains that enhance medicines and waters, making the land prosperous and granting splendor across the three seasons. Parjanya is likened to a barren cow and is also the cause of rain, taking forms as desired. Mother Earth receives juice from the heavenly father, thereby nurturing all living beings. The hymn recognizes Parjanya as the source of all living beings and worlds, and as the provider of water in three ways, raining on all sides. Parjanya is praised and asked to accept the worship, ensuring auspicious rains and fruitful medicines. The hymn concludes with a plea for Parjanya's water to protect for a hundred years, always following and supporting them.

Sukta 102, attributed to Rishi Vashisht by the young Agneya and dedicated to the deity Parjanya, in the Gayatri chanda, the hymn calls upon the praisers to sing the praises of the rain. This rain brings forth medicines, cows, horses, and other necessities. The hymn urges offering sacrifices in the fire to invoke this rain, praying that it provides abundant food and sustenance.

Sukta 103, attributed to Rishi Vashisht and dedicated to the deity Frogs (symbolizing rain), in the Trishup and Anushup chanda, the hymn compares frogs to fasting stotas who stay awake for a year, praising Parjanya. When divine water reaches the hidden rams in the lake, the frogs croak 'Medhak' like calves calling to their mother cows. During the rainy season, as forest dwellers provide water to thirsty frogs, they gather and move closer. Frogs of two species leap joyfully and favor each other when it rains. Like disciples imitating their teacher, frogs mimic each other's sounds. They jump on the water, chanting beautiful words, strengthening all parts of their bodies. The frogs, resembling cows and goats in sound, appear in various colors like smoke and green, and emerge from different waters. They surround filled lakes, reciting words like stotas in the Som Yagya called Atiratra. Frogs are guardians of divine laws, harmonizing with the seasons. At the year's end, freed by the rain, they bring wealth, extend lifespans, and bless with cows and plants during the rainy season.

Sukta 104, attributed to Rishi Vashisht and dedicated to the deities Indra, Soma, Agni, the Maruts, and others in earth and space, in the Jagati, Trishup, and Anustup chandas, the hymn fervently calls upon Indra and Soma to destroy the demons that thrive in darkness. These demons, gPankti ing in malevolence and hidden in the shadows, are to be eradicated by the combined might of Indra and Soma. The hymn begins by imploring these powerful deities to come forth and eliminate the demonic forces, ensuring that they are driven away or utterly destroyed.

Indra and Soma are urged to subjugate these demons, making them as invisible as charu thPankti n into the fire. The hymn emphasizes the need for constant enmity towards the maharathis, those demons with bitter speech and evil eyes who are enemies of the Brahmins. The call to action is clear: Indra and Soma must defeat these foes and maintain the safety of the righteous.

The hymn vividly describes the role of Indra and Soma in warfare, urging them to kill the demon that committed vile acts and to ensure that not a single monster is left. The hymn calls for their angry force to subdue all enemies, leaving no room for escape. Furthermore, the deities are asked to reveal violent weapons from both space and earth, using the power of the clouds to create thunderbolts that destroy demons. The invocation includes a plea for Agni to tear the sides of the demons with stones and weapons, causing them to flee in fear.

The hymn also reflects on the broader cosmic battle, asking Indra and Soma to bind the demons as tightly as ropes bind a horse. The worshipers seek protection from violent demons, hoping that sinners never find happiness or the opportunity to harm them. The hymn appeals to Indra to ensure that evil-speaking demons disappear as swiftly as water from a clenched fist. Those who slander or falsely accuse the devotees are to be cast away, punished for their misdeeds.

Agni is invoked to punish those who destroy food or harm livestock and children, ensuring that such evil-doers become rootless and violent, along with their progeny. The hymn calls for these demons to be cast down below the three worlds, with their fame and influence dried up.

The hymn acknowledges that false and true words often compete, and it is Soma who follows the truth and destroys falsehood. Soma is praised for tormenting sinful liars and ensuring that those who act deceitfully fall into their own traps. The worshipers declare their allegiance to the true gods, seeking protection from Agni's wrath against the liars.

The hymn further implores Indra to kill those wicked individuals who falsely label the devotees as demons, condemning them to the worst fate among all beings. Night-walking demons, hiding like owls, are to be cast into deep pits. Even the desert is invoked to catch Yagya-violent demons, ensuring their destruction. Indra is asked to fire his thunderbolt from space, protecting the devotees from all directions.

As the hymn progresses, it describes how Indra's violence against the violent is as decisive as an ax cutting wood or a mace breaking mountains. Indra is envisioned as coming to protect his worshipers by crushing the demons. The hymn details various forms taken by demons—owls, chickens, chakravak, and gridhra—and calls for their destruction by Indra's stone-made thunderbolt.

The worshipers express their desire to be protected from the surrounding demons, asking that the demons who question "What is that?" be driven away. They seek protection from both earthly and divine sins, hoping that Indra's might will sever the heads of violent demons, preventing them from seeing the rising sun.

The hymn concludes with a powerful invocation to Soma and Indra, praising their ability to care for everyone. The worshipers ask for Indra's vajra-like weapon to be fired at the demons, ensuring their complete destruction and securing the prosperity and safety of the devotees. This final plea underscores the belief in the deities' power to protect, providing a shield against all forms of evil and malevolence.

The Seventh Mandala of Rig-Veda concludes with this Sukta, emphasizing the unity of divine power and the importance of praise and worship in seeking divine blessings and protection.

NINE

THE ETERNAL ECHOES (THE LEGACY OF THE RIG-VEDIC WATERS)

As we arrive at the conclusion of this journey through the ancient hymns of the Rigveda, it is only fitting that we pause to reflect on the enduring legacy of these sacred verses. The Rigveda, hailed as the earliest scripture known to humanity, is more than just a religious text. It is a repository of profound spiritual, ecological, and philosophical wisdom, offering insights that remain relevant even in our contemporary world.

The hymns of the Rigveda, composed thousands of years ago by enlightened Rishis, transcend their historical context. They speak to the eternal truths that govern life, the cosmos, and the interplay between the human and the divine. The prayers, invocations, and rituals described in the Rigveda are not just acts of devotion but expressions of a deep understanding of the natural world and its sacredness. They reflect a worldview in which the divine is imminent in every aspect of creation, where the rivers, mountains, and forests are seen as embodiments of the divine, deserving of reverence and care.

The Rigvedic hymns, particularly those found in the family books of Mandalas 2, 3, 4, 6, and 7, are a testament to the Rishis' profound connection with the cosmos. These hymns reveal a sophisticated understanding of the universe, one that is both spiritual and scientific. The Rishis recognized that the forces of nature—the sun, the wind, the rain, and the rivers—were manifestations of divine power, essential for sustaining life on Earth.

In the first chapter of this book, we explored the eternal wisdom of Rigvedic prayers, comparing the old and new Mandala. The older Mandala, believed to be the original core of the Rigveda, are often more direct in their approach, focusing on the essentials of life—water, food, shelter, and protection. The newer Mandala, while still rooted in these basics, exhibit a more developed philosophical outlook, reflecting the evolution of Vedic thought over time.

Despite these differences, both the old and new Mandala share a common purpose: to establish harmony between the human and the divine, the individual and the cosmos. The Rig-Vedic prayers are not mere supplications for material benefits; they are a means of aligning oneself with the cosmic order, of ensuring that one's actions contribute to the balance and stability of the universe.

In the second chapter, we delved into the world of the Rig-Vedic gods, the deities who were invoked in the yajnas performed by the Rishis. These gods—Indra, Agni, Varuna, and others—are not distant, anthropomorphic beings but representations of natural forces and cosmic principles. The Rig-Vedic gods are deeply integrated into the fabric of the universe, with each deity embodying a specific aspect of creation.

Indra, the king of the gods, is the god of storms and rain, a force of nature essential for the fertility of the land and the survival of the people. Agni, the god of fire, is both the sacrificial flame and the fire within all beings, a symbol of transformation and purification. Varuna, the god of cosmic order, oversees the moral and physical laws that govern the universe.

The yajna, or ritual sacrifice, is central to Rig-Vedic worship. It is through the yajna that the Rishis sought to maintain the cosmic order, to ensure that the forces of nature continued to operate in harmony. The Rig-Vedic hymns are often structured around these yajnas, with the Rishis invoking the gods to bless the ritual, to accept the offerings, and to grant their favor.

However, the yajna is not just a ritualistic act; it is a microcosm of the universe itself. The fire altar represents the world, the offerings symbolize the elements, and the recitation of the hymns mirrors the creative power of the divine word. In performing the yajna, the Rishis were not just asking for the gods' blessings; they were participating in the ongoing creation and sustenance of the cosmos.

The third chapter focused on the Saraswati River, a central figure in the Rigveda and a powerful symbol of life, wisdom, and spiritual nourishment. The Saraswati, now largely vanished from the physical landscape, was once the mightiest river of the Vedic civilization. It was along its banks that the earliest hymns were composed, and it was to this river that the Rishis directed their most fervent prayers.

The drying up of the Saraswati is a poignant event in Vedic history, marking the decline of the civilization that flourished along its banks. Yet, the Saraswati's significance extends beyond its physical presence. In the Rigveda, the Saraswati is celebrated not just as a river but as a goddess, a divine mother who nourishes the earth with her waters and bestows wisdom upon those who seek it.

The prayers for the revival of the Saraswati, as explored in this book, are more than just appeals for the restoration of a physical river. They are symbolic of the Rishis' deep understanding of the interconnectedness of life, the recognition that water is life and that the loss of a river is the loss of a way of life. The Rishis' hymns to the Saraswati are calls to preserve the natural world, to honor the sources of life, and to recognize the sacredness of water in all its forms.

Chapters four through eight took us on a journey through the hymns of the five great Rishis—Gratsmand, Vishwamitra, Vamadeva, Bhardwaja, and Vashisht—whose compositions are preserved in Mandalas 2, 3, 4, 6, and 7 of the Rigveda. Each of these Rishis offers a unique perspective on the cosmic waters, the life-giving rivers, and the role of the divine in sustaining the universe.

Gratsmand, in Mandala 2, invokes the rivers with a sense of awe and reverence, recognizing their power to nourish and to destroy. His hymns reflect a deep connection to the land and its waters, a recognition of the essential role that rivers play in the cycle of life.

Vishwamitra, in Mandala 3, is best known for his Gayatri Mantra, a prayer for enlightenment and divine guidance. His hymns to the rivers are infused with a sense of urgency, a recognition of the precariousness of life and the need for divine intervention to sustain it.

Vamadeva, in Mandala 4, explores the relationship between fire and water, two seemingly opposing elements that are both essential to life. His hymns reflect a deep understanding of the balance that must be maintained between these forces, a balance that is essential for the continuation of life.

Bhardwaja, in Mandala 6, focuses on the role of the yajna in sustaining the cosmic order. His hymns emphasize the importance of ritual and prayer in maintaining the harmony of the universe, and the role of the Rishis in mediating between the human and the divine.

Vashisht, in Mandala 7, offers some of the most profound reflections on the nature of the divine and the role of water in the cosmic order. His hymns to the Saraswati are filled with a sense of longing and devotion, a recognition of the river's importance not just as a physical entity but as a symbol of spiritual nourishment.

The Saraswati River, central to Vedic culture, gradually dried up, leading to a significant cultural and geographical shift. This event marked a crucial turning point in Vedic history, leading to migrations and the eventual decline of the civilization that had thrived along its banks. However, the Rishis' response to this ecological crisis was profound, illustrating their deep connection to the land and its rivers.

The prayers for the revival of the Saraswati, explored in this book, reflect the Rishis' understanding of the river as more than just a waterway. The Saraswati was a source of life, knowledge, and spiritual nourishment. Its drying up was seen as a cosmic event, requiring not just physical but spiritual restoration.

The Rishis' hymns to the Saraswati are filled with a sense of longing and devotion. They are prayers for the river's return, but they are also prayers for the restoration of balance and harmony in the universe. The Saraswati, in these hymns, becomes a symbol of the interconnectedness of life, a reminder that the well-being of the natural world is essential for the well-being of humanity.

As we conclude this exploration of the Rig-Vedic hymns, it is essential to consider the lessons they offer for our contemporary world. The Rigveda, with its emphasis on the sacredness of the natural world, offers a model for living in harmony with the environment. The Rishis recognized that water is not just a physical necessity but a sacred element that sustains life and connects us to the divine.

In an age where the natural world is increasingly threatened by human activity, the Rig-Vedic hymns offer a reminder of the need to respect and protect the environment. The prayers for the revival of the Saraswati, the invocations of the Rig-Vedic gods, and the rituals of the yajna are all expressions of a deep ecological consciousness, recognition that the well-being of humanity is intimately tied to the well-being of the planet.

The legacy of the Rig-Vedic waters is eternal. The Rishis' prayers continue to resonate across the millennia, offering guidance and inspiration for the challenges we face today. The Saraswati may have vanished from the physical landscape, but its spirit lives on in the hymns of the Rigveda, a reminder of the sacredness of water and the need to preserve it for future generations.

In this concluding chapter, we have journeyed through the sacred waters of the Rigveda, exploring the prayers and rituals that connect humanity to the divine and the natural world. The Rig-Vedic hymns are not just a relic of the past but a living tradition that offers profound insights into the challenges we face today. The Rishis' prayers for water, their invocations of the gods, and their rituals of the yajna are all expressions of a deep understanding of the interconnectedness of life.

As we move forward, let us carry the lessons of the Rigveda with us, recognizing the sacredness of water and the need to live in harmony with the natural world. The echoes of these ancient hymns continue to resonate, guiding us toward a future where the sacred and the natural are one.